THE NATURE OF

RATIONALITY

THE NATURE OF RATIONALITY

Robert Nozick

PRINCETON UNIVERSITY PRESS

PRINCETON, NEW JERSEY

COPYRIGHT © 1993 BY ROBERT NOZICK

PUBLISHED BY PRINCETON UNIVERSITY PRESS, 41 WILLIAM STREET,
PRINCETON, NEW JERSEY 08540
IN THE UNITED KINGDOM: PRINCETON UNIVERSITY PRESS,
CHICHESTER, WEST SUSSEX

ALL RIGHTS RESERVED

LIBRARY OF CONGRESS CATALOGING-IN-PUBLICATION DATA

NOZICK, ROBERT.
THE NATURE OF RATIONALITY / ROBERT NOZICK.
P.   CM.
INCLUDES INDEX.
ISBN 0-691-07424-0
1. REASONING.   2. REASON.   I. TITLE.
BC177.N69   1993   128'.3—dc20   92-46660

THIS BOOK HAS BEEN COMPOSED IN ADOBE PALATINO

PRINCETON UNIVERSITY PRESS BOOKS ARE PRINTED
ON ACID-FREE PAPER AND MEET THE GUIDELINES FOR
PERMANENCE AND DURABILITY OF THE COMMITTEE ON
PRODUCTION GUIDELINES FOR BOOK LONGEVITY
OF THE COUNCIL ON LIBRARY RESOURCES

PRINTED IN THE UNITED STATES OF AMERICA

3   5   7   9   10   8   6   4   2

To Carl Hempel

AND TO THE MEMORY OF

Gregory Vlastos

CONTENTS

ACKNOWLEDGMENTS

THE FIRST two chapters of this book were originally delivered as Tanner Lectures at Princeton University on November 13 and 15, 1991. I had been a graduate student at Princeton, and the lectures were dedicated, as is this book, to my teachers there. Chapters 1 and 2 are reprinted with the permission of the University of Utah Press from the *Tanner Lectures on Human Values*, vol. 14 (Salt Lake City: University of Utah Press, © 1992). (Some additions and changes have been made in the versions printed here.) First drafts of these two chapters were written at the Rockefeller Foundation Research Center at Bellagio, Italy, in the summer of 1989.

Portions of Chapter 5 constituted the Walter C. Schnackenberg Memorial Lecture, given at Pacific Lutheran University in March 1990. Parts of Chapters 3–5 were given as a Centennial Lecture at the University of Chicago in May 1992.

I am grateful to the discussants of the lectures at Princeton—Gilbert Harman (who also read the complete manuscript), Clifford Geertz, Susan Hurley, and Amos Tversky—and also to Scott Brewer, Eugene Goodheart, David Gordon, Christine Korsgaard, Elijah Millgram, Bill Puka, Tim Scanlon, Howard Sobel, and William Talbott for their very helpful comments and suggestions. Special thanks go to Amartya Sen for many stimulating discussions of this material, inside classes we have taught together and out.

I am very grateful to Laurance Rockefeller for his interest in and generous support of this research project.

I thank my wife, Gjertrud Schnackenberg, who made the years during which this book was written so romantic and loving—and such fun.

INTRODUCTION

THE WORD *philosophy* means the love of wisdom, but what philosophers really love is reasoning. They formulate theories and marshal reasons to support them, they consider objections and try to meet these, they construct arguments against other views. Even philosophers who proclaim the limitations of reason—the Greek skeptics, David Hume, doubters of the objectivity of science—all adduce reasons for their views and present difficulties for opposing ones. Proclamations or aphorisms are not considered philosophy unless they also enshrine and delineate reasoning.

One thing philosophers reason about is reasoning itself. What principles should it obey? What principles must it obey? Aristotle initiated the explicit formulation and study of deductive principles, writers on science and probability theory delineated modes of nondeductive reasoning and support, Descartes attempted to show why we should trust the results of reasoning, Hume questioned the rationality of our doing so, and Kant demarcated what he held to be reason's proper domain. This delineation of reason was not an academic exercise. Discoveries were to be applied: people's reasoning was to be improved, their beliefs and practices and actions made more rational. Inquiring into the rationality of contemporary beliefs and practices carries risks, Socrates discovered. The traditions of a society sometimes do not withstand scrutiny; not everyone wishes to see the implicit examined explicitly. Even the simple consideration of alternatives can seem a corrosive undercutting of what actually exists, an exposure of arbitrariness.

Rationality fixed human distinctiveness, the Greeks held. "Man is a rational animal." The capacity to be rational demarcates humans from other animals and thus defines them. Human specialness has repeatedly been contracted since the Middle Ages—this was the first large statement about intellectual history that I recall reading. Copernicus, Darwin, and Freud taught us that human beings do not occupy a special place in the universe, they are not special in their origin and are not always guided by rational or even consciously known motives. What continued to give humanity some special status, though, is its capacity for rationality. Perhaps we do not consistently exercise this valuable attribute; yet it sets us apart. Rationality provides us with the (potential) power to investigate and discover anything and everything; it enables us to control and direct our behavior through reasons and the utilization of principles.

Rationality therefore is a crucial component of the self-image of the human species, not simply a tool for gaining knowledge or improving our lives and society. Understanding our rationality brings deeper insight into our nature and into whatever special status we possess. The Greeks saw rationality as independent of animality, certainly not its outgrowth. Evolutionary theory makes it possible to see rationality as one among other animal traits, an evolutionary adaptation with a delimited purpose and function.

This perspective can yield important consequences for philosophy, I believe. Rationality has not been merely the philosophers' special love and an important part of their subject matter; it has been their special tool for discovering truth, a potentially unlimited one. (In the *Critique of Pure Reason*, Kant gave reason a humbler function: not to cognize the heart of an independent reality but to know an empirical realm that it partially constitutes and shapes. Still, its valid scope remained extremely large.) If rationality is an evolutionary adaptation with a delimited purpose and function, designed to work in conjunction with other stable facts that it takes for granted and builds upon, but if philosophy is an attempt of unlimited scope to apply reason and to justify rationally every belief and assumption, then we can understand why many of philosophy's traditional problems have turned out to be intractable and resistant to rational resolution. These problems may result from attempts to extend rationality beyond its delimited evolutionary function. I have in mind here the problems of induction, of other minds, of the external world, and of justifying goals. I shall explore the consequences and implications of this evolutionary perspective later on.

In recent years, rationality has been an object of particular criticism. The claim has been put forth that rationality is *biased* because it is a class-based or male or Western or whatever notion. Yet it is part of rationality to be intent on noticing biases, including its own, and controlling and correcting these. (Might the attempt to correct for biases itself be a bias? But if that is a *criticism*, from what quarter does it come? Is there a view that holds that bias is bad but that correcting it is bad too? If it is held to be impossible to eliminate bias, then in what sense does charging bias constitute a criticism? And would such impossibility mean that there is some one particular bias that is intrinsically resistant to elimination or just that not all biases can be eliminated simultaneously?)

Charging a bias in existing standards does not show that one exists. That is done by using reasoning and evidence—hence using our existing standards—to reach the conclusion that these standards themselves, in some applications, show some particular specified distortions and biases. It is not sufficient merely to say that we (all) see the world through our conceptual schemes. The question is: In what specific ways, and by what exact mechanisms, do our particular conceptual schemes and standards distort? Once we are shown this, we can begin to make corrections. Of course, our current standards of rationality are not perfect—in what year should we suppose they became so? But they have real virtues, and to show that they are flawed requires rational argumentation of at least the same weight as those standards being attacked. Detecting particular such flaws is the necessary first step toward repairing them and toward formulating the standards of rationality more adequately. So evidence for charges of bias in standards should be welcomed and sought out. Standards of rationality are a means whereby we rise above, or check, our own particular hopes, wishes, and biases. It would be ironic and tragic if the current widespread criticism of standards of rationality had the effect of removing or undercutting one of the major ways through which humanity is able to correct and rise above personal and group bias.

The study of rationality, which is of such great evaluative and practical importance both personally and socially, has gotten transformed into a technical subject. Principles were sharpened to delineate valid reasoning and to capture the patterns of belief and action supported by reasons. Deductive logic was transformed by Gottlob Frege in the late nineteenth century and burst into technical elaboration in the twentieth. Systems of logic were developed and their own properties and limitations were explored using logical techniques. Probability theory led to formal theories of statistical inference, and mathematization permeated attempts to theorize about the rationality of belief and to formulate the rudiments of an inductive logic, or at least of inductive rules of acceptance. A sleek and powerful theory of rational action—decision theory—was developed in this century by mathematicians, economists, statisticians, and philosophers, and now this theory is applied in a wide variety of theoretical and practical contexts. (The apparatus of this theory provides the framework for the formal theory of rational strategic interaction, game theory, the formal theory of social choice and welfare economics, the theory of microeconomic phenomena, and elaborate theories of the political realm.) The relevant literature is sprinkled with, when not wholly engulfed by, forbidding formulas in unfamiliar symbolic notations that are elaborated into mathematical structures. I do not decry this turn. These current theoretical developments are continuous with the earlier motivations and concerns, and they carry the inquiry much further.

This book too will take account of such technicalities and propose some new ones in the two major areas covered by theories of rationality: rationality of decision and rationality of belief. We shall reformulate current decision theory to include the symbolic meaning of actions, propose a new rule of rational decision (that of maximizing decision-value), and then proceed to trace the implications of this rule for the Prisoner's Dilemma and for Newcomb's Problem. The rationality of belief involves two aspects: support by reasons that make the belief credible, and generation by a process that reliably produces true beliefs. (The evolutionary account I offer to explain the puzzling connection between these aspects reverses the direction of Kant's "Copernican Revolution.") I shall propose two rules to govern rational belief: not believing any statement less credible than some incompatible alternative—the intellectual component—but then believing a statement only if the expected utility (or decision-value) of doing so is greater than that of not believing it—the practical component. This twofold structure then is applied to issues about the "ethics of belief" and a new resolution of the "lottery paradox" is proposed. I also shall explore the scope and limits of instrumental rationality, the effective and efficient pursuit of given goals, and propose some new conditions on the rationality of goals. Because rational thinking also encompasses the formulation of new and fruitful philosophical questions and ideas, some heuristics for doing this shall be presented. Thus, this book is awash in technical details needed to push thinking on the fundamental issues of rationality further.

Yet there is some cause for concern. Until recently, questions about rationality had been the common possession of humankind, sometimes discussed in intricate trains of thought—no one could claim that Kant's *Critique of Pure Reason* is an easy book—but, nevertheless, largely accessible to intelligent people willing to make the effort. New thoughts on these questions were part of the general culture; they shaped the terms of discussion and debate, and sometimes even of sensibility (recall how greatly Kant's thought influenced Coleridge). Now things are different—and not just with the topic of rationality.

The most fruitful and interesting lines of inquiry about many topics of fundamental human concern have taken an increasingly technical turn. It is impossible now to discuss these topics adequately without a grasp of these technical developments, of the new questions they open, and of the ways some traditional positions are undercut. When the Encyclopedia Britannica recently published its (second) edition of "Great Books of the Western World," this occasioned some public controversy over the representation—or relative lack—of women and minorities, and over the putative elitism of any canon of great works.* What received no comment, however, was that many of the greatest intellectual works of the twentieth century were omitted, presumably because they were too technical for the intelligent generally educated reader.

The point is not just that interesting thoughts and results have occurred in this century that are inaccessible to large portions of even a well-educated population—that has been true since Newton. Rather, now these ideas concern topics we want and need to understand, topics we think everyone should understand. Yet without some technical familiarity, these topics cannot be understood or intelligently discussed. The very terms of evaluation have become technical.

Let me give some examples of topics that have undergone technical development. (1) The notion of the general welfare (and Rousseau's notion of the "general will") and an understanding of the purposes of democratic voting procedures have been transformed by Kenneth Arrow's Impossibility Theorem. This shows that several extremely natural and desirable conditions, which apparently should be satisfied by any procedure for determining the general welfare or the democratically most preferred alternative, cannot all be satisfied together. Something has to give. (2) Amartya Sen's work on the Paretian liberal paradox shows that a very natural interpretation of the scope of individual rights and liberties, and of how the choices of society should be rationally organized, cannot be easily fit together. These notions need a new structuring. (3) The fundamental nature of the physical world— the structure of space and time—cannot be understood apart from the technicalities (and mathematics) of space-time as presented in general relativity theory. (4) Similarly for the nature of causality and of the independent character of the physical world as these are depicted in the most precise and successful scientific theory we now possess, quantum field theory. (5) Discussion of the nature and status of mathematical truth—since the Greeks, the exemplar of our best and most certain knowledge—has been drastically transformed by Kurt Gödel's incompleteness theorems. (6) The nature of infinity and its various levels is now elaborated and explored in contemporary set theory. (7) Without the theory of how a price mechanism and associated institutions of private property make rational economic calculation possible, and the decades-long theoretical discussion of whether rational calculation was at all possible in a socialist society, one cannot under-

---

* I myself do not find a uniform edition of the works of many different authors, with the series title emblazoned more prominently than the titles of the individual works or the authors' names, a fitting presentation of the written accomplishments of the mind. It might be useful, however, for a group to publish a *list* of such books and to reprint those not easily available; different groups might publish different lists.

stand why it is that communist societies were so economically ineffec-
tive. (8) Concerning aspects of individual rationality and rational interactions among persons, there have been many theoretical advances:
decision theory, game theory, probability theory, and theories of statistical inference.

For each of these topics, this century has seen dramatic new results
and theories, ones that are difficult to understand or to discuss respon-
sibly without an understanding of the technical structures and details.
This is, I realize, a philosopher's list; social and natural scientists
would add further topics. That reinforces my point. The common culture of intelligent, educated, and serious people has lost its grip on
many topics that are central to understanding and thinking about society or people or the universe at large. The claim that there are complicated scientific factual issues for whose resolution we must turn to experts, experts who perhaps will disagree—for instance, issues about
the environmental effects of various practices—is familiar. What is
new is this: many of the very terms and concepts of evaluation and
understanding that *we* wish to use have themselves become technical.

I raise this issue without a solution to propose. Of course, exposi-
tions of these materials are needed for the general reader. But the
clearest of these, if it is indeed to convey the essential ideas accurately,
will involve some technical descriptions and developments—and thus
be limited in its readers. The task is even more difficult for a work
that presents and explores new ideas. I do not *want* the topic of rationality to be taken away from the general reader. Yet some ideas can be
stated, specified, or defended only in a somewhat technical manner. I
have tried to minimize these technical details, or at least confine them
to specific sections. For the intellectual health of our society—not to
mention the social health of our intellectuals—the fundamental ideas
must stay public.

THE NATURE OF

RATIONALITY

I

HOW TO DO THINGS WITH PRINCIPLES

W HAT are principles *for*? Why do we hold principles, why do we put them forth, why do we adhere to them? We could instead simply act on whim or the passion of the moment, or we could maximize our own self-interest and recommend that others do the same. Are principles then a constraint upon whim and self-interest, or is adherence to principles a way of advancing self-interest? What functions do principles serve?

Principles of action group actions, placing them under general rubrics; linked actions are then to be viewed or treated in the same way. This generality can serve different functions: intellectual, interpersonal, intrapersonal, and personal. I start with the intellectual.

Intellectual Functions

Consider judicial decisionmaking. In one imaginable system, a judge simply decides a case so as to yield what she thinks is the best or preferable result in that particular case. Another system of judicial decision involves principled decision: a common law judge is to formulate a principle to fit (most or almost all) precedents and a range of hypothetical cases, and then use this principle to decide the current case.* The attempt to formulate an acceptable general principle is a *test* of your judgment about the particular case: is there *some* adequate general principle—a principle that gives the right result in all established cases and obvious hypothetical ones—that also yields the result you want in this case? If you cannot find such a principle, reconsider what result you do want in this case.

Such a procedure is a test of a particular judgment on the assumption that any correct judgment is yielded by *some* true acceptable gen-

---

* My aim here is to highlight some general features that principles have outside of the legal realm by analogy to some aspects of judicial decision, not to present a complete picture of the functioning of legal institutions. What is illuminating is the analogy between how a current judicial decision is to be yielded by a principle that fits past precedents and how (outside the law) a principle is to yield correct judgments. That within the legal system *stare decisis* is itself a (higher-order) principle of the law that may sometimes conflict or compete with other principles need not concern us now.

eral principle, that true particular judgments are consequences of general principles applied to specific situations. Failure to uncover an acceptable general principle that yields some judgment in particular may mean that there is no such acceptable principle, in which case that particular judgment is mistaken and should be abandoned. Or perhaps you have not been astute enough to formulate the correct principle. We have no mechanical procedure to decide which explanation is correct.[1]

When you find a general principle or theory that subsumes this case, a principle you would be willing to apply to other cases as well, this particular judgment receives new support. Consider empirical data points a,b,c,d. If a straight line is the simplest curve through these, this supports the prediction that another point e, also on that straight line, will hold. It is not an easy matter, inductive logicians have discovered, to isolate and explain how a (relatively) simple lawlike statement can group existing data points so that inferences and predictions legitimately can be made to new points. Nevertheless, we do not doubt that data can support the hypothesis that a law holds and also support a prediction that a new point will accord with that law. Similarly, the simplest principle that covers acceptable normative points a,b,c,d also will support an additional judgment e (that fits this principle) as a correct normative point too. A theorist gains confidence in his particular judgment (or side in a controversy) when he can formulate a general principle or theory to fit it, especially one that is appealing on its face.[2]

Philosophers of science have tried to demarcate scientific laws from accidental generalizations. Accidental generalizations only happen to hold, or to have held, true. From such a generalization, for example, that all the coins in my pocket are dimes, one cannot infer a subjunctive statement such as: If there *were* an additional coin in my pocket now, it *would be* a dime. (From a scientific law, on the other hand—for instance, that all freely falling bodies fall a distance equal to $1/2gt^2$—we can infer that if some other object now at rest were in free-fall for t seconds it would travel a distance equal to $1/2gt^2$.) If all previous data fit a given generalization, we can plausibly infer that new data would fit it (and hence predict that new data that *will* be gathered will fit it) *only if* that generalization is of lawlike form and is a candidate for being a law. It is when data fall under a lawlike statement (or arise from several of them) that we can legitimately extrapolate to further cases. The features of a lawlike statement, those aspects that differentiate it from an accidental generalization, constitute our license to travel from given data to predictions or expectations about further data. Similarly, for particular normative judgments, what licenses us to travel to a further judgment on the basis of previous ones is that the previous ones all fall under a normative general principle. The features of a normative principle license a subjunctive inference to a new case that steps beyond the indicative instances that happen already to have fallen under it. Principles are transmission devices for *probability* or *support*, which flow from data or cases, via the principle, to judgments and predictions about new observations or cases whose status otherwise is unknown or less certain.

What features enable principles to transmit probability? The following features have been mentioned to distinguish scientific lawlike statements (or nomic universals) from accidental generalizations.[3] Lawlike statements do not contain terms for particular individual objects, dates, or temporal periods—or if they do, these statements can be derived from more general lawlike statements that do not. Lawlike statements contain purely qualitative predicates: stating the meaning of these does not require reference to any *particular* object or spatiotemporal location. Lawlike statements have an unrestricted universality; they are not simply a finite conjunction that was established by examining all cases. Lawlike statements are supported not just by instances falling under them but also by a linkage of indirect evidence.

These very same features might be what enables a normative principle to license the derivation of new judgments from previously accepted ones. Writers on ethics frequently state that ethical principles must be formulated using general terms only—no names of particular persons, groups, or nations. This feature might enable a principle to license an inference to a new case, hence enable new normative judgments to be supported by previous ones. A generalization lacking this feature of nonparticularity might be, at best, an accidental one, incapable of transferring support from some data to others. When moral principles are general and do not contain any nonqualitative predicates or particular names, rather than being a specifically *moral* aspect of the principles, this feature might link data or judgments together to support subjunctive inferences. It would be worthwhile to investigate how much of the "form" of moral principles is necessary for such linkage.

This does not mean these features are tagged onto weaker generalizations to make moral principles that perform inferential functions, any more than such features are tagged onto accidental generalizations to make scientific laws. One can hold that scientific laws and moral principles hold true apart from any constructions we add or any uses of them we make, that their independent truth is what makes these uses possible. Nevertheless, features such as generality, no proper names, and no positional predicates would not be specifically *moral* features but lawlike ones, necessary for anything to be a law, scientific or moral. In the appropriate context, features that are not specifically moral can have moral consequences.

A person may seek principles not only to test his own judgment or give it more support but also to convince others or to increase their conviction. To do this he cannot simply announce his preference for a position; he must produce reasons convincing to the others. Reasons might be very particular, but they also can be general considerations that apply well to a wide range of cases and point to a particular judgment in this instance. If these judgments in the other cases are ones the other person already accepts, then the general reasoning will recruit these cases as evidence and support for the judgment proposed in the present case. Principles or general theories thus have an interpersonal intellectual function: justification to another. Justification by general principles is convincing in two ways: by the face appeal of the principles and by recruiting other already accepted cases to support a proposed position in this case.[4]

In using a judge to illustrate the testing and support function of principles, I have imagined that her purpose is to arrive at the right decision about a particular case and that she treats the past decisions as (for the most part) right themselves. That is, I have treated a judge as structurally identical to a moral reasoner who wishes to decide what is right or permissible on this new occasion or situation and who utilizes her knowledge of what is right or permissible in other actual or hypothetical situations to formulate, test, and support a moral principle that yields a result for this situation.

Of course, a judge also is a figure in an institutional structure, and principled decisions that fit past cases may have a particular point within that institution. Legal theorists tell us that the doctrine of respecting precedents, *stare decisis*, can enable people to predict more exactly the legal system's future decisions and so plan actions with some confidence about their legal consequences.[5] For this effect, the precedents need not have been decided correctly or be followed with the goal of reaching a right decision; they are followed in order to yield a result that has been expected. Second, principled decisionmaking might be desired to constrain a judge's basis for decision. To be excluded are her personal preferences or prejudices, moods of the moment, partiality for one side in a dispute, or even thought-through moral and political principles that are personal to her. It might be held that a judge's own views, preferences, or even considered views should have no more effect than anybody else's—the judge was not given that institutional position to put her own preferences into effect.

A requirement that decisions be principled fittings to past precedents might be a device to *constrain* the effect of such personal factors, limiting their play or crowding them out *altogether*.

However, the analogy to science, where the aim is truth and correctness, casts doubt upon the last strong claim. Fitting the scientific data is a requirement, but this does not uniquely determine one lawlike statement (even apart from the leeway in the different ways a "best fit" can be defined). An indefinite number of curves can fit any finite set of data points; more than one will be lawlike. Hence additional criteria will be necessary to select which lawlike statement to accept tentatively and use in predicting. These criteria include simplicity, analogy to supported lawlike statements in related areas,[6] fit with other accepted theories, explanatory power, theoretical fruitfulness, and perhaps ease of computation.[7] Merely requiring that a prediction fit the past data according to some lawlike statement does not uniquely determine that prediction. How likely is it, then, that merely requiring that a judge's decision in a new case fit past decisions according to some principle will suffice to determine that decision uniquely? Indeed, we find judges enjoined to use additional criteria, including various "formal" ones.[8] We can raise analogous issues about ethics too. W. V. Quine holds that the totality of (possible) empirical data does not uniquely determine an explanatory theory. Are correct ethical principles uniquely determined by the totality of correct judgments about particular cases, actual and hypothetical, or does underdetermination reign there? In addition to fitting particular judgments, must a moral principle also satisfy certain further criteria?

There is a connection between using principles as devices for reaching correct decisions and using them to constrain the influence of undesired or irrelevant factors, such as personal preference. We want to decide or judge a particular case by considering all and only the relevant reasons concerning it. A general principle, which forces us to look at other actual and hypothetical cases, can help test whether a reason R we think is relevant or conclusive in this case really is so. Would R be relevant or conclusive in another case? If reasons are general, we can check R's force in this case by considering other cases. Moreover, deciding via a general principle can call our attention to other relevant reasons, ones we have not yet noticed in this case. Looking at another case where feature R does *not* have great force might lead us to notice another feature F that the present case has, and it is R and F together that have great force. (If we hadn't looked at the other case, we might have thought R alone was enough.) Including all the relevant reasons might help to ensure that *only* relevant reasons are used, *if* these fill the space and so crowd out irrelevant ones. And will we really be willing to accept the impact that an irrelevant reason imposed in this case also would have upon other cases and examples? Notice that this use of hypothetical or other actual cases to test a judgment in this case already assumes that reasons are *general*. If we assume that things happen or hold for a reason (or cause) and that reasons (or causes) are general, then a general principle, perhaps defeasible, can be formulated to capture this reason, to explain why an event the scientist studies occurs or why a particular judgment about a case is correct.[9]

Principles can guide us to a correct decision or judgment in a particular case, helping us to test our judgment and to control for personal factors that might lead us astray. The wrongness that principles are to protect us against, on this view, is individualistic—the wrong judgment in *this* case—or aggregative—the wrong judgments in *these* cases, which are wrong one by one. However, judgments together might have an additional wrong, a *comparative* wrong that occurs when cases that should be decided in the same way are decided differently. It has been held to be a maxim of (formal) justice that like cases should be decided alike; this general maxim leaves open which likenesses are the relevant ones.[10] Principles might function to avoid this injustice or disparity, not simply to get each and every case decided correctly by itself but to get relevantly similar cases decided similarly. But if I see films two weeks in a row, I need not decide which ones to attend on a similar basis. These two similar decisions, then, apparently do *not* count as like cases that must be decided alike. (The earlier decision may affect the later choice but does not constrain it.) What demarcates the domain within which the maxim of formal justice is to operate? As a moviegoer, I do not see my task in deciding which movie to attend (on either occasion) as that of reaching a *just* decision on that occasion. The issue of comparative injustice arises only in contexts that involve individual justice or injustice, however these latter contexts are marked. If case A, calling for a decision of justice, is decided wrongly, that is bad. If now case B, relevantly similar, is decided differently—that is, correctly—and *if* that decision introduces an additional bad into the world—not the result in case B itself but the comparative bad of the two cases being decided differently—and this bad stands over and above the badness involved when case A was decided incorrectly, then *this* context of justice is a comparative one, invoking the formal maxim of justice.* One function of principles, then, may be to avoid

* I have said that a necessary condition for invoking the formal maxim of justice is that the context is one in which a just decision is to be reached, but I have not claimed this is a sufficient condition. If there are individual decisions involving justice that do not have that comparative aspect, then a further criterion is needed to mark which contexts involving justice do invoke the formal maxim. In *Anarchy, State, and Utopia* (New

this particular type of injustice, ensuring that like cases will be decided alike. (Whether it would be better to decide both cases wrongly—avoiding the comparative injustice—or to decide one of them correctly—avoiding injustice in that individual case but incurring the comparative injustice—presumably will depend upon particular features of the situation and the cases.)

Interpersonal Functions

A principled person can be counted upon to adhere to his principles in the face of inducements or temptations to deviate. Not necessarily in the face of any possible temptation or of extremely great inducement—nevertheless, principles are some barrier to a person's following the desires or interests of the moment. A person's principles of action thus have an interpersonal function in reassuring others that (usually) he will get past temptations; they also have an intrapersonal function, helping the person himself to overcome temptation.

Consider first the interpersonal function. When (refraining from) an action is mandated by a person's principles, we can count on it more. Being able to rely to some significant extent upon his behavior, we ourselves can perform actions whose good outcome is contingent upon the principled person's specific behavior. Even were the future to bring him inducements to deviate, we can trust that he will not, and we can rely upon this in planning and executing our own actions. Otherwise we would have to behave differently, for the chance would be too great that this previous behavior would come to naught or to ill. With people personally close to us, we can rely upon their affection and continuing good motivations to produce coordinate actions; with others more distant, we rely upon their principled behavior.

Such considerations are familiar in discussions of contract law. Contracts enable a person to bind himself to carry out an action, thereby encouraging another to count upon this and thus perform an action that takes her out on a limb that would be sawed off if the first person

---

York: Basic Books, 1974), ch. 7, I presented a theory of distributive justice, the entitlement theory, which explicitly was not a patterned theory and did not involve comparisons among the holdings of different people. That is not to say, however, that the formal maxim would not apply to people's holdings arising in accordance with the *same* general principles (of justice in acquisition, transfer, and rectification). Hence, so far as that theory goes, in addition to the injustice of someone's holdings not arising through the operation of those principles, there could be an additional comparative injustice if another's holdings had so arisen (for example, the first is discriminated against by others who do not let those principles of justice in holdings apply to him).

failed to perform. Since the first person benefits from that second person's action, which would not be performed if the first person had not contractually bound himself to act, this first person is willing in advance to restrict himself to so acting in this case even should his future incentives change. For if his action was left dependent upon the vagaries of future fluctuations, the second person would not perform that complementary action which the first person now wishes her to do.

Principles constitute a form of binding: we bind ourselves to act as the principles mandate. Others can depend upon this behavior, and we too can benefit from others' so depending, for the actions they thereby become willing to undertake can facilitate our social ease and interactions, and our own personal projects as well.[11] *Announcing* principles is a way to incur (what economists term) reputation effects, making conditions explicit so that deviations are more easily subject to detection. These effects are significant for someone who makes repeated transactions with many people; others are assured that he will act a certain way (in order to avoid diminution of a reputation that serves him in interaction).[12]

These considerations can make a person want to *seem* to others to have particular principles, but why would he actually want to have them? For most of us, possessing principles may be the most convincing and the least difficult route to seeming to have them, but fiction and real life too abound with skilled deceivers. Suppose a person does want to have a particular principle, and not merely seem to, because this will function most convincingly for others and most easily for himself. *Can* he come to have that principle merely because of its useful interpersonal functions? Mustn't he believe the principle is *correct*? (Hence, doesn't the intellectual function play a role in the interpersonal function?)

And how reassuring would I find someone's telling me that he believes his holding a principle is indeed necessary to reassure me and others. "But *do* you hold it?" I would wonder. "And how strongly?" If he regarded the principle simply as a reassurance for others, even a very necessary and extremely useful reassurance, wouldn't I wonder about his continuing adherence in the face of momentary temptations or inducements to deviate? What I would want, I think, is for the person to believe the principle is *correct* and *right*. Of course, it is not enough that he think this now; his belief must be stable, not subject to overturn by the slightest counterargument or counterinducement. That's what would reassure me sufficiently so that I would run risks whose good outcome was contingent upon his good behavior. And I might be proficient at detecting genuine belief in a principle and be unwilling to run cooperative risks in its absence.[13]

Believing in the correctness of her principles, then, might be a useful trait for a person to have, making possible an expanded range of interactions with others and cooperative activities. This belief could be useful even if the notion of "correct principles" made no sense at all. For this—let us for the moment suppose—senseless belief, evidenced by her and detected by others, would be a reliable indicator to them of her future conduct and would lead them to do trusting actions that benefit her too. (Similarly, the belief that certain conduct is divinely prescribed and that all deviations will meet dire punishment might be a useful belief for people to have, whether or not it is true or makes any sense at all, provided it guarantees to others a person's continuing conduct.) This raises the possibility of a sociobiological explanation not of particular patterns of conduct but of the belief in an objective moral order. Believing in *correctness* might be selected for. (Might a belief in *deontological* principles serve a similar interpersonal function and so have been selected?)

If people are to be assured about my future conduct, it may not be enough for me simply to announce my principles; other people may need to see, upon occasion, that I actually am adhering to these principles. Yet the principles I think most correct or adequate may be difficult for others to observe in operation; those most adequate principles might respond to subtle contextual details, nuances of history or motivation or relationship not known to others or reliably checked by them. Justice, it is said, must not only be done but be seen to be done. Yet, what should occur when what can be dependably seen and recognized is less complex than (fully) adequate justice requires? The interpersonal function of assuring others that justice is being done or that principles are being followed might necessitate following principles that are less subtle and nuanced but whose applications (and misapplications) can sometimes be checked by others.*

Thus, there can be a conflict between fine-tuning a principle to a situation and producing public confidence through the principle. The more fine-tuned the principle, the less easily can its applications be checked by others. On the other hand, beyond a point of coarsening, a principle may fail to inspire confidence, not because it cannot

---

* David Kreps, *A Course in Microeconomic Theory* (Princeton: Princeton Univ. Press, 1990), p. 763, reports that Robert Wilson argues that publicly held accounting firms that perform external audits of businesses, in order to assure potential investors that the auditors themselves are not suborned by the firms they are auditing, must follow established rules for auditing, rules whose application can be externally checked, even if these practices do not provide the most revealing information about a business's finances. Because the application of these established rules *can* be checked, the auditing firm is able to maintain its reputation as an independent third party.

be checked but because its applications no longer count as desirable. It has been claimed—the matter is one of some controversy—that women's moral judgments are more finely attuned to situational details and nuances of relationship and motivation than are men's.[14] This difference, if indeed it holds, might be explained by the statistical fact that women less frequently make (or anticipate making) decisions in a nonfamilial realm where the basis or motives of decision are an object of suspicion. If in some (public) realm assurance must be given to others, anyone in that realm may need to bend (somewhat) to the dictates of what *can* provide assurance, and principles are one such device. Predictions have been made about the moral changes to be effected once large numbers of women enter previously male arenas— a good thing for very many reasons—but it is not certain that it is the arenas rather than the included women who will experience the greater change.

Another person's principles enable me to predict with reasonable (though perhaps not perfect) accuracy some aspects of his behavior and hence lead me to count upon those aspects. For that other person, though, his principles do not seem primarily to be predictive devices. Only rarely do people attempt to *predict* their own future behavior; usually they just *decide* what to do. Rather, the person's principles play a role in producing that behavior; he *guides* his behavior by the principle. My knowing of his principles affects my estimate of the likelihood that he will behave a certain way, my estimate of the probability of his behaving that way. *For him*, the principles affect not (merely) *estimates* of the probabilities but these very probabilities themselves: the principles are not evidence of how he will behave but devices that help determine what he will (decide to) do.[15]

Personal Functions

It is because principles of behavior have a personal (or an intellectual) function, apart from issues of social interaction, that they are able to perform and achieve their interpersonal function. (It might be enough for others to think, mistakenly, that principles do perform some personal function for someone.) This interpersonal function—reassuring others of our behavior in the face of temptations and hence leading them to choose to act coordinately with our actions—could not arise (as a solution in a coordination game) or be maintained without its basis in the personal matrix. What, then, are the personal and intrapersonal functions of principles, and in what ways do they achieve these?

Principles may be one way a person can define her own *identity*: "I am a person with *these* principles." Further, principles followed over an extended period are a way a person can integrate her life over time and give it more coherence. Some might say it is good to be principled because that is a way of being consistent. However, if actions are (logically) inconsistent in themselves or among themselves—going to the movie that day, and not going to the movie that day—then it is not possible to do all of them, and principles are not needed to avoid the inconsistency. Among actions that it is logically possible to do jointly, adherence to a principle adds no further logical consistency. An action *can* be inconsistent with a principle, and hence derivatively with the other actions that fit that principle. But if one wanted merely to avoid such inconsistency, that could be done by having *no* principles at all. Principles do knit one's actions together, though. Through them, one's actions and one's life may have greater coherence, greater organic unity. That may be valuable in itself.

What does it mean to define oneself or one's identity in terms of principles? Should we construe the self as a system of principles? These could include principles for transforming existing principles and for integrating new ones, thus for altering the self too in terms of principles. (If a person violated her principles, would that then threaten to destroy her self?) But continuing goals also would integrate a person's life and actions over time. Why define oneself by principles rather than goals? A person who doesn't *define* herself through principles nevertheless might *have* principles, not as an internal component of her identity but as an external constraint upon the actions of a separate, distinguishable identity. One thinks of the Kantian themes of self-creation and self-legislation. But if chosen goals can give self-creation, why is self-*legislation* needed? Does this role of principles depend upon controversial Kantian claims about what (and only what) gives rise to autonomous freedom?

These personal functions of principles concern one's life or identity as a whole, or at least extended parts of it. Principles also function for a person, more modestly, at the micro level. One intrapersonal function of moral principles is connected to our commitment to them. When we start long-term projects, there is the question of whether we will stick to them in the future, whether our—as some like to say—future selves will carry them out. Only if the answer is yes might it be worthwhile to begin a particular project, and beginning it might be rational only when we have some assurance it will continue. If my holding something *as a principle* now creates a greater cost to deviating from it in the future—that very same action would have less cost when it is no deviation from a principle—then a project that incorporates a current and longstanding principle will be one I am less likely to abandon, not because I have some additional principle to stick to my projects but because this project embodies a principle I (probably) will continue to have. Just as principles have an interpersonal function of giving assurance to another—she can count on my behavior in planning hers—so too they have the intrapersonal function of enabling me to count on certain behavior from my future self—when he too probably will have that principle. Therefore, I now can reasonably undertake some projects whose desirability is contingent upon certain future behavior by me.

Within the process of a person's decisionmaking, principles might function as an exclusionary or filtering device: in choice situations, do not consider as live options those actions that violate your principles. Principles thus would save decision effort and calculation time for a creature of "limited rationality." Yet the exclusion need not be absolute: if no sufficiently good action (above a certain level of aspiration) is found among the live options, a previously excluded action might be reconsidered.

Overcoming Temptation

The central intrapersonal function of principles I want to focus upon is their getting us past temptations, hurdles, distractions, and diversions. The psychologist George Ainslie has presented a theory of why we engage in impulsive behavior that we know is against our long-term interests and of the devices we use to cope with the temptations to such behavior.[16] Before we turn to Ainslie's work, some background is useful.

We care less about a future reward now, economic and psychological data show, than we will later when that reward eventuates: we "discount" the future. The current utility to us of receiving a future reward is less than the reward's utility will be when it occurs, and the more distant that reward, the less its current utility. This itself is an interesting phenomenon, and we may wonder about its rationality. In our plans and projects of action shouldn't we value a reward at all times as we would when it occurred? To be sure, we also want to take account of the uncertainty that we will survive until that time or that the reward will occur—each event may be less than completely certain. In our present calculations, then, we wish to use an expected value, discounting that future reward's value by its probability. But shouldn't the utility of actually receiving the reward remain constant, no matter when the time?

Time preference—the term some economists use for utility discounting of the future—may be evolution's way of instilling in creatures that cannot perform such anticipatory probabilistic calculations a mechanism to roughly the same effect. Innate time preference may be a rough rule of thumb that approximates the behavior or decisions that calculations previously would have yielded, at least with regard to those rewards (and punishments) affecting inclusive fitness; there may have been selection for such time preference.[17] A problem arises, then, for beings with the cognitive apparatus to take explicit account of the uncertainties concerning a future reward and to perform explicitly a probabilistic discounting of the future. If already installed in us is an innate time preference—evolution's attempt to perform the probabilistic discounting for our ancestors—and if, moreover, what we explicitly discount in our probabilistic calculations is the (already discounted through time preference) present value of the future reward, then what takes place will be a *double discounting*. And surely that is too much. It seems that beings who are sophisticated enough to realize all this and who perform expected-value calculations should use current estimates of what the utility of the future rewards will be when they eventuate (which then are explicitly discounted by the probabilities) rather than the time-preferenced current discounted values of those future rewards. Otherwise, they should skip the expected-value calculations and stick with the evolutionarily instilled time preference.[18] If pure time preference is a rational phenomenon in itself, however, and not *simply* an evolutionary surrogate for probabilistic discounting, and if such evolutionary shaping did take place, then the situation is more complicated.

The curves describing the time-preferenced discounting of future rewards need not be straight lines or exponential; they may be hyperbolic.[19] Ainslie noticed that two such highly bowed curves (as the hyperbolic) can cross, and he traced out the implications of this fact. (In Figure 1, the utility of a reward is measured on the y-axis; its utility for a person at a given time is measured by the height of its curve at that time. The curve slopes downward to the left because a future reward has a lesser value earlier.) Suppose there are two projects or plans of action leading to different rewards, where receiving the earlier possible reward, the smaller of the two, will preclude or thwart receiving the later larger one. A person proceeds along in time, staying with the project having the highest utility at that time. In the time interval A, the more distant reward has the greater utility; in the time interval B, though, the nearer reward has the greater utility. Since the larger reward can actually be collected only at the end of the time interval C, the person must get through that middle period B without turning to the smaller reward. This presents a problem: during that middle time interval the prospect of receiving that smaller reward *soon* has greater utility than the prospect of receiving the greater reward later.

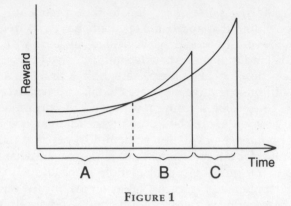

FIGURE 1

Why assume that the person *should* try to get past that intermediate time period; why shouldn't she take the smaller but more immediate reward?[20] What makes periods A and C, wherein the larger reward looms largest, the appropriate ones for deciding which choice is best? During them the person will prefer acting to gain the larger reward; during period B she will prefer acting to gain the smaller one—that is, one that is smaller when she gains it than the other one would be when she gained *it*. Where are *we* standing when we say that avoiding the temptation is the better alternative, and why is that standpoint more appropriate than the person's standpoint within the time interval B?

Here is a suggestion. The time interval B is not the appropriate benchmark for deciding what the person ought to do because B is not a representative sample of her view of the matter. The time intervals A and C sum to a longer interval. Moreover, when we add her judgments *after* the moment the rewards are to be realized and graph which rewards seem largest to her *then*, we find that soon after consuming the smaller reward she wishes she had not done this, but after consuming the larger reward (at the end of the time interval C), she continues to prefer having chosen that larger reward. I suggest that, often, what makes resisting the temptation and taking the larger reward the preferred option is that this is the person's preference for a majority of the time: it is her (reasonably) stable preference; the other is her preference at a nonrepresentative moment.[21] (Leaving aside any after-the-fact preferences, if the time interval B lasted for longer than the intervals A and C, would it be clear *in that case* that the temptation should be resisted?) Temptations should not always be resisted, just when the desire for the larger reward (including the preference after the fact) is the person's preference for the larger amount of time. This criterion is meant to be defeasible, not conclusive. It does have the virtue of staying close to a person's preferences (though it is not wedded to a particular local preference) in contrast to saying that it simply *is* in the person's interests to pursue that later larger reward (because of what the reward is) and so to resist the temptation, or saying that the relevant criterion is—and resisting temptation serves—the maximization of utility over a lifetime.[22]

Ainslie describes various devices for getting oneself past that intermediate period of temptation. These include: taking an action during interval A that makes it impossible to pursue the smaller reward during B (for example, Odysseus tying himself to the mast); taking an action during interval A (making a bet with another person perhaps) that adds a penalty if you take the smaller reward, thereby altering *its* utility during interval B; taking steps during A to avoid noticing or dwelling upon the virtues of the smaller reward during B;[23] and—our current topic—formulating a personal general principle of behavior.

A general principle of behavior groups actions; it classifies a particular act along with others. For example: "Never eat snacks between meals"; "Never smoke another cigarette." (One might think of principles as deeper and less mechanical than rules—this is the usual distinction in the philosophy of law literature—but for present purposes I do not make any distinction between them.) We might try to represent the effect of this principled grouping of actions within utility theory and decision theory as follows. By classifying actions together as of type T, and by treating them similarly, a principle links the utilities of these T-actions (or the utilities of their outcomes). It would be too strong to say that because of the principle all T-actions must have the same utility. One particular T-action also can fall under further types and principles that another T-action does not, so their utilities may diverge. What a principle sets up is a *correlation* among the utilities of the various actions falling under it. To state this at the level of preference: when acts of type T are ranked with other actions in a preference ordering, there will be a correlation among the rank orders of the T-acts. If, however, this correlation were the only effect that adopting or accepting principles had on the utilities of the actions falling under them, then principles would not be of help in getting us past temptations.

The mark of a principle ("Never eat snacks between meals"; "Never smoke another cigarette") is that it ties the decision whether to do an immediate particular act (eating *this* snack, smoking *this* cigarette) to the whole class of actions of which the principle makes it part. This act now stands for the whole class. By adopting the principle, it is as if you have made the following true: if you do this one particular action in the class, you will do them all. Now the stakes are higher. Tying the utility of this act of snacking to the disutility of all those acts of snacking in the future may help you to get through the period B of temptation; the utility for you now of this particular snack is altered. This snack comes to stand for all the snacks, and at this early point the current utility of being thin or healthy later far outweighs the current utility of those distant pleasures of eating; the current disutility of poor health or a poor figure becomes a feature of the currently contemplated particular act of snacking.[24]

But why assume that the person will formulate a principle during time period A rather than during period B? Why won't the person take the snack this time and formulate a principle to snack all the time or, more generally, a principle always to give in to immediate temptation? But formulating and accepting such a principle (alongside the action of taking the snack now) will not itself bring reward immediately or maximize reward over time. It does generally reduce delay in reward. But during period B, facing one particular temptation, do I want *always* to reduce delay for any and every reward? No. For although I am in that B period with respect to one particular reward, with regard to many other (pairs of) rewards I am in the A period (or the C period). With regard to these other, more distant pairs of lesser and greater, I do not now want always to take the more immediate reward, even though I do now wish to take one *particular* reward that is more immediate because I am in *its* B period. It is because temptations are spread out over time that, at any *one* time, we are in more A (or C) periods than B periods. Hence we would not accept a principle always to succumb to temptation.*

By adopting a principle, we make one action stand for many others and thereby we change the utility or disutility of this particular action. This alteration of utilities is the result of exercising our power and ability to make one action *stand for* or *symbolize* others. Violating the principle this one time does not necessitate that we always will violate it: having this snack does not necessitate that we will become continual snackers. Before we adopted the principle it was not true that doing the act this one time would involve doing it always. Adopting the principle forges that connection, so that the penalty for violating the

---

* The proponent of succumbing to temptation may reply, "You are saying that we don't *want* always to succumb to temptation. But you say a principle is the device to get us past what may be our current desire. So perhaps we need a principle to get us past the desire not always to succumb to temptation." Leaving aside the skirting of paradox, a principle is (most easily) adopted during a time period t when a contrary desire is stronger than the temptation is during t. (The temptation will reach full strength later than t.) And there will not be a time period when the desire *always* to succumb is not weaker than a contrary desire. (Or if such a temporary period did arise, any principle adopted then soon would be overturned on the basis of a later desire that was not just momentary.)

principle this time becomes the disutility of violating it always. It would be instructive to investigate precisely *how* we are able to do this.

The fact that we *can* has important consequences. We can so alter utilities (by adopting a principle and making one act stand for others), but we cannot do this too frequently and make it stick. If we violate a particular principle we have adopted, we have no reason to think the next occasion will be any different than this one. If each occasion is the same, and we do it this time, won't we do it on such occasions always? Unless we can distinguish this occasion from the later ones, and also have reasons for believing that this distinction will carry weight with us *later* so that we won't indulge once again by formulating another distinction which again we won't adhere to still later, then doing the action this time will lead us to expect we will continue to repeat it. (To formulate a distinction that allows this one act yet excludes future repetitions is to formulate yet another principle; we must have more reason to think we will adhere to that one than to this, or the reformulating will give no credibility to our abstention in the future.) Doing the act this one time, in *this* situation, means we will continue to do it in the future. Isn't this enough to alter the utility now of doing it this one time, attaching to this particular act now the disutility of all its future repetitions?

We expect that if we do it this one time, we also will do it repeatedly in the future. But does our doing it this once actually *affect* the future; does it *make* it more likely that we will repeat the action? Or does this action simply affect our *estimate* of how likely that repetition is? There are two situations to consider. If no principle was adopted previously that excluded the action, doing the action now may have a minor effect on the probability of repetition in accordance with the psychologist's "law of effect": positive reinforcement of an action raises its probability of occurrence in the future. And the estimate of the probability of repetition may be raised somewhat if this action is added to a number of similar ones in the past. If a principle was adopted previously, acting in violation of the principle will raise an observer's estimate and the agent's own estimate too of how likely she is to repeat this particular act. Also, the violation makes it more likely that she will. The principle has broken down; one bar to the action has been removed. Moreover, realizing this may discourage the agent and make her less likely to exert effort to avoid the action in the future. (Notice that an action that affects *her estimate* of the probability of similar future actions may then produce discouragement and thereby affect the actual probability of repetition.) Formulating a principle that would constitute an additional bar to the actions it excludes is a way of actually tying the effects of all to the effects of any (previous) one. The more one has invested in a principle, the more effort previously exerted in adhering to it, the greater the cost in violating it now. (For how likely is it that you will continue to adhere to another principle if you couldn't manage to stick to this one despite so much effort?) Moreover, adhering to the principle this time is a type of action subject to the law of effect: positive reinforcement makes it more probable that adherence to that principle will occur in the future.

The effects of violating a principle may be more general still, for the probability or credibility that you will successfully adhere to *any* principles at all in *any* arena (when faced with a temptation as strong as the one that caused you to succumb this time) may be affected. To be sure, you may try to demarcate and limit the damage to this *one area*, but this presents the same problem—one level up—as the attempt to limit the damage *within* this area to just *this one* violative act. Deontological principles may have the greatest weight when their violation directly threatens *any* and all principled action in the future: if I violate *this* principle (in this circumstance), how can I believe I will succeed in adhering to any (desirable) principle ever again? Someone might try, in an excess of Kantian zeal, to increase the potential effect of spreading disaster by formulating a (meta-)principle never to violate any principle. But even though getting any violation to stand for all might lessen the probability of any given one, the actual consequences of the slightest violation would get dangerously magnified. This is not to say that one violation of a principle, because one act stands for all, discharges a principle so that the person then can violate it freely and with impunity. One act has the disutility of all, but then so does the next, even if that first act has been done. This disutility can be escaped by dropping the principle, not by violating it; but one then faces the very disutility that adopting the principle was designed to avoid.

Because adoption of a principle itself is an action that affects the probability linkages among other actions, some care is appropriate in choosing which principles to adopt. One must consider not only the possible benefits of adherence but also the probability of violation and the future effects that violation would have. It might be better to adopt a less good principle (when followed) but one easier to maintain, especially since that principle may not always be available as a credible fallback if one fails to adhere to the more stringent one. (Also, one wants to adopt a principle sharp enough to mark its violations clearly, so one's future self cannot easily fudge the issue of whether the principle is being followed.) No doubt, a theory of the optimal choice of principles could be formulated, taking such considerations into account.[25]

A principle typically speaks of all the actions in a group, and it makes each present act stand for all. To perform its function of getting one past temptations such as that of the B period, it must speak of *all* the actions of a certain kind. We do not have principles that say *most* **P**'s should be **Q**'s or 15 percent of **P**'s have to be **Q**'s. (Or, if we do, they are not designed to cope with the same temptations.) Sometimes, though, all we need is to perform an action some or most of the time (for example, skipping desserts most evenings, paying most of our bills each month). The way we achieve this through principles is nevertheless to formulate a statement that speaks of "all," "each," or "every" and yet is coextensive with the mix we desire. *Each* month, pay most of your bills; *every* week, skip desserts most evenings; each year, go to some general faculty meetings. A teacher—not myself—whose principle it is not to give very many A's grades *every* class on a curve. Thereby, each week or month or class comes to stand for all. Thus, we can explain why principles that serve to overcome temptation concern all the members of a class, not just some. (A norm could concern itself with n percent, where n is not 0 or 100, but a principle cannot.) A principle has certain functions, and for it to perform these, one instance must stand for or symbolize all. The observed "all"-character of principles thus provides support for our view of the functions that principles have and the ways they perform them.[26]

Principles may seem crude devices for accomplishing our goals; their universal coverage—giving up *all* desserts, *all* diversions until the task is done—may be more than is necessary to reach the goal. The leeway in what the "all" covers (desserts, weeks) mitigates this somewhat, narrowing the overkill of principles. Still, some drawbacks will remain. If there were a clear threshold of n repetitions of an action, past which the consequences of continuing that action thwart the goal but before which the goal still can be reached, wouldn't a rational person perform the action precisely n times and then stop? (A more complicated statement is needed if each repetition increases the difficulty of reaching the goal.) No principle would be needed to exclude the $n+1$th action, since that action itself would have bad consequences on balance. This might be a theory of (approximately) when the person decides to stop smoking (or gaining weight, and so on) and hence of when she decides to institute a principle. Yet, given temptation, it is a principle that needs to be instituted *then*.

Sunk Costs

One method Ainslie mentions for getting past the tempting time interval B is this: *commit* yourself during the earlier interval A to seeking the larger reward during C and during B. One mode of such commitment is, during A, to invest many resources in the (future) pursuit of that larger reward. If I think it would be good for me to see many plays or attend many concerts this year, and I know that when the evening of the performance arrives I frequently will not feel like rousing myself at that moment to go out, then I can buy tickets to many of these events in advance, even though I know that tickets still will be available at the box office on the evening of the performance. Since I will not want to waste the money I have already spent on the tickets, I will attend more performances than I would if I left the decisions about attendance to each evening. True, I may not use *all* of these tickets—lethargy may triumph on some evenings—yet I will attend more frequently than if no tickets had been purchased in advance. Knowing all this, I purchase the tickets in advance in order to drive myself to attend.

Economists present a doctrine that all decisionmaking should pay attention to only the (present and) future consequences of various alternative actions. The costs of past investments in these courses of action already have been incurred. Although existing resources may affect the consequences of the various actions now open before me—already possessing the ticket, I can attend the performance without any additional future payment—and hence be taken into account through these consequences, the mere fact that costs already have been borne to further a certain project should not carry any weight at all as a person makes a decision. These costs, "sunk costs" as the economists term them, are a thing of the past; all that matters now is the future stream of benefits. Thus, sitting at home this evening, if I now would prefer staying home to going out and attending a performance (for no monetary payment), then this evening at home has higher utility for me than traveling out and attending the performance; therefore I should stay at home. It should make no difference that I already have spent money on the ticket for the performance—so runs the economists' doctrine that sunk costs should be ignored.[27]

This may be a correct rule for the maximization of monetary profits, but it is not an appropriate general principle of decision, for familiar reasons. We do *not* treat our past commitments to others as of no account except insofar as they affect our future returns, as when breaking a commitment may affect others' trust in us and hence our ability to achieve other future benefits; and we do *not* treat the past efforts we have devoted to ongoing projects of work or of life as of no account (except insofar as this makes their continuance more likely to bring benefits than other freshly started projects would). Such projects help to define our sense of ourselves and of our lives.[28]

The particular issue we have been discussing indicates yet another defect in the doctrine of ignoring sunk costs as a general principle of decision. The fact that we do not ignore sunk costs provides one way to get past the temptation during period B to choose the smaller but more immediate reward. Earlier, during time interval A, when we can clearly see the benefits of the larger but more distant reward, we can sink resources and effort into achieving that reward, knowing that when the time of temptation comes the fact that we do not want (and will not want) to have wasted those resources will count for us as a reason against choosing the smaller reward, adding to its disutility. If I know I will be tempted some evening in the future by the smaller immediate reward of comfort (not having to go out into the rain, and so on), yet I also know that now and afterward too I will be happy to have attended all those performances, then I can buy the tickets now, in advance, to spur myself to forgo staying home when that evening arrives.

Everyone sees succumbing to the smaller reward during time interval B as a problem, an irrationality, or an undesirable shortsightedness. The person herself sees it that way—beforehand and later, if not right then—and we see it that way too as we think about it. The economist also regards another type of behavior, the honoring of sunk costs, as irrational and undesirable. But we now see that this latter behavior, anticipated in advance, can be used to limit and check the first type of undesirable behavior (that is, succumbing to the smaller but nearer reward). We can knowingly employ our tendency to take sunk costs seriously as a means of increasing our *future* rewards. If this tendency is irrational, it can be rationally utilized to check and overcome another irrationality. If someone offered us a pill that henceforth would make us people who *never* honored sunk costs, we might be ill advised to accept it; it would deprive us of a valuable tool for getting past temptations of the (future) moment. (Might such a tendency to honor sunk costs, which can be adaptive, have been selected for in the evolutionary process?) Since taking sunk costs into account sometimes is desirable (so the economists' general condemnation is mistaken) and sometimes is not, the desirability of taking such a pill would depend upon the comparative numbers of, and stakes within, these two types of encountered situations.

Earlier, I mentioned that the more effort one has put behind adherence to a principle designed to get past temptations of the moment, the greater is the cost in violating it now. It is unlikely that you will manage to stick to another principle if you could not stick to this one despite so much previous effort. Realizing this gives you much reason to hold on to this one—it's the one life raft in sight—and therefore gives great weight to not violating it in the face of this particular temptation. Groupings of actions (in order to avoid immediate temptation) that we have succeeded in following thereby gain a further tenacity. Notice that this involves a sunk cost phenomenon. My reasoning behind sticking to *this* principle and its associated grouping involved saying that, if I could not stick to it despite so much previous effort, how could I hope to stick to another? It is only if I am someone who honors sunk costs that I will be able to make this argument; only one who thus honors sunk costs would have a reason to adhere now to his current principle for bypassing temptation, rather than succumbing this one time and then formulating a different principle, which too will fall when its time comes, perhaps on its very first test. It is sunk costs that make *this* principle the place to take a stand. (Do not argue that these are future-regarding considerations about the future consequences of the two different courses of action—sticking to the present policy versus succumbing to the temptation and then formulating a new policy—and hence that the person who does not honor sunk costs can go through the same line of reasoning; it is only because of the known tendency to honor sunk costs that one course of action will have, and can be seen to have, consequences significantly different from those of the other. Otherwise, why think it is less likely that I will follow the new principle after violating the old one than that I will continue to adhere to the old principle if I don't violate it now?) Might the known phenomenon of our honoring sunk costs play some role in our following principles we have just adopted? We now know that if we can manage to adhere to this principle for some time, the fact that we will have invested in it will provide us in the future, as honorers of sunk costs, with reasons to continue to follow that principle then—and that may give us some reason now.[29]

To these functions performed by our honoring sunk costs the economist might reply that, for an otherwise perfectly rational person, honoring sunk costs is not desirable at all; only someone with some *other* irrationality should indulge in it. This conclusion is not so evident, however, even leaving aside what was mentioned earlier: commitments made to other persons and past investment in our projects of work and life. For it might be interpersonally useful to have a means of convincing others that we shall stick to projects or aims even in the face of threats that seem to make this adherence work to our future disadvantage—as a way of discouraging their making or carrying out such threats.[30] This might be useful even if you have no other tendency to irrational behavior and the others you are trying to convince have none either.[31] Yet the theme of countering or fencing in one irrationality with another is worth marking. Can some other things that we think irrational—perhaps weakness of will, self-deception, or fallacies of reasoning—consciously be put to use to thwart or limit still other irrationalities or undesirable happenings? (And could a total package of such apparently irrational tendencies even work better together than the *total* package of apparently—when separately considered—rational tendencies?)

Let me mention one other technique a person might use to carry herself over that tempting time interval B where the smaller reward looms so large. She might consider what action she would recommend to another person in that very situation, someone whose well-being she cares about, and then adopt that advice for herself. Distancing oneself from the situation, looking at the diagram impersonally instead of simply looking ahead from one time point, might be a way to defuse the allure of the otherwise nearer (but ultimately smaller) reward. This procedure requires an ability to look impersonally at a situation you are in and to think that the same principle of choice should apply to yourself as to others, that you should do the very same action another should do in that situation. A strong predisposition to such an impartial attitude would be extremely useful in surmounting the B interval of the crossed curves, hence in maximizing a person's total reward. And this very disposition constitutes one component of ethical judgment: to apply the same principles to one's own behavior as to that of others.

There is one function of principles I have not yet mentioned: *drawing the line*. Principles mark a boundary beyond which we will not step—"this is where I draw the line!"—and we think, "If I don't draw it here, where *will* I draw it?" There may be no other obvious place in a gradient of situations, no obvious place within acceptable territory. (Or there may be another acceptable place, but we feel we will not succeed in drawing the line there.) This point is connected to the earlier mentioned function of principles, getting one past the temptation of the moment. In this case, however, it is not temptation but rather the *reasoning* of the moment that needs to be gotten past. If I reach *that* point, I will reason that there is no special reason to stop just then, so I had better stop much beforehand, where there *is* a clear line and a *special* one.*

---

* Thomas Schelling's theory of coordination games might usefully incorporate this notion of specialness. In attempting to coordinate with another, I am searching for an action we both will think is special (yet also desirable), and both will realize we both think it special—not simply striking, but special. When there are ten alternatives, nine of them extremely striking, the special one might be the one that is not—at least at the first level—striking at all.

Here is a coordination problem. Each of us independently is to pick a German philosopher from a certain period, and if we both pick the same one, each of us receives a large prize. The philosophers to be chosen among are Kant, Hegel, Fichte, Schelling, and Jacobi. Which one do you choose?

This, I think, is what enables principles to define a person. *"These* are the lines I have drawn." It is these lines that limn/delineate him. They are his outer boundaries. A person in very fortunate circumstances, then, who knows he won't actually get taken very far along any undesirable gradient, may not have to draw any specific lines. Thus, in this sense, he may not be as well defined as someone in less fortunate circumstances.

Symbolic Utility

We have said that by adopting a principle, doing the particular short-sighted action this one time in this situation now means that we shall continue to do it in the future. This act *stands for* all the others that the principle excludes; doing this one *symbolizes* doing the rest. Is this fact of *meaning, standing for*, and *symbolizing* constituted by the intertwining of the two strands of connection between doing the act now and repeating it in the future that we already have discussed? (Doing it now affects your estimate of the probability of doing it again, and doing it now alters the very probability of doing it in the future.) Or is symbolizing a further fact, not exhausted by these two strands but one that itself affects the utility of alternative actions and outcomes? Symbolizing, I believe, is a further important strand, one that an adequate decision theory must treat explicitly.

Freudian theory explains the occurrence or persistence of neurotic actions or symptoms in terms of their symbolic meaning. Producing evident bad consequences, these apparently irrational actions and symptoms have a symbolic significance that is not obvious; they symbolize something else, call it M. Yet merely having such symbolic meaning cannot alone explain the occurrence or persistence of an action or symptom. We have to add that what these actions and symptoms symbolize—that is, M—itself has some utility or value (or, in the case of avoidance, disutility or negative value) for the person; and moreover, that this utility of the M which is symbolized is imputed back to the action or symptom, thereby giving *it* greater utility than it appeared to have. Only thus can an action's symbolic meaning explain why it was chosen or manifested. Freudian theory must hold not only that actions and outcomes can symbolize still further events for a person but also that they can draw upon themselves the emotional meaning (and utility values) of these other events. Having a symbolic meaning, the actions are treated as having the utility of what they symbolically mean; a neurotic symptom is adhered to with a tenacity appropriate to what it stands for. (I am not aware of a clear statement in the Freudian literature of this equation or of the weaker claim that *some* of the utility of what is symbolized is imputed back to the symbol, even though some such version is presupposed, I believe, in some Freudian explanations.) Disproportionate emotional responses to an actual event may indicate that it stands for other events or occasions to which the emotions are more suited.[32]

For the symbolic action to get done, it must somehow come to have a higher utility, a higher number that represents the maximand, than the other actions available to the agent.[33] I have suggested how that happens. The action (or one of its outcomes) symbolizes a certain situation, and the utility of this symbolized situation is imputed back, through the symbolic connection, to the action itself. Notice that standard decision theory also believes in an imputation back of utility, along a (probabilistic) causal connection. By virtue of producing a particular situation for sure, an action comes to have—to have imputed to it—the utility of that situation; by virtue of probabilistically producing certain situations, an action comes to have—to have imputed to it—their utilities in the form of an expected utility. What the current view adds is that utility can flow back, be imputed back, not only along causal connections but also along symbolic ones.

One mark that it is an action's symbolic connection to an outcome that plays a central role in the decision to do it, rather than the apparently causal connection—I am thinking of cases where the agent does not think the action is itself intrinsically desirable or valuable—is the persistence of the action in the face of strong evidence that it does not actually have the presumed causal consequence. Sometimes a person will even refuse to look at or countenance this evidence or other evidence about harmful consequences of the action or policy. (On these grounds, one might claim that certain antidrug enforcement measures *symbolize* reducing the amount of drug use and that minimum wage laws *symbolize* helping the poor.) A reformer who wishes to avoid such harmful consequences may find it necessary to propose another policy (without such consequences) that equally effectively symbolizes acting toward or reaching the goal. Simply halting the current action would deprive people of its symbolic utility, something they are unwilling to let happen.

Of course, to give a particular symbolic meaning to an action A has causal consequences of its own, as it affects which actions we perform, and a purely consequentialist theory can say something about that. It can speak of whether giving such symbolic meaning (or, later, refraining from extinguishing that symbolic meaning) is itself a causally optimal action. But this view will be different from that of a purely consequentialist (nonsymbolic) theory of the action A itself, and it does not imply that we must assess the act of bestowing or tolerating symbolic meaning solely by its causal consequences.

Since symbolic actions often are *expressive* actions, another view of them would be this: the symbolic connection of an action to a situation enables the action to be expressive of some attitude, belief, value, emotion, or whatever. Expressiveness, not utility, is what flows back. What flows back along the symbolic connection to the action is (the possibility of) expressing some particular attitude, belief, value, emotion, and so on. Expressing this has high utility for the person, and so he performs the symbolic action.[34]

There may not seem to be much difference between these two ways of structuring our understanding of why one chooses to perform a symbolic action. Each will give a different explanation of why a symbolic act is *not* done. For the first, wherein utility is imputed back to the action along the symbolizing connection, this presents a puzzle. Presumably the symbolizing connection always holds, so that an action of handwashing always symbolizes removing guilt or whatever. Because this situation symbolized, being guilt-free, presumably always has high utility, if utility is imputed back, why won't the action of handwashing always have maximal utility, so that the person will always be doing it? (Apparently, this does happen with some compulsive handwashers, but not with all, and not with all actions done because of their symbolic meaning.) The expressiveness theory says that the possibility of expressing some attitude toward being guilt-free is always present, as a result of the ever-present symbolic connection, but the utility of expressing this may vary from context to context, depending upon how recently or relevantly one has expressed it, what one's other needs and desires are, and so forth. The utility of expressing that attitude or emotion competes with other utilities. The utility imputation theory will describe this differently. The absolute or relative utility of the symbolized situation can fluctuate for the person; the utility of being guilt-free can actually become less if the person recently has taken steps to alleviate guilt—there now (temporarily) is less to deal with. Or the utility of being guilt-free can remain constant while the utility of other competing goods, such as eating, temporarily rises to become greater than the utility of removing guilt. Each of these structures for understanding symbolic expressiveness will have some utility fluctuate—a slightly different one. What I want to emphasize now is the *importance* of this symbolic meaning, however it is precisely structured.

When utility is imputed to an action or outcome in accordance with its symbolic meaning—that is, when the utility of an action or outcome is equated with the utility of what it symbolically means—we are apt to think this irrational. When this symbolic meaning involves repressed childhood desires and fears or certain current unconscious ones, it may well result in behavior doomed to be frustrating, unsatisfying, or tormenting. Yet mightn't symbolic meanings based upon unconscious desires also add gratifying reverberations to consciously desired goods? In any case, not all symbolic meanings will be rooted in Freudian material. Many of these others too, however, will look strange to someone outside that network of meanings. Recall the dire consequences some people bear in order to avoid "losing face" or the deaths people risked and sometimes met in duels to "maintain honor" or in exploits to "prove manhood." Yet we should not too quickly conclude that it would be better to live without any symbolic meanings at all or never to impute utilities in accordance with symbolic meanings.

Ethical principles codify how to behave toward others in a way that is appropriate to their value and to our fellow-feelings with them. Holding and following ethical principles, in addition to the particular purposes this serves, also has a symbolic meaning for us. Treating people (and value in general) with respect and responsiveness puts us "on the side of" that value, perhaps allying us with everything else on its side, and symbolizes our intertwining with this. (Does it symbolize this to a greater extent than it actually intertwines us, or does a welcomed symbolic connection constitute an actual intertwining?) Kant felt that in acting morally a person acts as a member of the kingdom of ends, a free and rational legislator. The moral action does not *cause* us to become a (permanent) member of that kingdom. It is what we would do as a member, it is an instance of what would be done under such circumstances, and hence it symbolizes doing it under those circumstances. The moral acts get grouped with other possible events and actions and come to stand for and mean them. Thereby, being ethical acquires a symbolic utility commensurate with the utility these other things it stands for actually have. (This depends, then, upon these further things actually having utility for the person—a contingency Kant would be loath to rely upon.) There are a variety of things that an ethical action might symbolically mean to someone: being a rational creature that gives itself laws; being a lawmaking member of a kingdom of ends; being an equal source and recognizer of worth and personality; being a rational, disinterested, unselfish person; being caring; living in accordance with nature; responding to what is valuable; recognizing someone else as a creature of God. The utility of these grand things, symbolically expressed and instantiated by the action, becomes incorporated into that action's (symbolic) utility. Thus, these symbolic meanings become part of one's reason for acting ethically. Being ethical is among our most effective ways of symbolizing (a connection to) what we value most highly.

A large part of the richness of our lives consists in symbolic meanings and their expression, the symbolic meanings our culture attributes to things or the ones we ourselves bestow.* It is unclear, in any case, what it would be like to live without any symbolic meanings, to have no part of the magnitude of our desires depend upon such meanings. What then would we desire? Simply material comfort, physical security, and sensual pleasure? And would no part of how much we desired these be due to the way they might symbolize maternal love and caring? Simply wealth and power? And would no part of how much we desired these be due to the way they might symbolize release from childhood dependence or success in competition with a parent, and no part either be due to the symbolic meanings of what wealth and power might bring? Simply the innate, unconditioned reinforcers evolution has instilled and installed in us, and other things only insofar as they are effective means to these? These had served to make our ancestors more effective progenitors or protectors of related genes. Should we choose this as our only purpose? And if we valued it highly, might we not value also whatever symbolized being an effective progenitor? "No, not if that conflicted with actually being one, and in any case one should value only actually bearing or protecting progeny and relatives, and the effective means to this that evolution has marked out, namely, the unconditioned reinforcers, and also the means to *these*." (Notice, though, that having instilled desires that serve to maximize inclusive fitness does not mean that evolution has instilled the desire to be maximally inclusively fit. Males now are not, I presume, beating at the doors of artificial insemination clinics in order to become sperm donors, even though that would serve to increase their inclusive fitness.) But why is actually leading to something so much better than symbolizing it that symbolization should not count at all? "Because that's the bottom line, what actually occurs; all the rest is talk." But why is this bottom line better than all other lines?

In any case, if we are symbolic creatures—and anthropology attests to the universal nature of this trait—then presumably evolution made us so. Therefore, the attractive pleasures of symbolization, and sym-

---

* Notice that symbolic meanings might not all be good ones, just as desires or preferences might not be. The point is that a theory of rationality need not *exclude* symbolic meanings. These do not guarantee good or desirable content, however. For that, one would need to develop a theory of which symbolic meanings and which preferences and desires were admissible, using that to constrain which particular meanings and desires could be fed into the more formal theory of rationality.

bolic satisfactions too, are as solidly based as the other innate re-inforcers. Perhaps a capacity for symbolization served to strengthen other desires or to maintain them through periods of deprivation in reinforcement by their actual objects. Whatever the evolutionary ex-planation, though, this capacity, like other cognitive capacities, is not mired in its original adaptive function. It can be employed in other valuable ways, just as mathematical capacities can be employed to ex-plore abstract number theory and theories of infinity, although this was not the function for which they were evolutionarily selected. Once the capacity for symbolic utility exists, it may enable us, for example, to achieve in some sense—that is, symbolically—what is causally or conceptually impossible, thereby gaining utility from that, and also en-able us to separate good features from bad ones they actually are linked with, gaining only the former through something that symbol-izes only them.

This is not to deny the dangers opened by symbolic meanings and symbolic utilities. Conflicts may quickly come to involve symbolic meanings that, by escalating the importance of the issues, induce vio-lence. The dangers to be specially avoided concern situations where the causal consequences of an action are extremely negative yet the positive symbolic meaning is so great that the action is done never-theless. (Recall the examples of compulsive handwashing and drug prohibition.) A rational person would seek an (almost) equally satis-fying symbolic alternative that does not have such dire actual con-sequences. (This does not imply, however, that symbolic meanings always should be subordinate to, and come lexicographically after, causally produced outcomes.) Sometimes a symbolic connection will be thought better than a causal one. If an outcome—such as harming someone in revenge—is desired but seen as bad, it may be better for a person to achieve this symbolically than to inflict actual damage.[35] It would be nice to discover a general structural criterion about the kinds of links that establish symbolic meanings that can distinguish the good symbolic meanings from the bad, but perhaps we must simply be vigilant in certain kinds of situation—conflict is one—to isolate and exclude particular symbolic meanings. It may help that many undesir-able symbolic meanings are not in equilibrium under knowledge of their causes; if we knew what gave rise to these meanings, or the role they are playing in our current actions, we would not want to act upon them.[36] Some symbolic meanings do withstand these tests (for exam-ple, the symbolic meaning of a romantic gesture to the person you love). Perhaps the crucial thing is to stay aware of when meanings and connections are symbolic ones, keeping separate track of these and not treating them (unknowingly) as causally real. This would help with the many Freudian symbolic meanings that, when they enter into conscious deliberation as symbolic, lose their power and impact (if they are sufficiently "worked through").[37]

Symbolic meaning also is a component of particular ethical decisions. It has been argued that the symbolic meaning of efforts to save a known currently threatened person—a trapped miner, for instance—or of refusing to make those efforts affects our decision in allocating resources to current efforts to save versus accident-prevention measures. (This issue has been termed one of "actual versus statistical lives.")[38] It also has been argued that the symbolic meaning of feeding someone, giving sustenance, enters into the discussion of the ways in which the lives of direly ill people permissibly may be terminated—turning off their artificial respirator but not halting their food and starving them to death.[39] The political philosophy presented in *Anarchy, State, and Utopia* ignored the importance to us of joint and official serious symbolic statement and expression of our social ties and concern and hence (I have written) is inadequate.[40]

We live in a rich symbolic world, partly cultural and partly of our own individual creation, and we thereby escape or expand the limits of our situations, not simply through fantasies but in actions, with the meanings these have. We impute to actions and events utilities coordinate with what they symbolize, and we strive to realize (or avoid) them as we would strive for what they stand for.[41] A broader decision theory is needed, then, to incorporate such symbolic connections and to detail the new structuring these introduce.

Among social scientists, anthropologists have paid the most attention to the symbolic meanings of actions, rituals, and cultural forms and practices and to their importance in the ongoing life of a group.[42] So elaborate is their work that it is somewhat embarrassing to introduce a relatively crude and undifferentiated notion of symbolic meaning. Still, this notion has its uses, not served by nuanced and textured discussions that do not easily connect with formal structures. By incorporating an action's symbolic meaning, its symbolic utility, into (normative) decision theory, we might link theories of rational choice more closely to anthropology's concerns. There are two directions in which such a linkage might go. The first, the upward direction, explains social patterns and structures in terms of individual choice behavior that incorporates symbolic utility. This, the methodological individualist and reductionist direction, is not the one I am proposing here.[43] The second, the downward direction, explains how the patterns of social meanings that anthropologists delineate have an impact within the actions and behavior of individuals, that is, through their decisions that give some weight to symbolic utility. (Some anthropologists, as a matter of professional pride, seem not to be concerned with how the cultural meanings they delineate are mediated in individual behavior.)

How does the symbolic utility of an action (or of an outcome) work? What is the nature of the symbolic connection or chain of connections? And in what way does utility, or the possibility of expressiveness, flow through this chain from the situations symbolized to the actions (or outcomes) that do the symbolizing? Notice first that symbolic meaning goes beyond the way in which the adoption of principles makes some actions stand for others. There, an action stood for other things of the same type—other actions—or for a whole group of these, while symbolic meaning can connect an action with things other than (a group of) actions, for instance, with being a certain sort of person, with the realization of a certain state of affairs.

Some useful and suggestive categories have been provided by Nelson Goodman.[44] According to Goodman, A *denotes* B when A refers to B; A *exemplifies* P when A refers to P and A is an instance of P, that is, is denoted by P (either literally or metaphorically); A *expresses* P when A refers to P and A has the property P figuratively or metaphorically (so that P figuratively denotes A), and in exemplifying P, A functions as an aesthetic symbol. These relations can be chained together. A *alludes to* B when A denotes some C and that C exemplifies B, or when A exemplifies some C and that C denotes B. Even longer chains are possible,[45] some of whose links will be figurative or metaphorical. These chains, and others, can connect an action to further and larger situations or conditions, the ones it can symbolically represent or allude to (and so on), and the utility of these larger situations then provides the action itself with a *symbolic utility* that enters into decisions about it. These chains need not be very long: when A is in the literal extension of a term P and B is in that term's metaphorical extension, A might have B as part of its symbolic meaning. Sometimes an action may symbolically mean something by being our best instantiated realization of that thing, the best we can do.[46]

In what particular way is the symbolic utility (or expressiveness) of an action determined by the utility of that larger situation to which the chain connects the action and by the nature of the chain itself? Do shorter chains transmit more utility/expressiveness from the larger situation to the action itself? Is more utility/expressiveness lost, the more linkages there are? Do different kinds of linkage transmit differing proportions of (or possibilities of expressing) the larger situation's utility? (I am assuming that the symbolic utility of an action cannot be greater than the utility of the larger situation it is connected to by the chain and that it can be less.) Do only some symbolic connections induce the imputation of utility back, and what determines which ones these are? These questions all arise about situations of choice under certainty; further issues arise about choice under risk or uncertainty. Is there a probabilistic discounting along some particular chains? Do some kinds of larger situations, even when they are not certain to occur, transmit their full utility back to the action that might yield them? And, of course, the very fact that an action has particular risks or uncertainties associated with it may give it a particular symbolic meaning and utility, perhaps connected with being a daring and courageous person or a foolhardy one. Sometimes, though, the presence of probabilities rather than certainty may remove a symbolic meaning altogether. It is *not* the case that a half or a one-tenth chance of realizing a certain goal always itself has half or one-tenth the symbolic utility of that goal itself—it need not symbolize that goal, even partially. Here is another reason why symbolic utilities must be treated as a separate component of a theory of decision and not simply incorporated within existing (causal and evidential) decision theories. For such symbolic utilities do not obey an expected value formula. We might attempt to understand and explain *certain* of the observed deviations from an expected value formula and from the associated axioms of decision theory by attributing these to the presence of symbolic utilities. I have in mind here the Allais paradox, the certainty effect, certain deviations from Savage's Sure Thing principle, and so forth. There is a symbolic utility to us of *certainty* itself. The difference between probabilities .9 and 1.0 is greater than that between .8 and .9, though this difference between differences disappears when each is embedded in larger, otherwise identical probabilistic gambles—this disappearance marks the difference as symbolic.* A detailed theory of symbolic utility

---

* Or is it simply that some numbers are more prominent and that utility is affected by this prominence? Double-digit inflation has the symbolic meaning of inflation out of control, so there is more concern about a rise from 9 percent to 10 percent than from 16 percent to 17 percent; if we counted in base eleven, the (symbolic) line would be fixed elsewhere. In *Anarchy, State, and Utopia*, I commented on the significance of *eliminating* a problem completely, so that there is a greater difference between reducing the number of instances of an evil from one to zero than there is in reducing the number from two to one. I referred to this as a mark of an ideologue (p. 266); it is better seen as a mark of symbolic meaning.

Notice that the certainty effect, when it occurs, requires that utility be measured by a slightly different procedure than the usual one. In the usual procedure, two outcomes x and z are assigned utility numbers ordered in accordance with the preference between them, and the utility of any third thing y is found in accordance with the Archimedean condition. This conditions says that when x is preferred to y and y is preferred to z, then there is a unique probability p (between 0 and 1 exclusive) such that the person is indifferent between y for sure and an option consisting of a probability p of x and a probability $(1 - p)$ of z. When the person is fully satisfying all the Von Neumann–Morgenstern

awaits development. What we can do now is mark a place for it within the structure of a more general theory of decision, a place I will say more about in the next chapter.

Teleological Devices

Principles help you to discover the truth by transmitting evidential support or probability from some cases to others. Principles also help you to overcome temptation by transmitting utility from some actions to others. Principles are transmission devices for probability and for utility.*

Principles have various functions and effects: intellectual, intrapersonal, personal, and interpersonal. This is not to say that they have these effects in every possible situation. A temperature regulatory mechanism will work only within a certain range of temperature; beyond that range it will not be able to bring temperature back, and, depending upon its material, it may even melt or freeze. Why didn't evo-

---

conditions, there will be no problem; but when the certainty effect occurs, that intermediate certain option y will be assigned a misleading utility. A better procedure might be to measure utility without considering any certain outcomes, by embedding all of the preceding within canonical probability mixtures, for instance, with probability $1/2$. The person then would be asked to find the probability p such that he is indifferent between a $1/2$ chance of nothing and a $1/2$ chance of y, and a $1/2$ chance of nothing and a $1/2$ chance of (a probability p of x and a probability $1 - p$ of z). Thereby we control for the certainty effect. Of course, such a procedure can work only if it is not sensitive to the particular probability, in this example $1/2$, within the canonical probability mixture. It would have to be the case that the same results would be gotten with a wide variety of probabilities within the canonical mixture, perhaps with all but those within ε of 0 or 1.

* Must all principles transmit only one or the other of these, or can some principles transmit both? Should we speculate that there is *one* thing that all principles transmit, namely $p_i \times u^i$, probability *and* utility? There is no single term within decision theory to denote this weighted sum, $p_i \times u^i$, despite their very frequent travel together *as a unit*. Indeed, formal theories have to institute very particular procedures to disentangle them, procedures that frequently assume they have been successfully disentangled in specific cases and then employ devices to extend this to situations in general. We might learn something interesting by treating probability and utility as part of one integrated quantity—call it importance—and not separating these components too soon, by investigating what conditions this integrated quantity satisfies. (But is there an asymmetry at the beginning between the components, in that importance can be embedded in *probability* mixtures? Do we need to investigate the corresponding possibilities of utility mixtures, which may magnify or diminish the constituent importances? And might a temporal factor be included in the combination to begin with, only later to be abstracted out as a component? Is time-preference primarily a matter concerning probability or utility, or does temporal distance itself constitute a diminution in importance? Does the extension of a utility in time—not its displacement in time—magnify its importance?)

lution give us better regulatory mechanisms for body temperature? Given the small probability that such extreme cases will arise, that would be too costly in terms of energy and attendant sacrifice in other functions. A mechanism can perform its function pretty well, well enough, even if it will not work for some of the situations that might arise. Similarly for principles.

In order to justify a principle, you specify its function and show that it effectively performs that function and does this more effectively than others would given the costs, constraints, and so forth. We also can ask about the desirability of that function. Why should *anything* do that? A justification will show (or assume) that the function is desirable and does not interfere with other more desirable functions. Fully specified, a justification of a principle *P* is a decision-theoretic structure, with the principle *P* occupying the place of an action, competing with specific alternatives, having certain probabilities of reaching certain goals with certain desirabilities, and so on. (Our earlier discussion of factors that would be considered by a theory of the optimal choice of principles would fit into this decision-theoretic, teleological framework.)

A principle can be designed to cope with certain situations or to protect against *particular* dangers, such as giving in to temptations of the moment, favoring one's own interests, believing what one wants to be true. Hence, someone who doesn't face those dangers might have no need for *those* principles. And there might be devices other than principles to cope with such dangers. (Might a person cope with favoring her own interests not only through principles but also through empathic interaction with others and imaginative, full projection into their situations?)

We might ask whether the device of general principles itself has its *own* biases or defects. Putting things in terms of decision theory enables us to see principles as devices (that are supposed) to have certain effects—their functions—and hence not only to compare some principles with others but also to compare principles with other devices. Some goals might be impossible or very difficult for principles to reach, whereas other means might reach *those* goals more easily.

If one important goal is living together without a conflict so intense that it tears apart and destroys valuable social institutions, then when contending parties strongly put forward incompatible principles there may be no way to resolve that conflict by bringing the parties to agree to any third principle, much less to either of the original two. What may be needed is some compromise—but compromise is just what principles are not supposed to do! Hence a leader of an institution or a country may simply try to keep things going, to work out some arrangement to damp down people's fury so that institutional life can continue. To be sure, there may be a principle that recommends doing this, a principle to be applied to every situation of serious principled conflict that threatens to rend and make dysfunctional valuable institutions. The particular content of the compromise, however, may simply be determined by what the contending forces, given their respective powers, can manage to live with. That compromise need not itself be determined by principle in the sense that its details are taken to set a precedent for other similar situations.

This is not to recommend that political and institutional leaders be unprincipled. Perhaps they are to be principled in their decisions and actions except in those rare situations where the above-stated principle mandating (unprincipled) compromise comes into effect. (However, looking at the structure of the United States government, there seems to be a different division: some types of decisions—those made by the judiciary—are held to require principles, while the details of other decisions—those of the chief executive and legislature—generally are left to the play of various forces, with some oversight by the judiciary to ensure that certain general principles are not violated.) The only point I wish to make here is that the teleological device of principles may not be suited to each and every purpose.

Does this mean, then, that we must employ some principle to decide when to invoke a principle? And what makes *that* situation one to be guided by principles rather than by something else? The view that says everything is to be decided upon principle may happily propose that too as a principle. But is the view that says some things but not others should be decided upon principle a principled view itself—and must it be? Is there a *presumption* in favor of deciding things by principle that can be overcome by specific reasons favoring some other mode in that situation? If not, won't deciding some particular case on the basis of principle raise the question of why it was *principle* that was appealed to *then*? Might that have been done to bias the particular choice away from the result that some other mode would have produced? Or is there no presumption but simply a decision-theoretic account of when principles are appropriate, an account that itself uses some principle of decision theory and presupposes that for this one case at least, deciding when principles are appropriate, it is appropriate to use some principle, one of decision theory.

Another reason for thinking that principles of action have a teleological function is this. An actual case, for instance Nazi Germany, may thoroughly undermine or refute a principle P that would countenance or allow that. But why wasn't the hypothetical example enough? In 1911 couldn't one say: Principle P would allow, or even in certain circumstances would require, (somethng like) Nazi Germany. Therefore, P is false, unacceptable, evil?

However, if principles are only supposed to cover the cases that will, would, and could arise, then before the fact, if it is thought such a case is impossible (that the situation, motivations, or whatever that would lead to it could not arise or succeed), it might not be considered a *relevant* counterexample to that or any principle. But once it is discovered that human nature *can* do that—because it *did*—then the principle *P* that countenances it is refuted.

The consequences of people accepting and acting upon a principle can discredit the principle. "They acted on the principle *P*, and look at the horrendous situation to which that led." Someone else might say that they took the principle too far or took it in a wrong direction, that the principle itself did not *require* what they did. Nevertheless, the principle *P* is discredited. When everyone is revolted by the earlier consequences of following *P*, it is difficult for someone to say, "Let's follow *P* again, but this time in the right way." Why? Is it because *P* so easily *lent itself* to that way of acting, even when it didn't require that? That's what accepting *P* leads to when people, as people actually are, follow it.[47] If a principle is a device for having certain effects, it is a device for having those effects *when it is followed*; so what actually happens when it is followed, not just what it *says*, is relevant in assessing that principle as a teleological device.

But aren't principles also basic truths, which aid our understanding by subsuming instances (à la Hempel) and hence explaining why they hold? Here, again, principles might be considered to be devices with the *epistemological* function of producing understanding, and so even here we can ask (decision-theoretically) whether there are other routes to understanding, whether these others are better suited for some contexts or subjects, and so forth.

But might principles be what makes the particular truths true, what gives rise to them, in which case the primacy of principles would be *ontological*? If this does not simply repeat the epistemological function—we understand the particular truths best through principles—and if "giving rise to" is not a temporal relation and "makes it true" not a causal relation, then it is not clear exactly what the ontological thesis claims. In any case, we need not deny that the formulation of principles (of mathematics, of natural phenomena, of psychology) can bring coherence to these phenomena and depth to our understanding, whether the relation between the phenomena and the principles be ontological, epistemological, or some mixture. Hence, there is a further intellectual function to principles other than the one we began with—the transmission of support and probability—namely, to deepen and unify and make explicit our understanding of what the principles concern. (This function will produce tighter relations of support and probability. Might these *constitute* rather than result from the increased understanding?) The formulation of moral principles, thus, could deepen our understanding of moral action or moral facts and phenomena. Here, though, moral principles would have a status no different from the physical or psychological ones that describe phenomena but which there is no evident reason to act *on*. It might be said that although correct moral principles hold true—in that they *ought* to be followed—the only way to get them realized, that is, to be true of our actual behavior, is to try to follow them, to act *on them*. This is an empirical claim, one that would require evidence. Perhaps the principles we are able to formulate and follow are so far from what correct moral principles— more complex moral truths—would require that we would better conform to the latter by following routes other than trying to act on principle. It is, after all, an empirical question. In any case, that makes acting on principle, once again, a teleological device.

The term *principles* often is used to refer to something deeper and more general than rules. The principles are the general outlines within which the details find a place. In negotiations of agreements, these general outlines can be guidelines: the parties first agree to the principles that will govern the peace treaty between countries, the merger between corporations, the new school that will be established, and the details follow later. Agreeing to this general framework of principles can save time later if choices about details must be made only among alternatives that fit these general principles, so that not every possibility gets discussed and debated, not every issue gets reopened, and the agreed-upon principles themselves can be appealed to in resolving disputes. But the generality of principles is not confined to guiding actions. Titles of textbooks announce that they present the principles of economics or physics or psychology, the framework of general statements within which the details of the subject find their subordinate place. Perhaps there is guidance here too: the principles presented will guide readers' understanding of the subject's details.

If our cognitive abilities were limited in certain ways, there could be a difference between the principles that could guide our understanding of a subject and the true general statements (or laws) that underlie all the facts of the subject. The latter generalities might be too complex for us to understand, derive consequences from, or fit details within. Which, then, would be the principles of (for example) physics: the reasonably accurate generalities that we can understand and fit much within, or the precisely true and all-encompassing statements that we cannot comprehend or work with?

The Kantian tradition tends to hold that principles function to guide the deliberation and action of self-conscious, reflective creatures;

hence, principles have a theoretical and a practical function. We are creatures who do not act automatically, without any guidance. We could imagine having automatic guidance—would that make principles completely otiose for us?—or, more to the point, acting in a way that does not utilize guidance, for instance, at random. (Would acting completely at random suffice to free us from the domain of causality, the function Kant reserves for principles?) Doesn't this show that the purpose of principles is to guide us to something, whatever that is, that we would not reach by acting at random? And doesn't that leave principles as teleological devices? Kant, however, would also hold that principles are an expression of our rational nature, constitutive of rationality. To think or act rationally just is to conform to (certain kinds of) principles. Hence it would be a mistake to look only for the extrinsic *functions* that principles serve. If principles are something only a rational agent can formulate and employ, and if being rational is something we value, then following principles can symbolize and express our rationality. Principles thus might have high utility for us, not because of what their use leads to, but because of what that use symbolizes and expresses. To that extent, principles would not be solely teleological devices. But there would remain the question of why we so value our rational nature, and the acting on principles and reasons that expresses this, if our rational nature serves no further purpose. Why does the buck stop there?

Why are principles so intimately connected with rationality? And why do we value rationality? To speak of something, an action or belief, as rational is to assess the reasons for which it was done or held (and also the way in which the person took account of the reasons *against* doing or believing that). If reasons are, by their nature, general, and if principles capture the notion of acting *for* such general reasons—so that the person is committed to acting thus in other relevantly similar circumstances also—then to act or think rationally, one must do so in accordance with principles. But why should we believe or act rationally? One answer would be that we *are* rational, we have the capacity to act rationally, and we value what we are.[48] But if we are to step beyond simple self-praise, mustn't we invoke the functions served by believing or acting rationally? And why must reasons be general? Compare them with their most similar nongeneral relatives. To explain why we should use reasons rather than these alternatives, we must again invoke the functions of reasons.

Thus, the question turns from one about principles to one about rationality. What are reasons for? What is the function of rationality? Is rationality itself wholly teleological, wholly instrumental? These questions impel the later chapters.

II

DECISION-VALUE

A N ELABORATE THEORY of rational decision has been developed by economists and statisticians, and put to widespread use in theoretical and policy studies. This is a powerful, mathematically precise, and tractable theory. Although its adequacy as a description of actual behavior has been widely questioned, it stands as the dominant view of the conditions that a rational decision should satisfy: it is the dominant normative view. I believe this standard decision theory needs to be expanded to incorporate explicitly considerations about the symbolic meaning of actions, along with other factors. A useful entry into the inadequacies of the current standard theory is provided by Newcomb's Problem. My aim is to formulate a broadened decision theory to handle and encompass this problem adequately, and then to apply that broadened theory to illuminate the Prisoner's Dilemma, a problem that incisively sharpens issues about rational social cooperation and whether coercion (sometimes) is necessary to sustain this, and thus has propelled so much formal social theory recently.

Newcomb's Problem

Newcomb's Problem is well known, and I shall describe it only briefly here.* A being in whose power to predict your choices correctly you have great confidence is going to predict your choice in the following situation. There are two boxes, B1 and B2. Box B1 contains $1,000; box B2 contains either $1,000,000 ($M) or nothing. You have a choice between two actions: (1) taking what is in both boxes; (2) taking only what is in the second box. Furthermore, you know, and the being knows you know, and so on, that if the being predicts you will take what is in both boxes, he does not put the $M in the second box; if the being predicts you will take only what is in the second box he does put the $M in the second box. First the being makes his prediction; then he puts the $M in the second box or not, according to his prediction; then you make your choice.

* The problem was thought of by William Newcomb, a physicist, told to me by a mutual friend, and (with Newcomb's permission) first presented and discussed in Robert Nozick, "Newcomb's Problem and Two Principles of Choice," in *Essays in Honor of C. G. Hempel*, ed. N. Rescher et al. (Dordrecht: Reidl, 1969), pp. 114–146.

The problem is not only to decide what to do but also to understand precisely what is wrong with one of the two powerful arguments that conflict. The first argument is this: if you take what is in both boxes, the being almost certainly will have predicted this and will not have put the $M in the second box, and so you will almost certainly get only $1,000; whereas if you take only what is in the second box, the being almost certainly will have predicted that and will have put the $M into the second box, and so you will almost certainly get $M. Therefore, you should take only what is in the second box. The second argument is this: the being already has made his prediction and has already either put the $M into the second box or has not. The $M is either already sitting in the second box, or it is not, and which situation obtains is already fixed and determined. If the being has already put the $M in the second box, then if you take what is in both boxes you will get $M plus $1,000; whereas if you take only what is in the second box you will get just $M. If the being has not put the $M in the second box, then if you take what is in both boxes you will get $1,000; whereas if you take only what is in the second box you will get no money at all. In either case, whether the $M has been placed in there or not, you will receive more money, $1,000 more, by taking what is in both boxes. (Taking what is in both boxes, as it is said, *dominates* taking only what is in the second.) Therefore, you should take what is in both boxes.

Since 1969, when I first presented and discussed this problem, there has been much detailed investigation and illuminating theorizing about it.[1] In my initial essay, I distinguished those conditional probabilities that mark an action's *influencing* or *affecting* which state obtains from mere conditional probabilities that mark no such influence, and I suggested that, when it conflicts with the dominance principle, the principle of maximizing conditional expected utility should not be invoked if its conditional probabilities were of the second (nonaffecting, noninfluencing) sort. I supported this by intuitive examples. (These, because of an attempt to incorporate a certain reflexivity, are somewhat more complicated than the examples discussed by others afterward.) Linked genetic predispositions to a disease and to a career choice should not, I argued, lead someone to avoid one career since this raises the estimate of her chances of getting the disease—whether she actually does have that genetic makeup or will actually get the disease is not *influenced* or *affected* by the career choice. It did not occur to me to use this theme for the full and systematic development of competing versions of decision theory, causal and evidential, with their differing versions of the expected utility principle and even their differing versions of the dominance principle.[2]

The traditional principle of maximizing expected utility treats the expected utility of an action A, $EU(A)$, as the weighted sum of the utilities of its (exclusive) possible outcomes, weighted by their probabilities, which sum to 1.

$$EU(A) = \text{prob}(O_1) \times u(O_1) + \text{prob}(O_2) \times u(O_2) + \ldots + \text{prob}(O_n) \times u(O_n),$$

$$= \sum_{(i=1)}^{n} \text{prob}(O_i) \times u(O_i).$$

A more adequate principle, noticing that the outcomes need not be probabilistically independent of the actions, specifies the expected utility as weighted not by the simple probabilities of the outcomes but by the conditional probabilities of the outcomes given the actions. Call this the evidentially expected utility of A, $EEU(A)$.[3]

$$EEU(A) = \text{prob}(O_1/A) \times u(O_1) + \text{prob}(O_2/A) \times u(O_2) + \ldots + \text{prob}(O_n/A) \times u(O_n),$$

$$= \sum_{(i=1)}^{n} \text{prob}(O_i/A) \times u(O_i).$$

The causal decision theorists too use not simply the unconditional probability of the outcome but a probability relating the outcome to the action, this time not simply the conditional probability, $\text{prob}(O_i/A)$, but some causal-probabilistic relation indicating direct causal influence. The corresponding formula with these causal probabilities states the causally expected utility of act A, $CEU(A)$.

Despite these and other technical elaborations—backtracking subjunctives, explicit incorporation of tickles and meta-tickles, the ratifiability of decisions, and so forth—and despite attempts to show that the problem is irremediably ill defined or incoherent,[4] the controversy continues unabated. No resolution has been completely convincing.

Newcomb's Problem is a complicated one, other cases involve still further complications, the reasoning seems quite compelling on *all* sides—and we are fallible creatures. It would be unreasonable to place absolute confidence in any one particular line of reasoning for such cases or in any one particular principle of decision.*

---

* Some years ago in a graduate seminar, several students, particularly David Cope, queried how anyone could be certain either of causal or of evidential decision theory, given the strong arguments on both sides. I am grateful for this discussion, for it set me along the following train of thought. (But Howard Sobel writes me to say that things are not symmetrical, for it is only the causal theorists who have tried to produce arguments on their own side *and* to diagnose the [purported] errors of the opposing arguments, in line with the desideratum I proposed in my original article.)

The amount in the first box, the $1,000, has received little attention.[5] If the dominance argument—the second argument above—is correct, then you will be better off taking what is in both boxes even when the amount of money in the first box is much smaller, one dollar for example, or even one cent or a 1/10,000th chance of one cent. However, few of us would choose both boxes in such a case, granting *no* force to the other argument that if we take only what is in the second box we are almost certain to get $M. On the other hand, if the first argument above is correct and is understood as an expected utility argument (with the embedded conditional probabilities not needing to express any influence), then the amount of money X in the first box could be much larger than $1,000, yet the person would still choose to take only what is in the second box. Let us assume that the probability of the being correctly predicting your action (for each choice you might make) is .99. Where u denotes the utility function, the expected utility of taking only what is in the second box is $.99u(\$M)$, while the expected utility of taking what is in both boxes is $.99u(X) + .01u(\$M + X)$. If we suppose that the utility of money is linear with its amount in this range, then this expected utility of taking what is in both boxes is $u(X) + .01u(\$M)$. In this case, the expected utility of taking only what is in the second box will be greater than the expected utility of taking what is in both boxes if $.99u(\$M)$ is greater than $u(X) + .01u(\$M)$—that is, if $.98u(\$M)$ is greater than $u(X)$. On the assumption, then, that utility is linear with the amount of money, the person will choose to take only what is in the second box whenever the amount in the first box is less than $980,000. So, for example, in a choice problem having the same structure as Newcomb's Problem but where the first box contains $979,000 and the second box, as before, contains $M or nothing, the person would not take the contents of both boxes but only what is in the second box. No doubt, the utility of money is not linear with its amount in this range, but this is no great distortion for our purposes— it is the utility of $M+X$ that will be proportionally less than its monetary amount. The general point holds nevertheless: for very large amounts of money in the first box, $900,000 for example, provided the being is highly accurate in his predictions, a proponent of the first argument would take only what is in the second box. Few of us, however, would feel comfortable following the first argument in this case, granting *no* force to the other argument that we are better off in either case by taking what is in both boxes.

By varying the amount of money in the first box, we can make people extremely uncomfortable with their otherwise favored argument for choice in Newcomb's initial problem. People who initially chose both boxes are unwilling to follow the dominance argument when the amount in the first box is lowered to \$1; people who initially chose only the second box are unwilling to follow the expected utility argument (with conditional probabilities that do not mark influence) when the amount in the first box is raised to \$900,000. This suggests that no one has *complete* confidence in the argument he or she follows for Newcomb's initial example. No one is willing, unreservedly and across the board, to apply the reasoning that seems to move him or her in that case.

A person might have differing amounts of confidence in various principles of decision (and their associated arguments). For the moment we can restrict ourselves to just the two principles of maximizing (conditionally) expected utility, as these are formulated by causal decision theory and by evidential decision theory. These differing amounts of confidence might be represented by degrees of confidence between 0 and 1 inclusive that sum to 1, or by degrees that do not sum to 1 (leaving open the possibility that both of the principles are incorrect for a given case), or by confidence-weightings that are not degrees between 0 and 1. For some particular person, let Wc be the weight he or she gives to the expected utility principle of causal decision theory, and let We be the weight he or she gives to the expected utility principle of evidential decision theory. Let $CEU(A)$ be the causally expected utility of act A, the utility of that act as it would be computed in accordance with (some favored one of the versions of) causal decision theory; let $EEU(A)$ be the evidentially expected utility of act A, the utility of that act as it would be computed in accordance with evidential decision theory. Associated with each act will be a decision-value DV, a weighted value of its causally expected utility and its evidentially expected utility, as weighted by that person's confidence in being guided by each of these two kinds of expected utility.

$$DV(A) = Wc \times CEU(A) + We \times EEU(A).$$

And the person is to choose an act with maximal decision-value.[6]

I suggest that we go further and say not merely that we are uncertain about which *one* of these two principles, CEU and EEU, is (all by itself) correct, but that both of these principles are legitimate and each must be given its respective due. The weights, then, are not measures of uncertainty but measures of the legitimate force of each principle. We thus have a *normative* theory that directs a person to choose an act with maximal decision-value.

A maximizer of decision-value, if he gives nonzero weights to Wc and to We, will be led to shift his choice in Newcomb's Problem: from one box to two when the amount in the first box is raised sufficiently;

from two boxes to one when the amount in the first box is lowered sufficiently. Such changes are predictable for maximizers of decision-value. (Thus, the theory of maximizing *DV* has testable, qualitative, behavioral consequences, at least for those who conform to that normative theory.)

There are many different mathematical structures that would give *CEU* and *EEU* a role, but the *DV* formula is especially simple, and it would be premature to look now at anything more complicated. Of course, the weighted *DV* structure, all by itself, does not give anyone much guidance. How great should the weights be? Must a person use the same weights in all decision situations, or might the weights vary for different types of decision situation or, more systematically, according to where a decision situation falls along some dimension *D*— the further to the left the more plausible the use of one of the decision criteria (and hence the greater weight it receives), the further to the right the more plausible the use of the other one? I would welcome a theory to specify or restrict the weights, just as I would welcome a theory to specify or restrict prior probabilities within a Bayesian structure and one to specify or restrict the substantive content of preferences within the usual ordering axioms. Still, in each case the general structure can be illuminating.

That some weight is to be given to both factors, *CEU* and *EEU*, means that *EEU* will receive some weight even in decisions about cases where there is no causal influence of the act upon the relevant outcome, for example, the cases where a choice of a career indicates (but does not affect) differing probabilities of catching or already having a terrible disease. In my original article I thought it absurd to give such considerations any weight. Yet I knew that the evidential component of the *DV* formula has had major social consequences in human history, as the literature on Calvinism and the role that its view of *signs* (though not causes) of election played in the development of capitalism attests. (It can be a causal consequence of an action that a person believes something that act indicates but does not cause and is made happy by this belief. But someone who introduces this as a reason for doing the action must take care about countenancing such happy consequences as a reason for holding the belief.[7])

Theorists of rationality have been intent upon formulating the one correct and complete set of principles to be applied unreservedly in all decision situations. But they have not yet reached this—at any rate, we do not have complete confidence that they have. In this situation, won't a prudent and rational individual hedge her bets? I want to say more, namely, that no one of the principles alone is wholly adequate— it's not simply that we have yet to find the knockdown argument for the one that is correct. I do not say that the framework of decision-value alone will bring theorists to agree. They will continue to differ in the weights they assign to the specific decision principles, even were they to agree about which principles should be included. It is this dis-agreement about weights that explains the differing choices in Newcomb's Problem, but it is the fact that we do give *weights* (rather than sole allegiance to one principle) that explains the switching of the decision as the amount in the first box is varied. The *DV* structure represents the fact that each principle *EEU* and *CEU* captures legitimate reasons (of a sort), and we do not want to dismiss completely either sort.[8]

It is somewhat strange that writers on decision theory generally have shown such confidence in their views. For if we formulate the issue about the correct principle of decision as a decision problem, one about which principle of decision should be followed[9]—we might imagine that pills have been developed that can transform us into consistent followers of each principle—then it is not obvious what the contending principles of decision will answer. In particular, it is not obvious whether each will put itself forward as the preferred alternative. That depends upon what the world will be like. If it will offer many situations like Newcomb's Problem, with significant payoffs, then taking the *EEU* pill can be predicted to have better *causal* consequences, so that the *CEU* principle will recommend taking the *EEU* pill rather than the *CEU* pill. If on the other hand the world will offer many significant situations with the structure of my disease example or the many similar ones (Gibbard and Harper's Solomon example, and so on),[10] then the person following the *EEU* principle (without any "tickle" addition) will frequently forgo significant benefits (because of the misfortunes they portend). Since this can be predicted, the *EEU* principle itself will recommend taking the *CEU* pill as an act that has higher *EEU* utility than does taking the *EEU* pill. (In this case, the *CEU* principle also recommends taking the *CEU* pill. Is there an example where the *EEU* of taking the *CEU* pill is higher—and so the *EEU* principle recommends that—although the *CEU* of taking the pill is not higher, and so the *CEU* principle does not recommend taking it? Difficulties then would abound.) Just as there is no one particular inductive policy, no one Carnapian *c*-function, that is best or most effective no matter what the character of the world, so there may be no one best principle of rational decision.[11] And just as we want our inductive procedures to allow for learning, to contain parameters that get specified through some experience of the world, so too we want our principles of rational decision to contain parameters that can be specified to fit the discovered character of the world in which decisions are to be made. (In each case, evolution may have accomplished a significant part of the setting of parameters to fit the actual world, but this does not mean that we should expect our specific inductive policies or decision principles to be applicable in every imaginable science-fiction situation or that we should treat them as valid a priori.) The framework of decision-values, with its incorporated weights that can be altered over time, is one way that a fitting to the actual world can be accomplished.

The decision-value we specified was based upon the components *CEU* and *EEU*, but any alternative plausible principle of decision, or factor in decision, might be added as a term with its own associated weight. In particular, we could add to the formula the symbolic utility of an action, its *SU*, which incorporates the utility of the various outcomes and actions *symbolized* by the act, with its own associated weight *Ws*. (It is best not to try to incorporate symbolic utility alongside other utilities, because it may well not obey an expected value formula and because we might want to keep separate track of symbolic utility, since we think it appropriate to give this factor different weight in different kinds of choice situations.) The formula for the decision-value of *A*, *DV(A)*, then would become:

$$DV(A) = Wc \times CEU(A) + We \times EEU(A) + Ws \times SU(A).$$

It would be instructive to investigate the formal characteristics of this decision-value structure, it would not be surprising if this principle of weighted combination, like other criteria previously investigated in the literature of decision under uncertainty, sometimes failed to exhibit certain desirable features.[12]

Symbolic utility is not a different kind of utility, standing to standard utility in something like the way that metaphorical meaning stands to literal. Rather, symbolic utility is a different kind of *connection*—symbolic—to the familiar kind of utility. It stands alongside the already familiar connections, the causal and the evidential. The symbolic utility of an action *A* is determined by *A*'s having symbolic connections to outcomes (and perhaps to other actions) that themselves have the standard kind of utility, just as the *CEU* of *A* is determined by *A*'s causal-probabilistic connections to outcomes with the standard utility.*

---

* One further condition therefore needs to be imposed on the standard situation for measuring utility discussed in the footnote on pp. 34–35. That situation must be one where the actions have no relevant evidential or symbolic connections to utility outcomes. Utility is to be calibrated in causal contexts, where an expected-value principle is followed, and the (sanitized) utilities thus found are to be utilized in situations where actions also stand in evidential and symbolic connections to valued outcomes. However, the value of these latter outcomes is measured in situations that are wholly causal.

Should we ensure that these types of connection—causal, evidential and symbolic—are exclusive? The earlier formula for DV specified it as a weighted sum of CEU and EEU. Yet the EEU of an action includes its causal components, since the conditional probabilities of outcomes given actions, prob(O/A), which the EEU theorist utilizes, incorporate causal influences when such exist. In our weighted sum formula, then, should we not interpret the EEU as the expected utility represented by those (portions of) probabilities that are *not* (simply derivative from) causal ones? And similarly, shouldn't the symbolic utility SU of an action be its symbolic utility that is not (simply) derivative from and represented within those very causal and evidential connections?[13]

Should we incorporate still further components into the DV structure? One suggestion would be explicitly to include a component concerning the way an action fits into a person's self-image and is self-expressive. In fact, our three components already cover much of this territory. Although performing an action of the sort that would be done by a certain kind of person may not *cause* the agent to be this kind of person, it may symbolize his being that way, be some evidence that he is, and have the causal consequence of making it easier for him to maintain an *image* of himself as being of that kind. This last is a real causal consequence of an action and may have significant utility. Hence this kind of consequence—how doing a particular action affects the person's self-image—can play a significant, explicit role in an explanatory theory of that person's behavior, even though it is a type of consequence that the agent himself cannot easily take into account explicitly ("I am going to do A in order to make it easier to maintain my self-image as a person of kind K") without thereby diminishing that very effect.[14] We should not interpret expressiveness as exhausted by these other independent categories, narrowly conceived, for, as we said earlier, the categories of the symbolic and the expressive are intertwined.

If we array the category of the linguistic alongside the categories we already have as follows, causal/evidential/linguistic/symbolic, this suggests two questions. How does the symbolic differ in nature from the merely linguistic (the symbolic does lend itself more to utility being imputed back, but this need not happen every time)? And how might the linguistic arise out of the causal and evidential? When causal and evidential connections (which arise from a branching structure of causal and statistical regularities) are common knowledge, someone might intentionally produce an evidential sign of p in order to get another to believe that p. This would be a crucial step beyond a Gricean natural meaning, which is an evidential sign, to an intentional deployment to produce a belief in another, that is, part way to a Gricean non-natural meaning wherein this intention is intended to be recognized.[15] Such an evidential sign might be produced to induce a belief in a true p that the other person cannot independently observe right then. But also—perhaps equally likely—it might first have been produced to deceive the other person into believing p, on the basis of planted evidence, when p was false. The first statement that stood for something else might have been a lie, a faked natural sign. If language defined humanity, expressing humans' rational capacities and distinguishing them from other animals, then this would give an intriguing twist to the doctrine that we are born in original sin.

Prisoner's Dilemma

The Prisoner's Dilemma is a much discussed situation wherein each party's selection of a (strongly) dominant action, which appears to be the rational thing to do, leaves each of them worse off than if each had chosen the more cooperative dominated action. The combination of (what appears to be) their individual rationalities leads them to forgo an attainable better situation and thus is Pareto-suboptimal.

The general situation is named after one instance of it: a sheriff offers each of two imprisoned persons awaiting trial the following options. (The situation is symmetrical between the prisoners; they cannot communicate to coordinate their actions in response to the sheriff's offer or, if they can, they have no means to enforce any agreement they might reach.) If one prisoner confesses and the other does not, the first does not go to jail and the second will receive a twelve-year sentence; if both confess, each receives a ten-year prison sentence; if both do not confess, each receives a two-year sentence. Figure 2 represents the situation they face, where the entries in the matrix represent the number of years to be served in prison by the first and second prisoners, respectively).

		Prisoner II	
		Don't Confess	Confess
	Don't Confess	2, 2	12, 0
Prisoner I			
	Confess	0, 12	10, 10

FIGURE 2

Each prisoner reasons as follows: "If the other person confesses and I don't, I will receive twelve years in prison; whereas if I do confess, I will receive ten years. If the other person doesn't confess and I don't,

I will receive two years in prison; whereas if I do, I will receive no years at all. In either case, whichever thing the other person does, I am better off confessing rather than not. Therefore, I will confess." Each prisoner reasons in the same way: both confess and both receive ten years in prison. If both had not confessed, each would have received only two years in prison. Individual rationalities combine to produce a joint mess. And the situation is stable in the following sense: neither one has any incentive to perform the other (more cooperative) action, given that the other party is going to confess. Their actions of confessing are in equilibrium.

The Prisoner's Dilemma situation is an instance of a more general structure (see figure 3) in which each party has a choice between two actions—call them D for the dominant one, C for the cooperative—and has the following preferences among the possible outcomes a, b, c, and d of the combined actions. Person I prefers c to a to d to b, while person II prefers b to a to d to c. Since person I prefers c to a, and d to b, action D dominates action C, and he chooses to do D. Since person II prefers b to a, and d to c, action D' dominates action C', and she chooses to do D'. Together D and D' yield the outcome d, while both of them prefer the outcome a (which would result from C and C') to outcome d. Therefore, these simple facts about the structure of the 2×2 matrix and the structure of each person's preference ordering seem sufficient to mark a Prisoner's Dilemma situation.

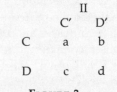

FIGURE 3

Some people have argued that a rational person in this situation, knowing that the other also is a rational person who knows as much about the situation as he himself does, will realize that any reasoning convincing to himself will be convincing to the other as well. So if he concludes the dominant action is best, the other person will as well; if he concludes the cooperative action is best, the other person will as well. In this situation, then, it would be better to conclude the cooperative action is best and, realizing all this, he therefore (somehow) does so. This type of argument has had a mixed reception.

The Prisoner's Dilemma parallels Newcomb's Problem, whether or not the two are (as some have argued) identical in all essential features. Both involve two arguments that lead to differing actions: one argument based upon the dominance principle interpreted in such a way as to be congenial to causal decision theory, the other argument based upon considering what each act would indicate (and what outcome therefore should be bet upon) in a way congenial to evidential decision theory. The argument that in the Prisoner's Dilemma you should expect that the other person will do as you do, even though your action does not causally affect what the other does, is allowed by the principle of maximizing the evidentially expected utility, where the conditional probabilities need not represent any causal influence. Causal decision theory recommends performing the dominant action; evidential decision theory recommends performing the cooperative action when you think the other party is relevantly similar to yourself. It need not be that you are certain you both will act alike; it will be enough if the conditional probabilities of the other party's actions, given your own, vary sufficiently. (Notice too that evidential decision theory might lead to performing the dominant action, if you believe the other party is likely to perform a *different* act than yours, or simply if her act is independent of your own but you ascribe sufficiently pessimistic probabilities to her chances of cooperating.) As was the case with Newcomb's Problem, our confidence in each of these positions may be less than complete, and we may want to give each some legitimate weight.

In the case of Newcomb's Problem, this multiple granting of legitimate weight (or, alternatively, the lack of complete confidence) showed itself in the switching of decisions when the amount of money in the first box was varied. (Yet the structure of the problem was kept constant as judged by the two competing principles of decision, which would have maintained their same decision through these changes.) In the case of the Prisoner's Dilemma, the question is what rational agents with common knowledge that they face rational agents should do. Proponents of the two differing arguments find that the abstract structure of figure 3 is sufficient to give their favored argument its compelling grip. All the dominance argument needs is that person I prefers c to a and d to b, while person II prefers b to a and d to c. All the evidentially expected utility argument about rational agents seems to need is that each has common knowledge that each is a rational agent and that each prefers a to d. If people do lack complete confidence in these arguments, however, we should find that variations in the amounts* of the payoffs within the abstract structure of figure 3 (while still maintaining the *order* of the persons' preferences) will produce changes in the decision people would make.

---

* More exactly—since utility is measured on an interval scale—in the ratios of differences in amounts. When the discussion to follow ignores this complication in the interests of lucidity, it can be suitably rephrased.

Suppose that utility is measured on an interval scale, unique up to a positive linear transformation, with an arbitrary unit and an arbitrary zero point, in conformity to some variant of the standard Von Neumann–Morgenstern axioms.[16] In the situation represented by figure 4,

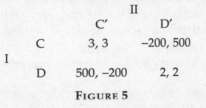

		II	
		C′	D′
I	C	1,000, 1,000	0, 1,001
	D	1,001, 0	1, 1

FIGURE 4

where the matrix entries are such utility numbers, we would think that cooperation is the rational choice. In general, when the cooperative solution payoffs are very much higher than the dominance ones, and when payoffs for the nonmatching actions offer only slight gains or losses over these two, then we strongly will think that cooperation is rational and will find that the dominance argument has little force. Alternatively, in figure 5, the cooperation solution is only slightly better

		II	
		C′	D′
I	C	3, 3	−200, 500
	D	500, −200	2, 2

FIGURE 5

than the dominant one, and the extreme values in the payoffs for the nonmatching actions diverge greatly. When we have no special ties to the other party or particular knowledge of the other party's probabilities of action, then we will think it is rational to perform the dominant action in the figure 5 situation, not running any risk that the other party will perform his dominant action, which he has a large incentive to do. (And if I go through this reasoning and think he also is very likely to be like me, then I may well settle upon the dominant action in this case, comfortable with the realization that he will also.)

These shifts in the decision one would make, which depend upon the (ratios of the differences in the) particular numerical utility entries in the matrix, are in accordance with the earlier principle of maximizing decision-value for people who give some weight to each of the particular principles *CEU* and *EEU*. At what precise point a person's decision will shift as the utilities are varied will depend upon how confident she is in each of these principles (that is, what weights she implicitly assigns to them) and also upon the probabilities she assigns to the other person's action being the same as her own. Notice, however, that even if this last is given a probability of 1, and even if the agent gives greater weight to the *EEU* principle than to the *CEU* principle, she will not necessarily perform the cooperative action. If the utility stakes are big enough and fit the situation in figure 5, that fact can combine with the weight that is given to the *CEU* principle, or with the dominance principle itself (in its causal variant), or with some other principle that gives weight to the security level, to yield a recommendation of the dominant action. Even absolute confidence that the other person will act as you do is not enough to guarantee your performing the cooperative action—in the absence of absolute confidence in, or weight to, the *EEU* principle.* (I have been assuming until now that it is one particular version of the *DV* principle, with its particular weights fixed, that a person applies in all decision situations. It might be, however, that for a given set of constituent principles of decision a person assigns them different weights depending upon the type of decision situation she faces. Still, each type of situation where more than one particular principle received positive weight would be fitted by some *DV* structure or other.)

In the previous section we incorporated the symbolic utility of doing an action, its *SU*, within the *DV* structure alongside *CEU* and *EEU*. It might be thought that if an action *does* have symbolic utility, then this will show itself *completely* in the utility entries in the matrix for that action (for example, perhaps each of the entries gets raised by a certain

---

* "But wouldn't a correct theory *insist* that when the probability is 1 that the other person will behave as you do, you *should* choose the cooperative action in the Prisoner's Dilemma situation, whatever the magnitude of the utility differences in the matrix? And so isn't this divergence an *objection* to the *DV* structure?" We might wonder, though, whether the person has (one level up) complete confidence in his probability estimate of 1 and whether that lack of complete confidence might affect his action in this high-risk situation. See Daniel Ellsberg, "Risk, Ambiguity, and the Savage Axioms," *Quarterly Journal of Economics* 75 (1961): 643–669.

Notice too that the argument proceeds too quickly from (1) common rationality, to (2) they will do the same thing, to (3) crossing out the upper-right and lower-left boxes in the matrix, representing divergent actions, to (4) arguing that, given that the choice is between the two remaining boxes, both should choose the one they prefer—each prefers—that is, both should do the cooperative action. Assuming common knowledge of rationality allows us to assume that we will reason in the same way and will end up doing the same thing. But perhaps *that* will result from each person reasoning about all four boxes in the matrix and each person concluding that in the light of the joint strategic situation presented by the full matrix, including all four boxes, I (and he or she) should do the noncooperative action, and so both persons end up in the lower-right noncooperative box—*thus* satisfying the condition that they act identically. Knowing in advance that we will do the same thing means that we know we will not end up in the upper-right or lower-left box. But this does not mean that we can therefore first delete them and then reason about the remaining situation. For perhaps the reasoning whereby we *will* end up performing the same action depends upon *not* first deleting those divergent corners.

fixed amount that stands for the act's symbolic utility), so that there need not be any separate *SU* factor. Yet the symbolic value of an act is not determined solely by *that* act. The act's meaning can depend upon what other acts are available with what payoffs and what acts also are available to the other party or parties. What the act symbolizes is something it symbolizes when done in *that* particular situation, in preference to *those* particular alternatives. If an act symbolizes "being a cooperative person," it will have that meaning not simply because it has the two possible payoffs it does but also because it occupies a particular position within the two-person matrix—that is, being a dominated action that (when joined with the other person's dominated action) yields a higher payoff to each than does the combination of the dominant actions. Hence, its *SU* is not a function of those features captured by treating that act in isolation, simply as a mapping of states onto consequences.[17] An act's symbolic value may depend upon the whole decision or game matrix. It is not appropriately represented by some addition to or subtraction from the utilities of consequences *within* the matrix. Many writers assume that *anything* can formally be built into the consequences,[18] for instance, how it *feels* to perform the action, the fact that you have done it, or the fact that it falls under particular deontological principles. But if the *reasons* for doing an act *A* affect its utility, then attempting to build this utility of *A* into its *consequences* will thereby alter that act and change the reasons for doing it; but the utility of *that* altered action will depend upon the reasons for doing *it*, and attempting to build this into its consequences will alter the reasons for doing that now doubly altered act, and so forth. Moreover, the utilities of an *outcome* can change if the action is done for certain reasons.[19] What we want the utilities of the outcomes to represent, therefore, is the *conditional* utilities of the outcomes given that the action is done for certain reasons.* This creates a problem for consequentialism in dealing with dynamic consistency issues; for it might be

---

* Or even the conditional utility of the outcome, given that the action is done for certain reasons *and leads to the outcome*. In the economic literature on auctions, it is pointed out that a person's estimate of the value of an outcome might change when he discovers that his particular bid was the winning one, when this indicates that other knowledgeable bidders had information or reached conclusions that led them to value the outcome less than he did. The ratifiability literature notes that the fact that "I decide to do A" can affect the estimate of the probability of a consequence *C* of *A*, in that prob(C/I decide to do *A*) is not equal to prob(C), while the auction literature notes that "my doing *A* is successful in bringing about *C*" can affect the utility of *C*, perhaps by altering the probabilities of other information that affects the utility of *C*. Thus, a fully formulated decision theory not only must employ conditional utility—see my *The Normative Theory of Individual Choice* (1963; rpt. New York: Garland Press, 1990), pp. 144–158—but the conditional utility it utilizes must be not simply u(outcome *O*/the action *A* is done) but rather u(outcome *O*/the action *A* is done, for reasons *R*, and this *A* done for *R* leads to *O*).

that the fact of having reached a particular subtree of the decision tree gives you information that alters the utility of a future outcome. If we attempt to cope with this by insisting that the utilities within the tree always be fully specified conditional utilities, then we cannot have the *same* outcomes at any two different places in the decision tree—to the detriment of stating general normative principles to govern such trees. (For *each* fact about an act, there might be a description that enables you to list that fact as a consequence of the act, but it does not follow that there is a description such that, for *all* facts about the act, that description incorporates them within the act's consequences. The order of the quantifiers matters.)

These considerations show that in Prisoner's Dilemma situations an action should be conceived as having a utility of its own, not simply as involving a constant utility addition *within* a row of its matrix.[20] But I wish to claim something stronger, namely, that this utility is a *symbolic* utility. I do not mean simply the usual kind of utility applied to an action rather than an outcome. This utility involves a different kind of connection. In some Prisoner's Dilemma situations, performing the dominated action—what is usually called the "cooperative action"— may have symbolic value for the person. It may stand for his being a cooperative person in interactions with others, a willing and non-carping participant in joint ventures of mutual benefit. Cooperating in this situation then may get grouped with other activities of cooperation that are not embedded in Prisoner's Dilemma situations. Hence, not cooperating in this particular Prisoner's Dilemma situation may come to threaten a person's cooperating in those other situations—the line between them may not be so salient, and his motivation for cooperation in the others may also be partly symbolic. Because he gives great utility to being a cooperative person, in a particular Prisoner's Dilemma situation he performs the dominated act that symbolizes this.*

This does not mean the person will look only at that act's *SU*. He also will consider its particular utility entries and how these are evaluated by the *CEU* and the *EEU* principles. The decision-value of the act for him will depend upon all three of these things—its *SU*, *CEU*, and *EEU*—and upon the weights he gives to these. Thus, the mere fact that he gives some (positive) symbolic utility to being a cooperative person

---

* Can we build this into the standard decision theory by saying that one constant consequence of his performing the dominant act in the Prisoner's Dilemma situation is that he will think of himself as a noncooperative person, and by then representing this in the game matrix by a negative addition, an addition of negative utility, all across the row for that action? Notice that this component of utility would be a function of his attitude toward that act as it stands within the structure of the whole matrix.

does not guarantee that he will perform the cooperative action in all Prisoner's Dilemma situations.

I do not claim that the only possible symbolic meaning relevant to the Prisoner's Dilemma situation is "being a cooperative person." Someone might think that performing the *dominant* action in such situations symbolizes "being rational, not being swayed by sentimentality." Thinking this quite important, he gives great symbolic utility (within his *DV* principle) to performing the dominant action, this in addition to the weight he gives to the *CEU* or dominance principle itself. Some writers on Newcomb's Problem who are proponents of the view that taking what is in both boxes is most rational overcome discomfort at the fact that they and people like themselves do worse on this problem than do maximizers of *EEU* by saying that its "moral" is: "If someone is very good at predicting behavior and rewards predicted irrationality richly, then irrationality will be richly rewarded."[21] I take it that such people give very great utility—is that a symbolic utility?—to being rational according to their best current estimate of what precise principles that involves. (It will be a subtle matter to distinguish between someone who gives weight to only *one* particular principle, *CEU* for example, and someone who gives some weight to *CEU* and also some lesser weight to *EEU* yet also attaches great symbolic utility—greatly weighted—to following her best *particular* estimate of what rationality involves.) One would guess that new complications would arise if following a particular decision principle itself has symbolic utility or if engaging in a particular kind of decision process or procedure does.

To say all this about symbolic utility is to say that our responses to the Prisoner's Dilemma are governed, in part, by our view of the kind of person we wish to be and the kinds of ways we wish to relate to others. What we do in a particular Prisoner's Dilemma situation will involve all this and invoke it to different degrees depending upon the precise (ratios of differences among) utility entries in the matrix and also upon the particular factual circumstances that give rise to that matrix, circumstances in which an action may come to have its own symbolic meanings, not simply because of the structure of the matrix.

We knew all this already, of course, at least as a psychological point about why people differ in their responses to Prisoner's Dilemma situations. However, the *DV* principle leaves room for general views about what sort of person to be, as this relates to and groups particular choices, not simply as a possible *psychological* explanation of why (some) people deviate from rationality, but as a legitimate component, symbolic utility, within their *rational* procedure of decision.

In a seminal paper on the repeated Prisoner's Dilemma, D. P. Kreps,

P. Milgrom, J. Roberts, and R. Wilson showed that your giving a small probability to my performing the cooperative action or your giving this to my believing that you will perform the cooperative action (or your giving a small probability to my believing that you will believe that I will perform the cooperative action) can be sufficient to make it rational for you to begin by performing the cooperative action, in order to encourage me in my cooperative actions or consonant beliefs.[22] If you believe I might do the cooperative action (or follow tit-for-tat), and you believe that I will continue to do so only if *you* behave a certain way, then you will have reasons to behave as I think you might, in order to encourage me to do the cooperative action.[23] If the situation is mutual, both will (under certain circumstances) perform the cooperative action. Now the *DV* structure, when it is common knowledge that both follow it, does (promise to) give some probability of each player believing that the other will believe that the first will perform the cooperative action, and hence some probability of each, of both, performing the cooperative action. (Notice that this point, and the remainder of this paragraph, does *not* depend upon the full *DV* structure, which includes a weighting for symbolic utility. The narrower structure first presented, with a weighting only of *CEU* and *EEU*, is enough.) And this results, not as a perturbation away from full rationality, and not as one's rational adjustment to the other's deviation from rationality (or to the other's belief that you might deviate from rationality), but rather as a part of common knowledge that all participants are *totally* rational. For if the principle of maximizing decision-value is a rational principle, normatively desirable, then if (as it appears to) common knowledge of *DV*-maximization gives some probability of each participant's performing the cooperative action, the argument of Kreps, Milgrom, Roberts, and Wilson applies even under common knowledge of full rationality.[24]

It would be nice to reach a sharper result than that the cooperative action will be performed if the causal, evidential, and symbolic utilities interact so as to lead to this. Under what conditions, for what specifications of weights within a *DV* structure for one (or both) of the participants, will a person choose to perform the cooperative action in the Prisoner's Dilemma situation or follow a tit-for-tat strategy in the repeated Prisoner's Dilemma?[25]

Here we can take only some tentative first steps in listing appropriate assumptions for deriving results. In addition to requiring that both players follow the *DV* principle, we can add the following extremely weak form of the assumption that each should expect the other player to behave as he himself does, to be fed into the *EEU* component. This weak predictive principle says that the evidential conditional probability that the other player will do act C', conditional on your doing C, is greater than the unconditional evidential probability that she will do C'; and similarly for her act D' conditional upon your own act D. A somewhat stronger principle, but still short of the symmetry assumption that the other rational player will act exactly as you do, would hold that these evidential conditional probabilities, for the first play, are greater than $1/2$. Another principle specifies that the person gives *some* symbolic utility (and some symbolic weight to that) to performing the cooperative act in the Prisoner's Dilemma situation. Moreover, we might assume that performing the dominant act D has a negative symbolic utility of its own, in addition to the absence of the positive symbolic utility of cooperating.[26] Let $S(A/B)$ be the symbolic utility of act A given that the other person does act B. If person **I** assigns positive symbolic utility to performing the cooperative action, then $S(C/C')$ is greater than or equal to $S(C/D')$, and each of these is greater than (the negative quantity) $S(D/D')$, which itself is greater than (the more negative) $S(D/C')$. When the Prisoner's Dilemma structure is repeated many times between the same two persons, the further possibilities of mutually beneficial cooperation affect the utilities within a current play, including the very first one. Moreover, the symbolic utility of an action will change from play to play, depending upon the past actions of the other party. We might see the symbolic utility of performing the cooperative action as declining the more the other party performs her dominant action, perhaps as declining proportionally to the ratio of the number of times the other party has performed her dominant action to the number of times she has performed her dominated one. Cooperating with *her* becomes less a symbol of being a cooperative person the more she has refused to cooperate. On the other hand, the more the other person cooperates, the more symbolic utility your performing the cooperative action will have. And a comparable condition now applies to the negative symbolic utility of performing the dominant act. This disutility also declines in absolute amount the more the other person performs her dominant action and increases in absolute amount the more she performs her cooperative action. The hope is that these conditions, along with other plausible assumptions, will lead to sharper results.

Finer Distinctions: Consequences and Goals

We have discussed three different modes of connection of action to outcomes—namely, causal, evidential, and symbolic—and have suggested that decision theory needs to use and explicitly recognize all three modes. Does decision theory also need finer discriminations *within* these categories? For example, some writers on ethics have claimed that different kinds of causal connections carry different weights in choice situations, even though the resulting probabilities may be identical. There is a significant difference, they claim, between bringing something about and allowing it to happen or abstaining from preventing it. (And we might consider further kinds of causal relation, such as facilitating or aiding an event's happening.) And some writers have formulated a doctrine of "double effect," holding that there can be a moral difference (sometimes sufficient to make the difference as to whether an action is permissible) between bringing something about when this results from intending to bring it about as an end or a means to an end and knowingly bringing it about but as a side effect of one's pursuit of some other goal. Admittedly, these are matters of some controversy,[27] yet it is striking that causal decision theory thus far has taken no notice of these arguably important distinctions; it proceeds instead with an undifferentiated notion of "causal influence." Should normative decision theory make room for such distinctions and give them a role, either in its first-person theory of choice or in its instructions for an adviser? One natural place these distinctions might enter is in the notion of conditional utility. Earlier, in speaking of auction theory, we noted that decision theory should speak of u(outcome O/A is done and A causes or succeeds in bringing about O). The precise kind of causal linkage between action and outcome within the last part of this condition might affect the utility of the resulting outcome O, that is, yield differing conditional utilities for O and hence sometimes produce different decisions within a principle that employs such conditional utilities. Or is the import of these distinctions wholly symbolic, so that by incorporating symbolic utility within our theory we already have made an adequate place for them?*

I suggest we see these distinctions not as dichotomies but as items arrayed along a (not necessarily continuous) dimension. Indeed, we have here not one dimension but two. The first involves the *importance* of the causal role of the action in relation to the effect or outcome or resulting state of affairs. Here we have (at least) seven relations an ac-

---

* Or, instead, are these distinctions framing effects, in the sense of Tversky and Kahneman, which show variance across (descriptions of) situations where there should be invariance? See Amos Tversky and Daniel Kahneman, "Judgment under Uncertainty: Heuristics and Biases," *Science* 185 (1974): 1124–1131; reprinted in *Judgment under Uncertainty*, ed. Daniel Kahneman, Paul Slovic, and Amos Tversky (Cambridge: Cambridge Univ. Press, 1982). Doesn't the relation of the bringing about/allowing to happen distinction to a baseline seem suspiciously like that of the gain/loss distinction to *its* baseline? This last, of course, is a favored example for framing effects.

tion may stand in to a state of affairs. In decreasing importance, the action may: (1) cause the state of affairs to occur; (2) aid or facilitate its occurrence; (3) remove a barrier to its occurrence; (4) permit or allow its occurrence; (5) not prevent and not avoid its occurrence (when some act available to you would have); (6) not aid or facilitate its non-occurrence (when some act available to you would have); (7) not aid or facilitate its nonoccurrence (and *no* act available to you would have).

The second dimension also involves the causal role of the action, in relation to the effect or outcome or resulting state of affairs, but this dimension marks not an act's importance but the causal *robustness* of the relation to that outcome. The idea is that when something is pursued as a goal, certain subjunctives hold true of the person. He would reorganize his behavior in order to reach the goal (or to have a better chance of reaching it). In slightly different circumstances, where *this* action would not reach that goal, he would do something instead that *would* reach the goal; he would tend to exclude alternative actions that have no possibility of reaching the goal. When something is merely a known side effect of the action, on the other hand, the person would not alter his behavior if it turned out that his (current or planned) behavior would not produce this side effect. Of course, if it instead produced another significant effect he wished to avoid, he might do so. It is a question of the *range* of the situations where the behavior would alter. Pursuit of something as a goal involves subjunctives across a wider range of circumstances than acting in the knowledge that something will result as a side effect of other goal pursuit. Between these two falls the case of aiming at something solely as a means toward the realization of some other goal. Here behavior would be reorganized in some situations to realize the means—unlike the side-effect case—but in a narrower range of possible situations than where the effect is an end or goal itself. (Consider, for example, that possible situation where this particular effect no longer serves as a means to the goal.)

Along this dimension of robustness of the causal role, we can distinguish (at least) six connections of a person and an action to an effect or outcome. The action can: (1) aim at the effect as an end; (2) aim at the effect solely as a means. Or it can (3) not aim at the effect at all. And among actions that do not aim at the effect, the person might: (3') know of the effect (which is not aimed at); (4') not know of the effect (which is not aimed at) that she should know of; (5') not know of the effect (which is not aimed at), and it not be the case that she should know of it. Or (6') the state of affairs (which is not aimed at) occurs by accident.

Using these two dimensions, and their categories, we can form a 7×6 matrix. (If the two dimensions are not completely independent,

some of the boxes may be impossible.) An action and a person's relation to its effect (or to the resulting state) will be specified by its location within the matrix, that is, by its position along the two dimensions.[28] Should decision theory take account of these finer distinctions
concerning the mode of causal connection of an action to an outcome
and, if so, how? Are there also finer distinctions *within* the evidential
and the symbolic connections that decision theory should mark and
take into account? (Mightn't the later categories listed on the robustness dimension that refer to knowledge better be placed along an evidential dimension?) I raise these questions not to answer them here
but to place them on the agenda.

The themes discussed in these two chapters about principles and
symbolic meaning apply to ethical principles also. When we appropriately group actions together in a class, one action comes to stand for
all, and the weight of all is brought to bear upon the one, any one,
giving it a coordinate (symbolic) disutility. Deontological constraints
might exhibit this same phenomenon. By grouping actions together
into a principle forbidding them—"do not murder"—an action is removed from separate utilitarian (or egoist) calculation of *its* costs and
benefits. The action comes to stand for the whole group, bearing that
weight. This need not happen in a way that makes the constraint
absolute, barring the action no matter what, but it constitutes a far
greater barrier to performing the action by throwing its greatly increased (symbolic) disutility into any calculation.[29]

Recall now our discussion in the first chapter of the symbolic meaning of following ethical principles. Ethical action can symbolize (and
express) being a rational creature that gives itself laws, being a lawmaking member of a kingdom of ends, being an equal source and
recognizer of worth and personality, and so forth. The utility of these
grand things, symbolically expressed and instantiated by the action,
becomes incorporated into that action's symbolic utility and hence into
that action's decision-value. Thus, these symbolic meanings become
part of one's reason for acting ethically. A person who maximizes an
act's utility broadly conceived, that is, who maximizes its decision
value (*DV*), may be led to perform ethical actions. This person would
be pursuing his *own* goals (which need not be *selfish* goals). In terms of
the categorization of Amartya Sen, he therefore would be engaged in
self-goal pursuit rather than in the activity of *not* marginally pursuing
his own overall individual goal.[30] But note that if falling into this further category of not marginally pursuing his own overall individual
goal itself comes to have symbolic utility to him, then it will enter into
his *DV*. At that point, when he acts taking account of this symbolic
utility, is he once again pursuing his own goal, that is, *his* revised *DV*,

so that his attempt (within the *DV* framework) to enter Sen's other category is doomed to failure? However we decide this, the more general point holds. Being ethical is among our most effective ways of symbolizing (a connection to) what we value most highly, and that is something a *rational* person would not wish to forgo.

We discussed various functions of principles in the first chapter. Accepting and adhering to a particular principle, we saw, could be considered to be a (general) act *A* and treated within a decision-theoretic framework that was largely instrumental. Now we have presented an alternative framework for decision theory, one that includes evidential and symbolic aspects, not simply causal instrumentality. Within that framework, an act of accepting a principle will have a decision-value *DV*, and it will be chosen (from among alternatives) when it has a maximal decision-value. This broader framework opens the way to a revised discussion of why we have principles at all—why if we have that one *DV* principle we also will have some others—and of why we have some particular ones.

III

RATIONAL BELIEF

WHEN is a belief rational? Why do we want our beliefs to be rational, how can we tell whether they are, and how can we improve their rationality?

Two themes permeate the philosophical literature. First, that rationality is a matter of reasons. A belief's rationality depends upon the reasons for holding that belief. These will be reasons for thinking the belief is true (or perhaps for thinking that it has some other desirable cognitive virtue, such as explanatory power). Second, that rationality is a matter of reliability. Does the process or procedure that produces (and maintains) the belief lead to a high percentage of true beliefs? A rational belief is one that arises through some process that reliably produces beliefs that are true (or that have some other desirable cognitive virtue).

Neither theme alone exhausts our notion of rationality. Reasons without reliability seem empty, reliability without reasons seems blind. In tandem these make a powerful unit, but how exactly are they related and why?

It is natural to think of rationality as a goal-directed process. (This applies to both rationality of action and rationality of belief.) The stereotype of behavior in traditional societies is that people act a certain way because things always have been done that way. In contrast, rational behavior is aimed at achieving the goals, desires, and ends that people have. On this instrumental conception, rationality consists in the effective and efficient achievement of goals, ends, and desires. About the goals themselves, an instrumental conception has little to say.* If rational procedures are ones that reliably achieve specified goals, an action is rational when it is produced by such a procedure, and a person is rational when he appropriately uses rational procedures.

---

* "'Reason' has a perfectly clear and precise meaning. It signifies the choice of the right means to an end that you wish to achieve. It has nothing whatever to do with the choice of ends." Bertrand Russell, *Human Society in Ethics and Politics* (London: Allen and Unwin, 1954), p. viii. "Reason is wholly instrumental. It cannot tell us where to go; at best it can tell us how to get there. It is a gun for hire that can be employed in the service of any goals we have, good or bad." Herbert Simon, *Reason in Human Affairs* (Stanford: Stanford Univ. Press, 1983), pp. 7–8.

This account of an action's rationality refers to the process or procedure by which it arose. However, the standard account of an action's rationality presented by decision theory refers only to the action's maximizing expected utility. But an action might reach goals or maximize expected utility without having been arrived at rationally. It could be stumbled upon by accident or done inadvertently or result from a series of miscalculations that cancel each other out. That action, then, would have been the best thing to do (given that person's goals), but it would not have been done rationally.

Hence, it seems that decision theory too must refer to the process or procedure by which the action is generated in order to be a theory of rationality. The expected-utility (or the DV) formula marks an action as best. An action is rational when it is generated by a process that tends to produce the best actions, the ones with maximal DV. (To be sure, decision-theoretic considerations also enter in assessing the optimality of that process.) Decision theory by itself is a theory of best action, not of rational action. When we think of applying decision theory, we tend to ignore this. For won't an action thus arrived at be generated by a process that reliably yields best actions and so be rational when done? This is an *empirical* claim, though. Decision theory delineates the best action, but we might be unreliable appliers of that theory: we might tend to ignore certain factors, make mistakes in calculation, or otherwise misapply the theory. Another procedure might actually yield a much higher percentage of best actions, even though it is decision theory that provides the *criterion* of best action.[1]

The rationality of a belief, too, can be thought of in such instrumental terms. In this case, the particular goals are specified: truth, the avoidance of error, explanatory power, and so forth. Let us suppose for the moment that there is just one cognitive goal: believing the truth. A rational belief, then, would be one that was arrived at by a process that reliably yields true beliefs. This process includes not simply the acquisition of a new belief but also the way in which an existing belief is maintained, dropped, or revised.[2] For the most part, though, I will focus only upon acquisition.

Questions have been raised about the context in which reliability is supposed to obtain. Is a procedure to be reliable only the times it actually is used, or reliable all the times it could be used in the world as it is, or reliable also in worlds similar to the actual one, or reliable in worlds that in general are as we believe the world to be (whether or not that belief is correct)?[3] There also are questions about the degree of reliability that a rational procedure must have. Must it be the most reliable procedure available, or can a belief be rational when it arises from a quite reliable procedure that is not the very best? Must the procedure be more reliable than not, or can a belief about the explanation of a phenomenon be rational when it arises through the most reliable procedure available for arriving at correct explanations, even though that reliability is less than 50 percent? And in assessing a procedure, mustn't we look not simply at the percentage of times the procedure gets things right but also at what happens when the procedure gets things wrong and at how bad that resulting situation is? Just as the rational action is not always the one that yields the highest probability of a desired result, the rational procedure to use is not always the one that yields the highest chance of achieving the goal. Here enter the familiar considerations of decision theory.*

* The modern source of reliability views is Charles Peirce, who spoke of the validity of rules of inference ("leading principles") in terms of the percentage of times that, when their premisses are true, their conclusions are true. Deductively valid rules score 100 percent, while valid inductive rules would show a very high percentage. See Charles S. Peirce, "The Fixation of Belief," in his *Collected Papers* (Cambridge, Mass.: Harvard Univ. Press, 1931–1958), 5:223–247, reprinted in *The Philosophy of Peirce: Selected Writings*, ed. J. Buchler (New York: Harcourt, Brace, 1950), pp. 5–22. Notice that a high percentage, in Peirce's sense, is not sufficient to justify *application* of the rule of inference. Suppose that usually when a statement of type p is true, a corresponding statement of type q also is true. (We could formulate this as a statistical statement about percentages or with probabilities.) Does that mean I can reliably infer q from p and count on being right (roughly) that percent of the time? No. It might be the case that when I believe a statement of type p, the corresponding type q statement usually is *not* true. After all, my occasions of believing a type p statement are not a random sample of the situations when p is true, and they might not be a representative sample, perhaps because of a bias of the evidence coming to me or because of a bias in me. Even when there is a true statistical statement of the form, "Usually when I *believe* a statement of type p, a statement of type q is true," it still might be the case that when I infer q from believed p, q usually is false. For the times when I infer q from p (or make any inference on the basis of p) need not be a random or representative sample of the times when I believe p. Do we need instead to say, "Statistically, usually when I believe p and I infer q from p then q is true"? And is it that statement which licenses the inference to q? But infer in accordance with *which* rule of inference? Do we need to specify within the rule itself that *this* is a representative case where type p is true, believed, and used as a basis of inference in accordance with *this* rule? With an inference based upon a universally true leading principle, we need not worry about the particular occasion of our inference. But with one based upon a statistical principle, we need to worry about whether *this* occasion of inference is a representative one.

The root idea behind a reliability analysis of rationality is that rationality applies, in the first instance, to a process or procedure and, derivatively, to a particular inference, belief, or action as an instance of that procedure. The instance inherits its rationality from the procedure it instantiates. When the desirable trait of the procedure is its reliability, its yield of a high percentage of true beliefs, then the procedure is likely to yield a true belief. Does this tell us, of a particular belief yielded by the process, that *it* is likely to be true? That belief or inference falls under many possible procedures, and it falls into many other classifications as well. To infer that it has a particular probability of being true from its membership in a class—in this case, the class of beliefs yielded by a partic-

It seems that the two themes, reasons and reliability, can easily be connected: you more often arrive at a true belief if you hold your belief for supporting reasons. By giving reasons the major role, we make the processes that form our beliefs reliable.

But what makes something a reason, and why does believing for reasons contribute to holding true beliefs? Why should the goal of belief be truth? Would someone be irrational whose beliefs were formed by processes that (reliably) reached other goals, such as making him happy or well liked? Can we find precise rules or conditions to specify which beliefs are rational and which irrational?

Cognitive Goals

When a belief is rational because it was arrived at (and maintained) by a procedure that reliably and efficiently achieves certain goals, what are those goals? Usually, it is said that the goals are *cognitive* ones— believing the truth, avoiding error, or perhaps a wider mix, including explanatory power, testability, and theoretical fruitfulness.[4] The notion of a cognitive goal itself is not so well bounded. Truth, yes, and also explanatory power, theoretical fruitfulness, and scope. But is simplicity a cognitive goal? Ease in computation? Is mystic insight into the nature of God a cognitive or a noncognitive personal goal? And which is enlightenment, as this is construed in Eastern theories?

The primary cognitive goal discussed by philosophers is truth. Why is truth a goal? One answer is that truth, or believing the truth, is intrinsically valuable. All truth? I find that I do not at all mind the thought that I have some false beliefs about some matters—about some state capitals, for instance—and there are many truths I do not care to know at all—those stating the precise number of grains of sand on each beach in the world. Not every fact is worth knowing or even

---

ular procedure—given general probabilistic information about that class, is to make (what the probability literature terms) a *direct inference*. Since particular instances can fall into many different reference classes, it is a delicate matter to formulate the criteria for the validity of a direct inference that yields a (detachable) probability judgment about a particular case. See C. G. Hempel, "Inductive Inconsistencies," in his *Aspects of Scientific Explanation* (New York: Free Press, 1965), pp. 53–79; Henry Kyburg, "Randomness and the Right Reference Class," *Journal of Philosophy* 74 (1977): 501–521; Isaac Levi, *The Enterprise of Knowledge* (Cambridge, Mass.: M.I.T. Press, 1980), chs. 12, 16. On the reliability account of the rationality of a belief or inference, these delicate issues do not concern merely the formulation of the correct principles for one particular kind of inference; they infect the very notion of rationality itself. For the rationality of particular instances is *defined* in terms of a direct inference from probabilistic information about a class.

worth having a true belief about, although particular purposes may give such knowledge a point. Some things *are* worth knowing for themselves, I think—for instance, deep truths that explain a range of facts, *the* grand explanatory theory if there is one, the truth about how the universe originated. Certainly, we may become intellectually curious about a particular range of facts.

It seems reasonable to think that our original interest in truth was instrumentally based. Truths served us better than falsehoods and better than no beliefs at all in coping with the world's dangers and opportunities.* Perfectly accurate truth was not necessary, only a belief that was *true enough* to give (more) desirable results when acted upon. What was needed and wanted were "serviceable truths," and to be serviceable a belief need not have been precisely true.** Truth, then, would be rather like what John Rawls has called a primary good, something that is useful for a *very* wide range of purposes—almost all—and hence will be desired and bring benefit (almost) no matter what our particular purposes might be.[5] So we might desire true beliefs and come to be concerned with truth because true beliefs are useful for a very wide range of purposes. Yet that would leave our concern with truth instrumental—at least originally.[6]

Was William James right, then, in saying that truth is what works? We might see James as depicting the *value* of truth, not its nature. Rather than hold that truth simply is "serviceability," we can construe truth as that property—whatever it is—that underlies and explains serviceability. If one property underlies the serviceability of various statements about different subjects, that property will have to be very general and abstractly stated. The various theories of truth—correspondence, coherence, and so on—then would be explanatory hypotheses, conjectures about the nature of the property that underlies and explains serviceability.†

* The instrumental basis of our interest in truth is not that people desired to believe truths because they recognized that this would be instrumentally useful. Rather, it is this: because of the usefulness of believing approximate truths, some concern for truth in belief was evolutionarily selected for, as was some curiosity to seek out truths. Some explicit instrumental desire for truth also might develop, though.

** Against the view that we believed *p* and cared only whether it was, and would continue to be, serviceable, someone might argue that what we believed was, "It is approximately true that *p*," and *this* we wanted to be precisely true. But not every approximation will be serviceable in every context. So perhaps what we believed was, "*p* is serviceable," and it was this that we wanted to be precisely true. Yet why think that this shows we cared about truth rather than about serviceability?

† And if it turns out that the serviceability of different kinds of statement is explained by distinct properties?

Generally, believing a false statement lowers one's ratio of true beliefs; but in some circumstances belief in a falsehood might help someone to maximize that ratio. (If he believes this one false thing, I will tell him many truths he otherwise could not find out. Or I will give him a scholarship to college, where he will learn much. If he believes, falsely, that he did very well on a particular test, he will be motivated to learn, successfully, many true statements.) Is it rational for him to believe this one false statement, to follow a process that yields this belief? A statement can be believed through a process that maximizes the ratio of true beliefs yet itself be unlikely. If the cognitive goal is to maximize the ratio of true beliefs, then this false belief, derived through a procedure that effectively serves this goal, is rational. But if the cognitive aim of truth expresses itself as a constraint applying to this particular case—"do not believe anything false"—then this false belief does not serve that aim and so is not rational.[7]

These two forms are not the only ones the aim can take. Amartya Sen has proposed a structure wherein both kinds of goals—the agent's not doing something of type T himself this time, and also maximizing the amount of non-T done by all—are given separate weight (as part of a maximand that can include other goals as well).[8] Within this structure, an agent's cognitive goals will include both believing the truth (avoiding belief in a falsehood) this time and maximizing her ratio of true beliefs. Thus, there are (at least) three different ways to pursue the cognitive aim of truth: as a side constraint, as a goal of maximizing the ratio of true beliefs, or as this goal weighted with the goal of avoiding a false belief this time. Hence, it is not enough to say that a belief is rational when it is arrived at by a procedure that effectively and efficiently achieves the aim of true belief. Which structure is to be used in assessing a procedure as rational, or are there three distinct and legitimate notions of rationality, each appropriate for different purposes?

Situations in which it seems clear that believing the truth will *not* serve a person's other important goals have been discussed in the literature under the rubric "the ethics of belief." For instance, a mother is presented with courtroom evidence that her son has committed a grave crime, evidence that convinces everyone else but, were she to believe this, that would make her life miserable thereafter.[9] Is it rational for her to believe her son is guilty? A Bayesian analysis might show that she should arrive at a different conclusion than others do: she knows more about her son than they do and so may reasonably start with a different prior probability. But let us suppose that her different prior probability is based simply upon her love for her son and upon her unwillingness to believe that he could be guilty of such a crime. Still, it might be argued that she is rational in believing him innocent, because believing this will maximize her expected utility, taking all of her goals into account—and isn't that the criterion of a rational action?[10] Similarly, a person might take into account the likely negative moral effects upon himself of believing certain propositions—for instance, that there are heritable differences in intelligence among racial groups—and on this basis refrain from examining certain evidence or forming particular beliefs. (These negative effects would be ones not subject to the person's volitional control or ones controlled only with great difficulty or at great cost.)

We might distinguish (1) the proposition that p being the rational thing to believe from (2) believing p being the rational thing to do. The expected-utility account might apply to (2), by considering believing p as an action available to the parent; but it seems not to apply to (1), at least with regard to *all* the goals that the parent might have. For (1)— the proposition that p being the rational thing to believe—it seems that only evidential considerations should weigh. And even if the account of evidential considerations turns out to be instrumental, the relevant goals must be *cognitive* ones only—and the parent's happiness, however important, is not a cognitive goal.[11]

However, if cognitive goals themselves have a wholly instrumental basis and justification, wouldn't it be rational to "look through" the cognitive goals to the ultimate purposes they are meant to serve? When those purposes clearly are not served, shouldn't we ignore the cognitive goal and pursue the ultimate purposes more directly? (If so, the proposition that her son is innocent might turn out to be the rational thing for the mother to believe.) The notion of what proposition it is rational to believe, notion (1) above, might instead be *defined* in terms of *cognitive* goals, but wouldn't that arbitrarily truncate the notion? Do cognitive goals, even if once instrumentally based, come to have an authority of their own, even against the ultimate purposes that gave rise to them as goals?[12]

Holistic views of belief claim that the addition of any particular belief creates rippling effects throughout the body of beliefs. It modifies many other beliefs, it alters the prior probabilities of many hypotheses that enter into future Bayesian calculations, it poses new and recalcitrant problems for the overall explanatory unification of one's beliefs, and so forth. It would be unwise, then, to look solely to the immediately gratifying personal effects of believing something. The far-flung effects of introducing this one belief will be impossible to calculate, especially if one must also alter one's general procedures of belief formation to accommodate this. Even at the personal level, there is a strong presumption that the immediately beneficial effects will be outweighed by the rippling consequences of other resulting false beliefs and the further consequences of holding these.

Yet in any one case, the good personal effects of believing a certain statement may be clear, and it may be very tempting simply to go ahead and believe it, whatever the evidence. To avoid such a strong and salient particular temptation, dangerous if followed frequently or even that once, a person might adopt a *principle* to believe only what is true, only what the evidence shows to be (probably) true. According to our account of how principles help one to avoid temptations, by adopting this principle, believing a falsehood this particular time comes to stand for many instances of believing falsehoods; believing the truth this time comes to stand for many instances of believing truths. Believing a particular truth comes to have a symbolic utility not tied to *its* actual consequences. Cognitive goals might come to have an independent authority, even in situations where the *local* consequences of ignoring them are more beneficial. I shall return to issues about the ethics of belief later in this chapter, in the section "Rules of Rationality."

Responsiveness to Reasons

The rationality of a belief may derive from the process by which that belief is arrived at and maintained, but not every (conceivably) effective way of arriving at true belief would mark a belief as rational. If being knocked on the head or ingesting mescaline were a way of arriving at true beliefs about a certain topic—a topic other than whether one had been knocked on the head or ingested that substance—then that belief itself would not be a rational one. (For one who knows this, however, it might be rational to choose to be knocked on the head in order to gain that true belief.) The rationality of a belief is connected to a dense network of reasoning, inference, and evaluation of evidence in chains of overlapping statements. Observation may feed into this network, but at some level of description the process is propositional. This shows that rationality is not simply *any* kind of instrumentality. It requires a certain type of instrument, namely, reasons and reasoning. Suppose, then, that a particular procedure is a reliable way to arrive at true belief. If an action or belief yielded by that procedure is to be rational, not only must the procedure involve a network of reasons and reasoning, but this also must be (in part) *why* the procedure is reliable. The reasons and reasoning contribute to the procedure's reliability.[13]

Rationality involves not simply doing or believing something because of the reasons *in favor of* it but also taking into account (some) reasons *against* it. Karl Popper emphasized the importance, within science, of searching for data or evidence against a hypothesis or theory. Confirmations, he noted, are easy to find. The mark of a scientific theory is that it excludes certain evidence or facts, and we test a theory by searching in those areas where it is most likely to turn out false, not by gathering more instances where it is likely to be true.[14] This is a salutary emphasis, even if we do not endorse Popper's view that there are no reasons *for* (and do not hold that the only reasons for are reports of failure to find reasons against). Rationality involves taking account of reasons for *and* against. The belief or action must not merely be caused (in the right way) by reasons for and against; it must be *responsive* to these reasons. Over some range of variation in the nature or force or balance of these reasons, if the reasons were different, then the action or belief would be different.[15] The belief or action must be positively responsive: if the reasons are stronger, the belief must not disappear or be weaker; if the reasons are weaker, the belief must not get stronger.

The typical article in a philosophy journal is structured to induce rational belief in readers. Usually, a philosophical proposition or thesis is propounded as worthy of belief, and reasons for and against it are considered. Among the reasons in favor of the thesis are: general and acceptable statements from which it follows; other acceptable things it fits in with or alongside of; its consequences, which are acceptable and so support it; instances of it or examples that fit it and so provide some evidence for it. Among the reasons against the thesis that are considered are: possible objections to it (these are replied to, weakened, undercut, or somehow avoided); possible counterexamples (these are neutralized *or* used to modify the thesis into another proposition that is not subject to that counterexample, so that now it is the modified statement that is propounded as worthy of rational belief). One reason against a thesis p deserves separate mention: that an alternative proposition q, the best or most plausible alternative to p, may be more worthy of rational belief than p is. The practice is to raise particular objections to q, difficulties or counterexamples that are deemed sufficient to eliminate it or show why it should not be accepted. Rarely is it said that the objections to q are no worse than those to p but that p has better reasons in its favor. And more rarely still is q given the same full-scale examination that p receives. Still, all this adds up to a sustained consideration of the reasons for and against the thesis, leaving the reader in a better position to believe it rationally.

Perhaps we should say first that rationality involves being responsive to relevant factors, to all and only the relevant factors. It is an additional thesis that the relevant factors are *reasons*. It is a still further thesis—one that may not hold in all domains—that these reasons divide neatly into the two categories of *for* and *against*. But in what way, exactly, is a rational belief responsive to all the reasons for and against, in what way is the credibility of the belief determined by the reasons for and against it? It would be much too simple to say that a person holds beliefs so as to maximize the *net* weight of the reasons for his beliefs, that is, the measured weight of the reasons for the belief minus the measured weight of the reasons against that belief. There could be some interaction between the reasons for and against. Or the weight of particular reasons for something might depend upon which reasons against they were conjoined with; even whether something *is* a reason for might depend upon what reasons against there are.

Moreover, the particular weight a reason has may depend upon other factors that are not themselves reasons for or against. A statement r may be a reason for believing S, yet q may undercut r as a reason, not by being a reason for thinking that r itself is false or that S is, but by being a reason for thinking that (in this context) r is a weaker reason for S or is no reason at all.[16] (Correspondingly, there might be things that increase the weight of reasons: aggravators.) Hence, the net weight of the reasons for is not fixed by the component reasons alone; that value depends upon what undercutters (and aggravators) are around.

This suggests the formulation of a neural network model of reasons for and against. A reason r for statement S sends a signal along a channel with a certain positive weight to the S-node. A reason r' against S sends a signal to S along a channel with a certain negative weight. An undercutter of r as a reason for S will send a signal along a channel with a certain weight to reduce the weight (perhaps to zero) on the channel between r and S. The result of this network is a credibility value for statement S. (We shall explore this structure further in the next section.) There is room within this framework for many kinds of reasons with differing weights. Thus we might hope to capture many methodological maxims from the philosophy of science literature, either within the network or as an emergent phenomenon of the total network.

What the rational person cares about, though, is the truth. He uses the net balance among the reasons he has or knows of to estimate or predict this truth. It may not be reasonable, however, to estimate the truth by a direct extrapolation from the net balance among the reasons we have, for those reasons may be a biased indicator of that truth. The process by which reasons come to us may differentially admit certain kinds of reasons, those that point to the truth of the statement but not those that point to its falsity. Hence it would be unwise to base our belief only upon the reasons we have without also considering the representativeness of those reasons.

Here is a somewhat artificial but suggestive picture. Think of a person's reasons as a sample of the totality of relevant reasons concerning statement *S*. This totality may include the facts that others know of, the facts that could be ascertained, and so forth (with perhaps some restriction to exclude the statement *S* itself, even if someone else knows it, and also some other statements entailing *S*). The question, then, is whether that person's reasons are a biased or unrepresentative sample of the totality of reasons. The person herself may have some additional reason to think this bias exists.* I do not claim that the rational person will first use the net balance among the reasons she has to estimate the net balance among the reasons there are and then go on to apply that result to estimate the truth. But the rational person will try to be aware of whether the reasons she has are a biased indicator of the truth and will accordingly shape her estimate of the truth from the reasons she has. If she judges her reasons to be unrepresentative in some particular direction, she will correct for this. When rationality evaluates reasons, it is concerned not only with the force of the reasons but also with their representativeness.

It is in this sense that rationality involves some degree of self-consciousness. Not only reasons are evaluated, but also the processes by which information arrives, is stored, and is recalled. A rational person will try to be alert to biases in these processes and will take steps to correct those biases he knows of. In assessing the import of the information he has, he also will consider what *different* information could have arrived and how likely it is that it would have arrived, given var-

---

* But if we include this last reason within our reasons for and against, can we then do the straight-line extrapolation? However, this last reason may not concern *x* directly as a reason for or against some conclusion about it; because it concerns rather our processes of gaining information, it is best treated at another level.

Bernard Williams holds that the only reasons for action that are relevant to a person are those he already has or those he could arrive at by sound deliberation from his existing desires, preferences, and evaluations (if given fuller information). See Bernard Williams, "Internal and External Reasons," reprinted in his *Moral Luck* (Cambridge: Cambridge Univ. Press, 1981), pp. 101–113. These internal reasons are connected to his existing motivations. But when a person asks himself, "What should I do?" he needn't be asking what best serves his current motivations or the ones he would have if he were better informed. He may know that others' motivations might differ and be better than his own in some respects. His own may have been thwarted by a particularly deprived or brutalized childhood, or a particular situation may have instilled certain motivations in him. What he wants to know is what are the *best* reasons, and he may give others' opinions on this some weight. (Would Williams say that this assumes a particular existing internal motive, namely, to do what is supported by the best reasons?)

ious facts. This is one lesson of the three-prisoners problem*[17] and is an additional bar to Rudolf Carnap's project of developing an inductive logic to specify, in general, the degree of confirmation of hypothesis h on evidence e.[18] If a person's sources of information are such that even if p were false they would not (or would be unlikely to) deliver that information, then from the fact that he receives no such information he cannot conclude that p is true. He must consider that his sources of information are biased in favor of announcing "p."[19] I shall say more about the issue of bias in reasons later.

Rules of Rationality

Philosophers traditionally have sought to formulate rules for rational belief, for the rational inference and acceptance of deductive conclusions and for rational (nondeductive) ways of arriving at belief. They seek rules with an appealing face, which recommend themselves to reason by their content and also yield the inferences and beliefs we are most confident of, rules that might be applied to sharpen our ways of arriving at and evaluating beliefs.[20] If the rationality of a belief, however, is a function of the effectiveness of the process that produces and maintains it, then there is no guarantee that optimal processes will employ any rules that are appealing on their face. Those processes instead might involve scorekeeping competition among rival rules and procedures whose strengths are determined (according to specific scoring procedures) by each rule's past history of participation in successful predictions and inferences. None of these rules or procedures need look reasonable on their face, but, constantly modified by feedback, they interact in tandem to produce results that meet the desired external criteria (such as truth). The theory of that process, then, would be not a small set of rules whose apparent reasonableness can be detected

---

* The people who reach the wrong result about the three prisoners-problem—that each of the two remaining prisoners has a one-half chance of being executed—do so by applying some rule or principle that seems evident to them, an insufficiently subtle rule or one they apply with insufficient subtlety. We should realize that we too can be in this situation, even with some rule that is the very best one we currently can state, and so not be too quick to use a rule to override a statable reason (for example, "You already knew that one of them would not be executed, and so . . . "). There is room here also for an investigation in the style of Amos Tversky and Daniel Kahneman to determine what particular general heuristic is being used by those misled by the three prisoners problem. See Tversky and Kahneman, "Judgment under Uncertainty: Heuristics and Biases," reprinted in *Judgment under Uncertainty: Heuristics and Biases*, ed. Daniel Kahneman, Paul Slovic, and Amos Tversky (Cambridge: Cambridge Univ. Press, 1982), pp. 3–20, and see also their other essays in that volume.

so that a person then could feasibly apply them but a computer program to simulate that very process.[21] More radically, it is possible that no rules are symbolically represented, even in a weighted competition, but that any "rule" emerges as a regularity of behavior of a parallel distributed processing system whose matrix of weights determining activation of output or intermediate vectors is modified repeatedly by some error-correction rule.[22] If the most effective processes for reaching cognitive goals are of these kinds, then the type of normative rules that philosophers have sought to formulate will not succeed in demarcating rationality of belief. They will not themselves be components of that process, and conscious application of them will not be the best route to true (or otherwise desirable) belief.

In the study of reliable processes for arriving at belief, philosophers will become technologically obsolescent. They will be replaced by cognitive and computer scientists, workers in artificial intelligence, and others.* Our understanding thereby will progress, but the nature of this understanding will change: computer simulations will replace (a theory presenting) structurally revealing rules with a face validity that people can appreciate and apply.[23] This will be useful to us—machines will be produced to do intricate tasks—but it will not be what philosophers earlier had hoped for: rules and procedures that we ourselves could apply to better our own beliefs, *surveyable* rules and procedures—I take the term from Ludwig Wittgenstein—that we can take in and understand as a whole and that give us a structurally revealing description of the nature of rationality. (Consider the difference between traditional strategic advice for playing chess and a program that learned *only* through the results of its past moves through some feedback scorekeeping procedure. Such a programmed machine might end up playing very well, but we would not understand how it did this in any particular game; from it we would learn no particular rules we could follow to improve our own play. The elaborate system of weights the program has arrived at may not be formulable in terms of concepts available to us, in a way that we can understand.) The machines these programs inhabit, however, might become useful external

---

* The literature marking this transition already is enormous. For general reflections, see Clark Glymour, "Artificial Intelligence Is Philosophy," in *Aspects of Artificial Intelligence*, ed. James Fetzer (Dordrecht: Kluwer, 1988), pp. 195–207. My point is not one about the demarcation of academic disciplines. Of course, some people now trained in philosophy will shift their work to these areas, and in the future some people who would have entered the subject of philosophy will enter these other areas. The interesting point concerns the changed nature of the theoretical goal and of the kind of understanding that results. Still, philosophers' conceptual analyses of what is involved in various domains and tasks might help workers in artificial intelligence and cognitive science to avoid paths of research that cannot succeed.

aids for bettering our beliefs. (I can believe a calculator's answer to a question without understanding why that is the correct answer.)

Suppose that the most reliable processes of arriving at belief involve such scorekeeping procedures and continual revision of weights; the only rules are ones that determine what enters the competition with what strengths and how those strengths get modified by the ascertained results of using the competition's winner.* (Here is a rule: If you've overshot your target, modify slightly downward all positive weights that interact with positive quantities; if you've undershot, modify slightly upward all positive weights that interact with positive quantities; continue these modifications until you exactly hit the target, then stop. No doubt, this is an admirable form of rule—particular specifications will say exactly what modifications in the weights are to be made—but it is not a principle of rational belief of the kind previously sought. Nor is the "bucket brigade algorithm" for the apportionment of credit,[24] though it deals with more rulelike entities than does the delta rule.) Even so, it might be said, the philosophers' principles have an illuminating function, namely, to describe the *output* of these feedback processes (scorekeeping processes that modify their weights according to past performance in actual predictions and inferences). Some principles may *define* cognitive goals and hence specify the target at which the processes are aimed, but the (extant) principles might not further describe that output any more illuminatingly. In advance, we will not know whether various philosophical principles (that do not just define the cognitive goals) will accurately describe the output of the most effective processes for achieving those goals.

For instance, consider the frequently proposed normative requirement that a person's body of beliefs be consistent and deductively closed (that any logical consequence of things believed also be believed). Perhaps the most effective procedures for arriving at a high ratio of truths (and relatively few falsehoods) will yield a set of beliefs that is inconsistent. Hence, if that high ratio of truths is to be maintained, the set of beliefs had better not be deductively closed. To require in advance that no rules be used for generating beliefs that are known to lead (in some circumstances) to inconsistency might prevent us from arriving at a very large number of true beliefs. When such rules are used, though, steps must be taken to limit the consequences of the inconsistencies that might arise. We may look for an acceptable

---

* "But would we trust the verdict of such a device when it conflicts with our intuition about a particular case or proposition?" I certainly would trust the recommendation of a very experienced chess-playing machine, whose moves are the result of weightings modified in accordance with some error-correcting rule, over my own best choice of move, even if I myself can see no rationale for its recommendation.

way to avoid inconsistency, but in the meantime we will engage in damage control, isolating inconsistencies and taking steps not to infer any and every arbitrary statement from explicit contradictions.[25] In everyday life we do this with equanimity—we happily acknowledge our fallibility and affirm that one of our beliefs, no doubt, is false. Science embodies a strong drive to attain consistency, but scientists too will bide their time, refusing to renounce the many exact predictions of a theory known to generate inconsistencies or impossible values (witness the use of "renormalization" in quantum-mechanical calculations).

Nevertheless, there remains a role—a more modest role—for the philosopher's traditional endeavor to formulate explicit principles of rational belief. The verdict of a particular explicit principle P that it is rational (or irrational) to believe a statement q can be one output among others in a process of belief. The verdict of principle P will not be determinative of belief all by itself but will feed into later stages of the belief-forming process and will have its weight (in future belief formation) modified by the perceived outcome of accepting or rejecting that statement q and acting accordingly. Such a rule or principle P might be a processing unit, one among many others, within a parallel distributed processing system, and its output—whether a verdict of rational or irrational, a Bayesian probability, or whatever—might be propagated forward to play a role in activating some next unit, until eventually a result, belief or not, is reached and its further result is ascertained.* The weight assigned to principle P's connections to fur-

---

* Proponents of parallel distributed processing systems have tended to hold that rules emerge as a result of the shifting assignment of weights and need not themselves be symbolically represented anywhere—they emerge, I am tempted to say, by an invisible hand process. Here "rules" are embodied in a pattern of connectivity among processing units. Other places where rules may be sought are in the output function for each unit, the propagation rule for propagating patterns of activities through the network, the activation rule for combining the inputs impinging on a unit with the current state of that unit to produce a new level of activation for the unit, and a learning or error-correction rule whereby patterns of connectivity are modified by experience. (Here, I follow the list of aspects of a parallel distributed processing model in D. E. Rumelhart, G. E. Hinton, and J. L. McClelland, "A General Framework for Parallel Distributed Processing," in *Parallel Distributed Processing: Explorations in the Microstructure of Cognition*, ed. Rumelhart and McClelland [Cambridge, Mass.: M.I.T. Press, 1986], p. 46.) It is at this last place, the learning rule, that one might expect to find some symbolic representation. In any case, my remarks here are meant to show how, within a general framework of some parallel distributed processing model, a rule might have a function; I do not make the strong assumption that no rule is represented except as in a pattern of connectivity. For criticisms of the adequacy of connectionist psychological theories that do not symbolically represent rules, see the essays in *Connections and Symbols*, ed. Steven Pinker and Jacques Mehler (Cambridge, Mass.: M.I.T. Press, 1988).

ther components within this overall system would then be modified by feedback from the ultimate results, in accordance with some learning rule. (Perhaps some details of principle P also would get modified, thereby producing a new principle P'.)

My remarks here are not an endorsement of the (stringent) research programs of proponents of parallel distributed processing and are not tied to them, despite the current popularity of such connectionist theories.[26] Later I will suppose that specific rules deliver an output into a complicated feedback process, and it is no part of my concern that these rules themselves be emergent as a regularity in a parallel distributed processing system rather than symbolically and explicitly represented themselves. For my purposes, what is most suggestive about parallel distributed processing is the general framework it presents: multiple units feeding forward into further units (whose actions are determined by what feeds into them) in accordance with a matrix of weights that is modified by some feedback (error-correction) rule. Some of the units within such a network may themselves be *rules*. But they will exhibit relations among themselves similar to the ones shown among nonrule units in the parallel distributed processing structure.

Within this general framework, we may say that the traditional philosopher hoped to formulate a principle whose output would completely determine the later state of belief by being the sole input of any weight to the belief unit. In a parallel distributed processing system, a component such as a principle might come to have this strong role without starting out that way; over time the weights of all other (independent) components whose outputs impinge on the belief unit might come to be zero. (So this general framework leaves room for the traditional philosopher's hope but does not depend upon it.) Even short of this strong role, however, an explicit principle can be of help, its verdict part of the (most) reliable process for arriving at belief. Explicit principles should be taken with a grain of salt.

The various methodological maxims presented in the philosophy of science literature might be embedded within this general framework. Some of these maxims might be components within the system, having a gradually modified weight; some maxims might be emergent as descriptions of the system's operation rather than as components within it.[27] I have in mind maxims such as these: the evidential support is greater when the evidence is more varied (where variety is judged by categorizations embodied in your other beliefs); simpler hypotheses are to be preferred; a theory or hypothesis inherits the evidential support of the theory it supplants; predictions of new phenomena add more credibility than derivations of known ones; ad hoc hypotheses are to be avoided; control for all other variables that might well affect the result; the more precise the prediction that is borne out, the more confirmed is the hypothesis.

We have seen how an explicit principle can play a useful role in producing a true belief (or a belief that satisfies some other appropriate cognitive goal). But can an explicit principle help us to *understand* the nature of a rational belief? One way to understand the rationality of a belief is simply to regard it as the result of a certain type of process—for example, a parallel distributed process (to take what is the worst case for the understanding given by explicit principles). Or we can understand it in more detail as the result of this particular process, with all parameters, functions, and transition rules specified. (Compare: current animal and plant life is what arose from the continual operation of these particular Darwinian processes; current wealth and income distribution in a market society is what arose from the continual operation of these specified processes.) We may want to understand something else, though: namely, the patterns currently shown by the results of these processes, to the extent that they do exhibit a pattern that can be described. How do current organisms function? What is the pattern of the distribution of income and wealth and with what factors is this correlated? What does the set of rational beliefs look like? Yet, if rationality aims at truth, the principles for arriving at rational belief may not be the best description of what rational beliefs are like. The best short description of what the set of rational beliefs looks like might be our most compendious description of the set of truths—the largest one we can describe simply without encountering diagonalization problems. This will not be identical to the set of rational beliefs—we often believe falsehoods, and there are some truths we do not believe—but it may be the best short, intelligible description we can offer, and some of its mismatch will be reduced by the fact that *we* are offering the description, and so our description of the set of truths will include errors too, in the direction of our set of beliefs.

What we may want, though, is neither of these things—not a description of the patterns in the current time-slice of our rational beliefs, not a description of the process by which the current beliefs arose. Rather, we may want a description of the relation of our current rational beliefs to their source, a structurally revealing and relatively brief description of how the content and structure of our current rational beliefs is related to the content and structure of where they came from. What is the pattern of *this* connection? There may be no such thing to understand. Undergirded and established by the competitive scorekeeping feedback process, this connection may exhibit no other revealing pattern, even to a rough approximation. (Then, there will not be something we don't understand. There will be no such thing to un-

derstand.) But if there is such a pattern to the connection, or to successive stages of it, then we should be able to formulate that pattern in
some explicit principle. Such a principle also can help in deciding what
credence to place in the things that others tell us by showing the relation of what they say to what it is based upon.*[28]

Now, I would like to describe *one* component of the network of
many components with varying weights (in accordance with some
feedback rule) that is to determine our belief. It will be helpful to begin
with Bayes' Theorem. This theorem, very easily derived from the axioms of probability theory, states what the probability of an hypothesis
h on evidence *e* should depend upon. We can make of this theorem not
simply a complex formula but an intuitive statement.

How likely is the hypothesis *h* on the data *e*? Well, how likely is it
that the data arose via the (truth of the) hypothesis? How likely is it
that the fact that *e* is due to the holding of *h*? This is not simply the
probability that if *h* were true, it would give rise to *e*. Let us, temporarily, write *this* probability as prob(*e:h*). That is how likely the data *e* is,
given that *h* is true—here I spoke loosely—how likely *e* would be *if h*
were true.

To find out how likely it is that the data *e did* arise via the hypothesis
h, we have to consider not only prob(*e:h*) but also how likely *h* itself
is. That *e* arose from *h* may be unlikely, even when prob(*e:h*) is very
high, if prob(*h*) is very low. The probability that a horn would blow

---

* There are other possible routes to evaluating another's reliability that do not speak
of what patterned connection demarcates his beliefs, for instance, statistics about his
reliability. But, in general, these will be hard to come by. Yet "Why do you think so?"
might admit of a relatively easy and revealing answer. His saying, "I've had a lot of
experience with these things, and I can tell," also might be helpful. In current terms, he
tells us that his current weights, and therefore responses, have been shaped by and ben-
efited from much feedback. This would be reassuring, provided we think that the statement is of a kind that such a system could learn to recognize the truth of.

A process can be reliable in eventually arriving at the truth about a subject matter—it
eventually settles into a true belief in a high percentage of the cases—even though this
takes it a long time. If within this process beliefs also are arrived at along the way, modified by feedback, and so on, then many of these earlier beliefs will have been false. A
current belief may have arisen by a reliable process—one that eventuates in truth a high
percentage of the time—but at a stage of the process that does not give *it* a probability
of being true greater than 1/2. Is it rational now to believe *it*? One suggestion is to build
the process into some external device and refrain from believing something until that
device stably settles upon a belief. (Our reliable procedure then is *that* one.) Yet this
option might be unavailable to us. Perhaps the process can be carried on only in our
heads, and the feedback works only upon what we actually believe. To run this process,
then, a process that is eventually reliable, requires us actually to have many beliefs along
the way that are not reliably true. (Science would be an example of this if scientists must
believe its current results in order to do normal science, generate anomalies that require
a new theory, and so on.)

outside at this very moment is very high if there were a cabal of hidden Alpha Centurions with large powers who most desired for me to hear a horn right now. The probability of that latter hypothesis itself is minuscule, however, and the hypothesis does not gain significantly in probability by its ability to account for that particular hornblowing. It is $\text{prob}(e{:}h) \times \text{prob}(h)$ that represents how likely it is that e arose via the truth of h, how *absolutely likely* it is that e arose via the truth of h.

But what does this tell us about how likely h is or would be on the basis of e? We know the absolute likelihood that e arose via h, but there also is a chance that e arose from some *other* hypotheses $h2, h3, h4, \ldots$ We want to look not only at the absolute likelihood that e arose from h but also at the *relative* likelihood that it did. What *percentage* of the likelihoods of all the (other) ways that e could have arisen is the likelihood of its arising via h? (It is more convenient mathematically to delete that parenthesized "other.") The *relative* likelihood that e arose from h is the ratio of the absolute likelihood that e arose via h to the sum of the absolute likelihoods that e arose in *all* the different ways it could arise. It is this relative likelihood that e arose from h that seems to tell us how likely h is on the data e. Let us rename the hypothesis h we have been concerned with, $h1$. Then the probability of $h1$ on the basis of e seems to be

$$\frac{\text{prob}(e{:}h1) \times \text{prob}(h1)}{\sum_{(i=1)}^{n} \text{prob}(e{:}hi) \times \text{prob}(hi)}$$

And this seems to tell us how probable $h1$ is given e. For it tells us how probable it is that e arose from $h1$, as compared to all the ways e could have arisen. Thus we seem to have an intuitive derivation, or at least explanation, of Bayes' Theorem.

But it is not exactly Bayes' Theorem we have arrived at. Our probabilities that if a hypothesis were true, it would give rise to evidence e, $\text{prob}(e{:}h)$, are not the conditional probabilities of Bayes' Theorem. These latter are simply the probabilities that the evidence holds true, given that the hypothesis does, whether or not the hypothesis *gave rise to* that evidence, whether or not there is any (probabilistic) subjunctive connection between the hypothesis and the evidence. What we have been led to is a causalized or subjunctivized version of Bayes' Theorem. To emphasize that these probabilities of subjunctives are not the standard conditional probabilities, let us write the probability that if h were true, e would be true as: $\text{prob}(h{\rightarrow}e)$.

The above version needs to be modified somewhat, and not just typographically. For although we have considered the different hypotheses that might have given rise to evidence e, we have not yet considered the possibility that e might have occurred spontaneously, without (probabilistic) cause or generating hypothetical fact. This too needs to be taken account of. (Here we may consider the chance hypothesis about e, written as Ce, simply as the denial that there is any hi such that hi did, probabilistically, generate e.) Thus, our formula becomes the following.

$$\text{Measure}(h_1/e) = \frac{\text{prob}(h_1 \to e) \times \text{prob}(h_1)}{\sum_{(i=1)}^{n} \text{prob}(hi \to e) \times \text{prob}(hi) + \text{prob}(Ce)}$$

What is it that this measure measures?[29] Does this formula fix the measure of $h1$ on e as a conditional probability, interpreted as betting odds in a conditional bet, or does the formula fix some other quantity, such as the degree to which e supports $h1$, or the probability that if e were true $h1$ would be true, $\text{prob}(e \to h1)$? A preliminary question to investigate is what are the properties of the ratio on the right-hand side of the formula, does that ratio behave like a probability, and so forth.

There is a philosophical literature on explanatory inferences, "inferences to the best explanation."[30] To say there is such a principle of *inference* is to claim that the goodness of h as an explanatory hypothesis is sufficient to determine h's credibility as a belief. Something weaker seems true, though: namely, h's goodness as an explanatory hypothesis is one factor that enters into fixing and assessing h's credibility.[31] The above ratio would appear to be useful in specifying and analyzing this one factor. How good h is as an explanation of e will depend, at least, upon the probability that if h were true e would be true, and upon the prior probability of h; it is plausible that the dependence upon these will be upon their product. Hypothesis h provides a better explanation than another hypothesis hi, all other things being equal, if this product for h is greater than that product for hi.

We would not always want to infer what is the very best explanation, however. Suppose there were eight possible ones hi, where the $\text{prob}(hi \to e)$ is the same for each hypothesis hi, and $\text{prob}(h1)$ is only a shade greater than one-eighth while the probabilities of $h2, \ldots, h8$ are each a (smaller) shade less than one-eighth. It may be that $h1$ is the best explanation, but nevertheless it is not such a good one. This is indicated by $h1$'s small ratio, as measured by the right-hand side of our equation. Of course, the previous explanatory successes of an hypothesis will be important, and these will affect its prior probability as it enters into this formula. Other explanatory features may affect that prior probability as well. So perhaps the ratio in question measures the degree of explanatory support for $h1$ by e.* In assessing a hypothesis's explanatory status, it is relevant to consider more than one single fact e that is to be explained: which hypothesis gains the greatest explanatory support from the totality of the facts to be explained?[32] Within a multicomponent network that feeds forward with varying weights (such as a parallel distributed processing network), this explanatory value of h would be *one* factor feeding into h's total credibility.

Let us imagine a network that incorporates a weighting of many factors—including Bayesian probabilities, explanatory value (as represented by the Causalized Bayesian formula), Popperian methodological maxims, and an assessment of undercuttings—and feeds forward to result in a *credibility value* for a statement h. View this as an ideal assessment that duly weights all of the reasons for and against h.[33] My hunch is that, within this system, the rich hypotheses get richer. New data will not count as evidence for every hypothesis that fits them. They get corraled by the most credible of these hypotheses and thus add to *its* credibility but not to that of the other hypotheses. (This might be instantiated in a system where existing hypotheses bid for the support of new data; the hypotheses already rich in credibility have an advantage in such bidding.) When the previously most credible hypothesis is rejected for some reason, its supporting data then become available for another hypothesis.[34]

This processing system is a learning system; its weights are modified by feedback. Where does this feedback come from? Corrections of the system's predictions and expectations may result from an external teacher entering corrected values, or from sensory input different from that predicted, or from registered internal disharmonies that reduce the strength of each participating component.[35] The particular error-correction rule will vary from system to system, perhaps within a system from task to task, and the rule itself may compete with other error-correction rules in a feedback system subject to some further error-correction rule or even to one of those very competitors.

A person, considered as such a system, presents several aspects relevant to assessing her overall rationality. Does she have a good set of weights and strengths? Does she have a detection system that registers appropriate information for the purpose of feedback? Does she have an error-correction rule that modifies weights in an efficient way? And (perhaps) does she have some procedure for revising the structure of

---

* That is, the degree of explanatory support e gives to $h1$, given the hypotheses that have been formulated and that are known of. Some *other* hypothesis $hn+1$ that had not yet been formulated also might explain e, and this hypothesis is not included in any factor in the denominator of the formula, including the last factor that e occurs by chance. So the ratio is a measure of the degree of explanatory support of $h1$ by e, *relative to* our current formulation of admissible alternative explanatory hypotheses.

the whole network? The whole system can be rational without any one of these aspects being optimal. Perhaps there are more efficient error-correction rules that converge more quickly to appropriate weights that will not stand in need of correction, but the system will be (somewhat) rational if the existing rule at least makes (small) modifications in the right direction, with the right sign. How the component parts interrelate in the functioning of the system as a whole is what needs to be considered.

Thus far we have imagined a system that generates credibility values, giving a score for each statement h that is being assessed. How is this resulting credibility value of h to be used in arriving at belief about h? What will the rule of acceptance be?

The first rule of acceptance is this:

Rule 1: Do not believe h if some alternative statement incompatible with h has a higher credibility value than h does.

Credibility values are unlike probabilities in that the credibility value of h and that of not-h need not sum to any fixed value. However, when not-h has a higher credibility value than h does, Rule 1 tells us not to believe h. (But since many factors enter into determining the credibility value, such as explanatory power, do not assume that the relatively unspecific not-h always will have a higher credibility value than h does.)

Notice that this rule applies also when the alternative statement incompatible with h is not some alternative hypothesis at its level but rather some counterevidence g to h, strictly incompatible with h—a Popperian falsifier. In this case, if the credibility value of g is greater than that of h, then h is not to be accepted. Such apparent disconfirmation may not be conclusive, though, for g's credibility value may be less than h's, and indeed may be diminished through h's increasing the weight of some undercutter of g.[36]

Rule 1 eliminates some statements and leaves us with a set of candidates for current belief, namely, those whose credibility value is not topped by some statement incompatible with them. Among these admissible candidates, which shall be believed? Shall we believe all of these, or rather all those that remain after some further pruning procedure for removing inconsistencies? I do not believe we should follow this maximalist policy about belief. Rather, at that point, we should follow a decision-theoretic calculation about the desirability of holding that belief, a calculation that includes *practical* objectives and utilities, not simply cognitive ones. (I do not say we should explicitly make such a calculation; rather, we should act in accordance with it, revising our action if deviation from the calculation is brought to our attention.) That is our second rule of acceptance.

Rule 2: Believe (an admissible) h only if the expected utility of believing h is not less than the expected utility of having no belief about h.*

Thus we have a two-stage procedure: the first weeds out lesser credibility values, and the second determines belief among the statements that remain by considering the consequences (broadly conceived) of such belief. This procedure has much to recommend it. Under it, a person is excluded from holding cognitively inferior beliefs (as judged by their credibility value). However, he does not have to hold any belief about the matter at all. Whether he does will be determined by his objectives and goals, practical, theoretical, and social.

Consider again the case of the mother of the convicted felon. Let us assume that the credibility value for her of her son's guilt is greater than that of his innocence—her greater knowledge of her son does not actually reverse the credibility values others find. Believing in his guilt, however, even if this belief were accurate, would have great disutility for her. According to the two-stage principle proposed here, it is irrational for her to believe her son is innocent. (That her son is innocent is not a rational thing for her to believe—Rule 1 excludes that belief.) Yet it is not irrational for her *not* to believe that her son is guilty; it is not irrational for her to have no settled belief about the matter. (But what if the mother would be made decidedly miserable if she does not hold the belief that her son is innocent? Here we can invoke our earlier distinction. That he is innocent is not a rational thing for her to believe; but believing that might be the best, and hence the rational, thing for her to do.) What if the evidence of guilt were *overwhelming*? But how stringent the standards are that must be met before we believe a particular thing may be, in part, up to us. We decide what level of evidence, what amount of credibility, it will take to convince us; and how high we set that level may depend upon many factors, including the utility to us and to society of holding certain beliefs. (The mother need not set the standard so that nothing can satisfy it. Perhaps she can decide to believe in her son's guilt only if she has a direct and overpowering experience of God directly speaking to her of the son's guilt.) That we can choose how high to set the standard does

---

* A more stringent rule would require that the expected utility of believing h be greater than that of having no belief about h. The difference is over whether we should believe h when there is an exact tie between the expected utility of believing h and the expected utility of having no belief about h. We might think that in this case we should believe it because believing the truth has a value—but wouldn't this value already be included in the utility calculation that, by hypothesis, yields a tie? Or we might think that in this case we should not believe it because holding a belief itself has costs (we have limited storage capacity or mental energy or whatever)—but, again, won't these costs already have been included in the utility calculation?

not mean we can choose arbitrarily. Principles and requirements of consistency may be involved: cases that the person regards as similar might have to meet the same standard; the stringency of the standard might have to vary directly (and never inversely) with the cases' positions along the relevant dimension (for example, the amount of utility consequent upon the belief), and so on.*

Notice that a statement is excluded as a candidate for belief in the first stage only when its credibility value is less than that of some incompatible statement.[37] A candidate for belief need not have maximal credibility overall, though. Its credibility value may be less than that of some other, not incompatible statement. Notice too that when a statement is rejected for belief in the second stage—believing it is not desirable for practical reasons—that statement still remains active in the first stage to exclude statements of lesser credibility incompatible with it.** Under this principle, belief is a combination of the theoretical and the practical, with the theoretical coming (lexicographically) first.

That the first stage is an eliminative one captures the feeling that, with regard to rationality of belief, "irrationality" is the primary notion—in J. L. Austin's (sexist?) phrase, the one that wears the pants. It is clear that many things are irrational to believe. It is less clear that some beliefs are so credible that they are mandated by rationality, so that it is irrational not to hold them when you hold no belief about the

---

* The courtroom spectators may tell the mother, "We deem the evidence sufficient to make it *irrational* not to hold the belief that your son is guilty." The mother and these spectators agree that the lesser credibility statement (that the son is innocent) is not to be believed, but they disagree about what credibility value necessitates belief in his guilt. The mother may ask how they decided where to set the threshold of evidential sufficiency. If, as seems plausible, the setting of their threshold was determined by the average effects of their holding certain sorts of beliefs according to the dictates of that threshold, cannot the mother reply that the effects for her are not the average ones, and that if *their* average effects had the magnitude of her actual ones, they too would have set a more stringent threshold. Why then should her belief be mandated by the standard appropriate to their different situation? (The members of the jury, after all, appropriately set their threshold at a different place than the average spectator does.)

** Suppose p has a higher credibility value than q does, and q has a higher credibility value than r does; suppose also that p is incompatible with q, q with r, yet p is not incompatible with r. Is r an inadmissible candidate for belief because of q and application of the first rule, or shall r be admissible because the q that otherwise would exclude it is itself an inadmissible candidate for belief because of p and application of the first rule? Must what eliminates a statement via the first rule itself be admissible according to that first rule? It would be interesting to explore each of these directions in developing the system.

Does Rule 2 mandate that every change in a situation or a context necessitates that a person recalculate the expected utility of each belief (and each nonbelief) that he holds? Here the distinction between acquiring and maintaining or changing a belief is useful. Inertia rules unless there is some particular reason to change.

matter at all. In some contexts a person might, without irrationality, impose more stringent standards of belief than others do and hence hold no belief where they hold some.

Rule 2 does not mandate a belief as rational. If a statement passes the first test—no incompatible statement has a higher credibility—then Rule 2 tells us *not* to believe that statement if the expected utility of doing so is less than the expected utility of having no belief about the matter at all. Thus, Rule 2 tells us when not to believe a statement; it does not tell us when to believe it.

But if a statement does pass the test of Rule 1, and if the utility (for that person) of believing this statement is greater than the utility of having no belief about the matter at all, then won't it be irrational for the person not to believe that statement? (I have ignored until now the possibility that two incompatible statements might tie in credibility, each untopped by any other incompatible statement. Each is left as a possible candidate for belief. In such situations, the decision-theoretic calculation must compare the utility of believing each one not simply to that of holding no belief about the matter at all but also to the utility of believing the other. If once again there is a tie, perhaps either one will do.) No benefit is gained by abstention from belief, and some benefit is lost—such is the verdict of the practical calculation. If a statement is sufficiently credible—that is, no less credible than some incompatible statement—*shouldn't* a person believe it if a decision-theoretic calculation would recommend doing this? We could transform the more stringent version of Rule 2 into a sufficient condition for belief.

Rule 2′: Believe (an admissible) h if the expected utility of believing h is greater than the expected utility of having no belief about h.

I am reluctant to accept this rule, however, without a more detailed understanding of how the credibility values operate. Can the credibility of a statement be greater than that of any incompatible statement and yet be quite low? (Unlike probabilities, the credibilities of exclusive and exhaustive statements need not sum to 1. So couldn't a statement be more credible than its negation and yet have quite low credibility?) In that case, there should be no mandate to believe it (in the absence of some pressing need to hold a belief about the matter.)

This suggests another requirement upon rational belief: Believe a statement only if its credibility is sufficiently high.[38] How high is high enough will vary, depending upon the kind of statement this is, whether it is a report of observation, a statement of theoretical science, a belief about past historical events, and so on. Thus,

Rule 3: Believe an (admissible) h only if its credibility value is high enough, given the kind of statement it is.

What sets the level for each kind of statement? Is it the level that maximizes the utility of holding beliefs of that kind (when the beliefs are held according to Rule 3)? Thus, there would be two utility calculations: the first about a particular belief as mandated by Rule 2, the second about a kind of belief to set the credibility level used in Rule 3. But since statements can be classified in various ways, what determines the specification and shape of the relevant kind? Unless there is some limitation on what counts as a kind, the utility calculation threatens to collapse Rule 3 into Rule 2.[39]

Passing the tests of these three rules—supposing the third rule can be specified adequately—does give us a sufficient condition for rational belief. Thus, we have Rule 4: Believe a statement if it is not excluded by any of the first three rules. (We already have: Believe the statement only if it is not excluded by any of the first three rules.) More explicitly,

> **Rule 4:** Believe a statement h if there is no alternative statement incompatible with h that has a higher credibility value than h does, and the credibility value of h is high enough, given the kind of statement that h is, and the expected utility of believing h is at least as great as the expected utility of having no belief about h.

(Again, a more stringent rule would require that the expected utility of believing h be greater than that of having no belief about h.) Rule 2 was formulated using the standard framework of decision theory and speaks of expected value. If our earlier discussion is correct, a decision-theoretic calculation should maximize the decision value of an action, a weighted sum of its causal, evidential, and symbolic utility. Thus, the second rule is more adequately formulated as follows.

> **Rule 5:** Believe (an admissible) h only if the decision-value of believing h is at least as great as the decision-value of having no belief about h.

In deciding what to believe, we are to take into account not just the causal consequences of holding this belief but also the symbolic utility of holding it as well as what believing it evidentially indicates. (Rule 4 should be reformulated accordingly to speak of decision-value rather than expected utility.)

Earlier, I said that a rule for generating beliefs need not guarantee the consistency of all the resulting beliefs, and even may demonstrably lead to inconsistent beliefs under some circumstances—in which case steps are taken to isolate and limit the results of inconsistency. Consider Henry Kyburg's much-discussed example, "the lottery paradox."[40] A lottery is to be held, and you know that one of the million lottery tickets will be drawn as the winner. For any given ticket, the probability is overwhelmingly high that it will not be drawn. If a statement's having a sufficiently high probability is sufficient for (rational) belief, then for each ticket, you believe it will not be drawn; so you believe ticket 1 will not be drawn, you believe ticket 2 will not be drawn, . . . , and you believe ticket 1,000,000 will not be drawn. Yet you do believe the lottery will be held and so *some one* ticket will be drawn. Hence you believe that ticket 1 will be drawn or ticket 2 . . . or ticket 1,000,000 will be drawn. This set of beliefs is inconsistent. Some philosophers have concluded that this example shows that a rule that recommends believing something merely because its probability surpasses a certain very high value is inadequate. Moreover, if the rule goes on to say that one should believe something *only if* its probability surpasses that value, then one will not always believe the conjunction of two things one believes, for that conjunction will have a lesser probability than each of its noncertain conjuncts and hence in some cases will fall below the cutoff probability for belief.

The view we have presented does not make probability the sole determinant of the credibility value of a statement. Yet our view does face this type of issue. Whenever each of two statements is to be believed, is their conjunction also to be believed? Can inconsistencies be shown definitely to result from the structure presented here, and, if so, what rules are to be invoked to limit their effects? (Our discussion can proceed in terms of Rule 2' rather than the more complicated Rule 4; any sufficient condition for belief will face similar questions.)

Someone who applies Rule 1 (along with the provision for ties) will not come to believe two statements she knows to be inconsistent. Yet, because it is not a mechanical matter to recognize inconsistencies, there is no guarantee that a sincere applier of this rule will not be led (unknowingly) to inconsistent beliefs. Once the inconsistency is recognized, though, Rule 1 holds that the statement with lesser credibility is not a candidate for belief. Since this rule focuses upon alternatives to a statement that are inconsistent with it, its accurate application guarantees that a person's beliefs will be pairwise consistent. The person will not hold two beliefs, $h1$ and $h2$, that are inconsistent with each other. But what about larger circles of inconsistency? In the lottery paradox, we have the statement that one ticket among the million will win and the individual statement for each ticket that it will not win. Any two of these million and one statements are pairwise consistent—both can be true together—but not all of the million and one statements can hold true. These form an inconsistent set.

We have not required, though, that the total set of beliefs be consistent, merely that beliefs be pairwise consistent. If you want a very high ratio of true beliefs, believe each of the million and one statements; you will be right one million times. "But if the set is inconsistent, you know that you definitely will be wrong one time," someone will object. True, but in another case mightn't I be rational in choosing to have my beliefs formed by a process that I know will give me one false belief every million and one times, not as a matter of logic—these million and one beliefs all are consistent—but as a matter of fact? How are things changed, how is the desirability of following the belief-forming procedure changed, if the one error is guaranteed as a matter of logic, because the beliefs are inconsistent? To be sure, when I know the beliefs are inconsistent, I had better be sure not to use them all as premisses in an argument that might play upon the inconsistency; but this is a matter of isolating the results of the inconsistency.

In this situation we cannot conjoin beliefs indefinitely to arrive at new beliefs. The knowledge that a particular statement—for instance, a conjunction—is inconsistent will (within the network of factors that determine credibility) feed into the statement's resulting credibility value to give it minimal credibility. (This will depend also, of course, upon the score of the feeding statement that the conjunction *is* inconsistent.) The denial of the conjunction known to be inconsistent will be incompatible with it and always will have a higher credibility score. Hence, by Rule 1, that inconsistent conjunction is not an admissible candidate for belief.

How far up toward the inconsistent conjunction can we travel, though? How many consistent statements might we conjoin together and believe? In the lottery situation, Rule 1 (and the rule for ties) prevents us from moving up to each of two distinct conjunctions that are inconsistent with each other—for example, the statement that one ticket will win but that it will not be among the first 500,000, and the statement that one ticket will win but that it will not be among the second 500,000. Moreover, in these lottery cases, the more we conjoin, the less the credibility of the resulting conjunction. (The probability lessens, and this is *one* factor affecting the resultant credibility.) At some critical mass, the conjunction's credibility will drop below that of some competing statement incompatible with it, and hence it will not be an admissible candidate for belief. If the situation is symmetrical with regard to credibilities, we will be left with a number of similarly structured conjunctions, each an admissible candidate according to Rule 1. But Rule 2' need not endorse every maximal such conjunction, even leaving aside the question of ties. What payoffs really will depend upon believing such a maximal (consistent) conjunction? (Remember that some smaller conjunction consistent with this maximal one will have a yet higher credibility.) When we apply Rules 1 and 2' in the lottery situation, and we operate with credibilities (not simply probabilities), we might expect something like the following.

The person believes some ticket or other will win. Name a ticket, though, and he believes it will not win. For any given ticket, he believes it will not win. Name any two tickets, and he believes that neither will win. For any pair of tickets, he believes that neither member of that pair will win. Similarly for trios. At some point it becomes vague. Definitely, for a large n-tuple, he does not hold the belief that no one ticket in that group will win. He does not believe that no one of the first 900,000 will win. He does not even believe that no one of the first 499,999 will win. So where does his belief stop? What does it matter? In a particular situation there may be a point to his having a belief in some substantial conjunction or other, and in *that* situation whether he holds that belief will be determined by the utility of holding it. Now that—up until the previous sentence at least—sounds very much like my situation with regard to the lottery.*

If our beliefs may be inconsistent—though the rules will operate to attempt to keep them pairwise consistent—how are we to isolate the damage such inconsistency might cause? It is well known that from an inconsistency any and all statements can be deduced by using standard logical rules of inference. (From p & not-p, we can deduce that p. From p we can deduce that p or q for any arbitrary statement q. From p & not-p, we can deduce that not-p. From p or q and from not-p, we can deduce that q. Moreover, we need not start with the explicit contradiction p & not-p as a conjunction; start simply with the two distinct statements, the statement that p, and the statement that not-p, and the deduction proceeds largely as before.)

There are various devices one might use to avoid this escalation of belief. I suggest that for belief legitimately to be transferred from premisses to conclusion in a deductive inference not only must each premiss be believed but also the conjunction of the premisses must be believed. (Or, at least, the conjunction of the premisses must not be disbelieved.) This gives us a sixth rule for belief, applying to deductive inferences.

> **Rule 6:** Believe q because it is inferred from premisses $p1, \ldots, pn$ in an explicit deductive inference only if each of these premisses pi is believed *and* only if their conjunction $p1$ & $p2$ & $\ldots$ & pn also is believed.

When we assess a statement as a candidate for belief, Rule 1 bids us to determine whether there is some other statement incompatible with the first that has a higher credibility value. There is no assumption of some uniform credibility threshold that each admissible candidate must pass. Statement $s1$ might be excluded as a candidate for belief

---

* I do not see it as an especially pressing matter to remove the vagueness about the size of the acceptable conjunction any more precisely than the decision-theoretic calculation does. What has interested people about the lottery paradox is not its *sorites* aspect: precisely how many grains of sand make a heap?

by some incompatible statement s2 that has a higher credibility value, yet statement s3, unrelated to but with a lower credibility value than s1, might be admissible for belief because no statement incompatible with *it* has a higher credibility value. The credibility threshold is a comparative one; hence, it will be different from one context to another as these involve different kinds of competing statements with differing credibilities.

Rules 2 and 5 hold that the consequences of believing an admissible statement are to determine whether it is believed. Any complete theory will allow *some* consideration of what believing *p* involves. For believing *p* (for certain reasons or as the result of a certain procedure) will be another fact in the world, if it happens, and that fact may have a significance of its own. The conditional probabilities of various statements may change, including that of the very statement *p* that we are concerned with; the conditional probability of *p*, given the various reasons for it and given that you believe *p* for those reasons, may be different from the conditional probability of *p* on those reasons alone. Or believing *p* may have causal consequences that change what holds true in the ensuing situation.[41]

Rule 5 goes beyond this, though, adding a consideration of the causal, evidential, and symbolic utility of believing *p*. These utilities cannot make an inadmissible hypothesis admissible for rational belief. (On the other hand, though *p* may not be the rational thing to believe, Rule 5 does not deny that believing *p* still might be the rational thing to do in some circumstances, that is, believing an inadmissible *p* might have the highest expected utility or decision-value.)[42]

Just as someone might avoid investigating certain subjects in a given society because of what he predicts will be the harmful social consequences of the results—some true belief but also much distortion and misapplication—so too someone might avoid believing something because of the effect he predicts this belief actually will have upon himself, upon his character and mode of behavior. This would not require him to hold the opposite belief, just not to hold this one. Similarly, someone might avoid a belief because of what this would indicate about himself, even without causing that, and because of what certain beliefs stand for and symbolize.

Belief

Why do we *believe* anything at all? What do beliefs do for us? What functions do they serve? Why do we (want to) have beliefs at all? It is because the world changes in nonregular ways that organisms need adaptive mechanisms to respond to local circumstances; the whole job cannot be done by permanent structure and prewired responses (such as circardian rhythms adapted to the stable regularity of day and night)?[43] Operant conditioning of behavior gives organisms some adaptability, but it has two drawbacks: it does not yield immediately new and appropriate behavior in new situations or sufficiently rapid extinction of old, previously reinforced but no longer appropriate behavior; and it does not yield new and distant behavior in environments unless this new behavior is linked to present behavior by some continuous chain of reinforcement.[44] Beliefs are changeable, and when they are based upon reasons and upon reasoning to new conclusions, on a balancing of reasons for and against, they can be attuned to match new or changing situations and then usefully affect the behavior of an organism facing such situations.

But why is it necessary to *believe* any statement or proposition? Why not simply assign probabilities to each and every statement without definitely believing any one and, in choice situations, act upon these probabilities by (perhaps) maximizing expected utility? Such is the position of radical Bayesianism, and it has some appeal.[45] The first propositional result of sensory stimulation might be (shifting) probability judgments, without any need to formulate pure statements representing this sensory stimulation as evidence (certain or probable) for other statements. Because we are unwilling to act upon what we "believe" in all circumstances, betting our life upon each particular belief, isn't it more accurate to treat all these judgments simply as *degrees* of belief, assignments of probabilities to statements? Without any notion of belief, one need not formulate rules of acceptance for what is to be believed—a difficult task. All that is needed are rules for the continuing modification of probabilities.

Moreover, the cost of radical Bayesianism is not so apparent. According to it, the scientist, or the institution of science at a time, does not accept or believe theories or lawlike statements; rather, Carnap tells us, science assigns these statements particular degrees of probability. Previously, we thought the scientist believed these statements, at least *tentatively*. But this century's philosophy of science reiterates continually that scientific theories and formulated laws are at best only highly probable. How, then, can it contest the view that this is all that science *tells* us? (Is it any more plausible to say that science tells us that certain things definitely are true but that its statement when it tells us this is at best only probably correct?) And if you say that *you* definitely do believe something, and do not simply have some degree of belief in it, the radical Bayesian will translate this as your having a degree of belief of 1 in it: being willing to offer infinite odds, or any finite odds, in its favor, being willing to bet anything upon it. (And if you are not, he will be at a loss to understand the content of your claim to believe it rather than merely to have some degree of belief in it.)

Despite these apparent strengths, it is unclear that this position of radical Bayesianism can be formulated coherently. Probabilities of statements (rather than simply beliefs in them) are to be applied in choice situations, but a choice situation is one a person *believes* he is facing, that is, one where he believes that he can perform various alternative actions $A1, \ldots, An$, believes that $A1$ can have various possible outcomes Oi (perhaps depending upon which state of the world Sj obtains), and so on. To be sure, the person then acts upon probabilities, $\text{prob}(Oi/A1)$ or $\text{prob}(Sj/A1)$, but these occur *within* a structure of beliefs about the situation of choice. Can these latter be not simply beliefs but rather probabilities applied to statements? But the very setup of theories of personal probability and utility, or the background commentary they require, involves the existence or attribution of *beliefs* to the person whose choices are taken to indicate preference or probabilistic judgments. Without those beliefs about the situation he was in, his choices would not indicate these particular preferences or probabilistic judgments. The theoretical definition of these latter notions presupposes attributing certain beliefs to the person.

This point applies also to the prime argument of the Bayesian— whether "radical" or not—that degrees of belief should satisfy the axioms of the probability calculus. This is the "dutch book argument": if degrees of belief represent willingness to bet at certain odds, and the degrees of belief do *not* satisfy the probability axioms, then the person will be willing to enter into a series of bets from which she cannot win any money and may lose some. But for this argument to work, the person must *believe* that she is facing such and such a betting situation; if she does not, she will not bet or behave appropriately. For the bets she is willing to make will depend upon her *beliefs* about the structure of the (betting) situation, her beliefs about precisely what payoffs will obtain under precisely what eventualities, and so on. If she merely thinks it is highly likely that she faces a particular betting situation, yet there is some probability that her actions will lead to outcomes different from those the structure of the bet prescribes—for instance, that there is a probability of .01 that if she announces she will bet on statement p, angels will decend and transform the world—then over many such situations she will not conform to the axioms of the probability calculus with respect to the statements that appear (to the outside observer) to be the only relevant ones in the bet. Only if she believes the betting situation to hold can the dutch book argument reach its conclusion.

The radical Bayesian might reply that references to beliefs are necessary to explain or define his notion of degrees of belief (personal probability) and to state his dutch book argument, but that nevertheless beliefs do not exist. Degrees of belief do—and such degrees of belief can and should be postulated as explanatory factors in accounting for people's behavior. It was only for our guidance and understanding of what is postulated, he says, that he presupposed beliefs, but that ladder must be kicked away after it is climbed.

The radical Bayesian also faces formidable practical complexities. The task of assigning probabilities to each and every well-formed statement and combination of statements is overwhelming. Beliefs can cut down on this task if probabilities need not be assigned to whatever is incompatible with your beliefs—if all these are automatically ignored or assigned a probability of zero.

Isaac Levi, a critic of radical Bayesianism, has maintained that beliefs function as a standard of serious possibility. Once something comes to be believed, all possibilities incompatible with it can be ignored. Beliefs can be reexamined; but while they are held, they are treated as certain, as having no serious possibility of being in error.[46] Levi's theoretical structure is impressive in many ways, but this treatment of belief gets him into convoluted difficulties. The inquirer, for some reason, may cease being certain of his belief that p; but while he holds it, he is certain of it, and he is to examine reasons for becoming uncertain of p while in the midst of believing p and hence believing that p has no serious possibility of being false. Levi moves through this minefield, but the path is circuitous and implausible.[47] The mines were created by the structure of his own view; it is difficult for an outside observer to believe that trip really was necessary.

How can we wend our way between the mere degrees of belief of the radical Bayesian and the too tenacious and obstructive beliefs depicted in Levi's theory? Here is a (very) tentative suggestion. A belief excludes possibilities in a (type of) context. In another type of context, those very possibilities would not be excluded. I believe my new junior colleague is not a child molester. (Asked to list the people in the philosophy building who are not child molesters, I unhesitatingly place his name on the list.) Now the context changes; I need someone to watch my young child for two weeks. A mistake here would be serious—the stakes have escalated. Now I think more carefully. It is not that I did not believe in my colleague's innocence before. In that context, for those purposes, I did believe it; I did not consider, or assign a probability to, the possibility of his being a child molester. In this context, with higher stakes, I consider what probability that might have.

The radical Bayesian will welcome this. "Just as I thought," he says. "You never simply believed it; you always assigned some probability to it." Perhaps the situation is this. I assign probabilities to statements only when what is at stake warrants this, only when the probability times the utility that is involved would be sufficiently great. (Being sufficiently great may be a matter not of its absolute magnitude but of the proportion of the total magnitude that it might be—five dollars might make the difference in deciding whether to order a dish in a restaurant but not in deciding whether to purchase a car.) I first make a *rough* estimate of whether the magnitude *could* be sufficiently great, and only if so do I actually assign a probability to the event or statement. (We already have argued, though, that the radical Bayesian cannot say this about *every* belief.)

There may be relevant contextual features other than the utility that is at stake. Certain enterprises, such as scientific and scholarly publishing, may incorporate professional standards that a manuscript must meet to be put forth. Perhaps these more stringent intellectual norms are based eventually upon some general argument about what might be at stake—you do not know who will be acting upon your published information in what circumstances. Or perhaps these norms help to define the nature of that enterprise, contributing to the kind of knowledge we gain from it.

For everyday belief, Rule 1 provides a sufficient standard of credibility, namely, that nothing incompatible is more credible. (This is not sufficient for belief, though; at least the test of Rule 3 also must be passed.) For acceptance within science, however, a more stringent standard of credibility is applied: a statement may be required to reach a certain level of credibility, not simply to be more credible than any incompatible alternative. Or shall we simply say that this situation will be fixed by Rule 3 as applied to scientific contexts? Rule 3 itself is contextual. The scientific standards, once they are known, tend to be extended to—some might say "invade"—other contexts, first to public contexts involving issues of social policy and then even to interpersonal or personal ones.

Only recently has it become clear that in making claims about the effectiveness of medications, one must back these by double-blind experiments; if the patient or the judge of (putative) improvement knows whether the medication has been received, this can contaminate the results. Double-blind experimentation now constitutes a standard in assessing reasons and evidence in this area. (This change is an application of a constant standard, I think, that mandates that all relevant variables be controlled for. The change came in discovering that new variables were relevant.) The most stringent standard is not appropriate in every area: I reasonably can make an everyday causal statement even though I have not performed a double-blind experiment to back it up.

How stringent the standards should be for assessing reasons will depend upon what is at stake, how important or serious a mistake would be, how much energy, time, and resources would have to be devoted to employing procedures that satisfy stricter standards, the general nature of the enterprise, and so forth. If there are different procedures $P1, \ldots, Pn$ that satisfy standards of differing degrees of stringency, we may treat the question of which procedures to use as itself a decision problem, calculating the costs and benefits of each procedure in its specific context.[48] But what standards or procedures shall we use in making this calculation? Are we doomed to an inescapable and objectionable circularity? To answer the theoretical question of which procedures are best applied in which situations, I think we want to use the most stringent procedure that satisfies the most stringent standards in order to get a once-and-for-all answer that does not depend upon the exigencies of our particular situation right now. (That is what marks this theoretical context.)

Not only is belief tied to context, so is rationality. To term something rational is to make an *evaluation*: its reasons are *good* ones (of a certain sort), and it meets the standards (of a certain sort) that it *should* meet. These standards, we have said, may vary from area to area, context to context, time to time. We therefore should be careful in concluding that someone is being irrational simply because his reasons do not meet the most stringent standards we can formulate. They may meet the standards appropriate to their context, the standards the most stringent theory would recommend there. It might be irrational for him, the most stringent theory itself might hold, to meet more stringent standards there.

If something is fully rational when it meets all of the standards (of a certain sort) concerning reasons that it should meet, there also may be a graded notion, one that speaks of degrees of rationality or of rationality in certain respects, when something meets some of the standards but not all, or meets some to a certain degree but not completely.

In certain contexts, certain things are taken for granted. These things set the framework within which a person is acting or choosing, within which he attempts to maximize some function or have his action exhibit a certain property. For a person to take some statement q for granted in context C is for him to stand upon it in C as he attempts to maximize some function. He is not doing calculations to get *to* q; he is attempting to travel *from* q to reach somewhere else. In context C we take q for granted, and in this context we arrive at belief r, and we now can take *it* for granted, but only in contexts like C in which it is appropriate to take q for granted. Because q was tied to C, r does not float free of what was taken for granted in C in order to reach r.[49]

Beliefs are tied to contexts within which possibilities incompatible with them are excluded or deemed unworthy of consideration—let us call this view "radical contextualism."[50] (Whether or not any belief is to be taken for granted in all possible contexts may be left open.) We can identify beliefs more fully by a pairing $[bi, Cj]$. This pair indicates that it is true of me that I will take bi for granted when (I believe) I am in Cj. I now am such that this is true, though I could change so that it no longer holds true. The pairing indicates a disposition I currently possess.*

Beliefs affect actions insofar as they embody expectations about what the results of these actions will or would be. After an action is done, these expectations will (seem to) be borne out or not, to varying degrees, and these results then will modify the beliefs embodying those expectations. Beliefs about the world feed forward into actions, and the (perceived) results of these actions, along with other perceived facts, feed back, positively or negatively, upon the beliefs. The Bayesian also accepts such feedback upon probabilities, leading to their revision, perhaps in accordance with conditionalization. Yet such feedback also marks a distinction between radical contextualism and radical Bayesianism. Radical contextualism ignores certain possibilities in certain contexts. These possibilities the radical Bayesian identifies as having a probability that, when it weights what is at stake, yields a product that, given the magnitudes otherwise involved, is too small to affect the decision—so he too (he claims) can justifiably ignore them. At the Bayesian's feedback stage, however, it seems these probabilities must be revised and "updated" along with all the others, and this will involve significant computational effort. The radical contextualist, on the other hand, continues to ignore these possibilities, afterwards just as before, at least while he continues in this context.[51] (In another context, those possibilities and their probabilities might need to be considered.)

Are there general principles about which kinds of belief it is appropriate to take for granted in which contexts? But within what context are such principles being stated, and what is being taken for granted there? Would such principles have an intellectual rationale? Or could they simply be ones that were instilled in our ancestors and happened to work well enough to be passed on? Would we expect evolution to instill a mechanism for contextual belief, or one for noncontextual belief that fit a wide variety of contexts well enough to be selected for? However the theory of contextual belief eventually develops, there is

---

* Notice that radical contextualism, unlike the sociology of knowledge, does not undercut itself. Let RC be the doctrine of radical contextualism: all beliefs are held in a context. When someone believes RC, he too is in a context, call it Cj, and within this context he takes RC for granted, excludes possibilities incompatible with it, and so on. He need not think he would believe RC in all contexts. A statement S saying that S is valid in exactly contexts Ci is itself safe, provided it stays within Ci.

a phenomenon of belief it encompasses, and hence there will be room for questions about the rationality of belief. The radical Bayesian will not succeed in making the topic disappear, I bet.

Bias

We have said that a rational person will not simply extrapolate from the net balance among all the reasons she has to a conclusion about the truth. She will consider the possibility that the reasons she is aware of are not a representative sample of all the reasons there are. A rational person, then, will be self-conscious about possible biases in her own intellectual functioning and in the information she receives.

Amos Tversky and Daniel Kahneman discuss the way in which people sometimes estimate the frequency of a class by the ease with which instances can be brought to mind.[52] For example, people guess that more words sampled at random from an English text will turn out to have "r" as their first letter than as their third letter because it is easier to call words to mind by their first letter. Yet the frequency of words with "r" as the third letter in the sample of words people think of is not representative of their frequency in the larger population of words. There is a bias in the way information comes to mind.

Psychologists also have noticed that in assessing or supporting a belief, we do not use or call up from memory a random or representative sample of the relevant evidence we possess. Evidence we have encountered most recently or most strikingly will weigh more heavily with us. It also may be that when we gain a new bit of information that tends to support a particular hypothesis or belief, it calls up from memory consiliant information that also fits in with and supports that same hypothesis. (Current evidence of poor visual acuity reminds you of those occasions in your past when you did not see things very well.) This information all fits into a pattern, an edifice of support, so that even if one strut drops away—even the strut that originally called forth the others—the remaining ones are sufficient to support and maintain the belief or view. This phenomenon may underlie the role of lies and slander in political life. Not only does the truth never catch up with false information—something we already knew—but even when it does catch up and that particular bit of information is removed, the effects of that information's having circulated are *not* thereby removed but continue. (A political candidate might have aides knowingly slander an opponent, confident that when the particular lies are exposed and even repudiated by him, they still will have done their work.)

This explanation of why beliefs do not bounce back to their previous state after the falsity of some information underlying them is revealed[53] has implications also for the effects of *true* information that tends to support a hypothesis. That too will call up in memory other consiliant information that supports that hypothesis, while it will not similarly call up information that tends to count against that hypothesis. Thus, there will be a tendency to overestimate how likely or well supported a hypothesis is, in the absence of procedures designed specifically to call up and consider countervailing evidence. The evidence upon which we base our beliefs is not (in general) a random sample of the relevant evidence available to us or of the evidence that we already (in some sense) possess. A striking and salient presentation of *some* evidence will produce biases in the recall of other evidence and hence biases in the resulting beliefs.[54] Hence, it is especially important in assessing a possible belief not merely to consider the evidence for and against that we have thought of but to make particular and systematic efforts to call up all the relevant evidence, for and against, that we have.[55]

Beyond the possibility that the information we call to mind is not a representative sample of the information we already have, the information we have may not be a representative sample of the information there is. The relative frequency with which certain kinds of information come to our attention through the press or broadcasts, for example, may not be representative of all the information there is about a subject. Political or ideological bias in the news source can make it less likely that information pointing against the bias will be presented, and certain kinds of information can simply be harder to uncover or not be printed because editors judge that the public will find such information uninteresting or unbelievable. A bias in the kind of information (for or against a particular conclusion about a particular subject) that will find its way to us through our sources is represented not in the prior probabilities of that kind of information holding but in the *conditional* probabilities of that kind of information being presented by the source, *given* that it holds. What we should conclude about the truth on the basis of the information we have depends in part upon what different information would have flowed to us (through our sources presenting information and reasons) if the net balance among all the reasons there are were quite different. (The Bayesian framework seems an apt one for representing these issues.) In thinking about the possible bias of human sources, we must also consider the motivations and incentives of these sources.*

* Some writers on physics report to us that physics supports a spiritual view of the universe, but what is the nonexpert to think if these writers themselves thirst for such spiritual lessons? To what extent do their reports result from what the facts most plausibly show and to what extent from their own wishes and desires? What would be impressive is some physicist reporting *in distress* that, despite what he wished were the case,

Rationality in belief and action depends upon some self-consciousness in judging the process by which we come to have our reasons. A rational person will use *some* procedures to operate upon and correct other of her procedures, to correct biases in the sampling and evaluation of reasons and in the procedure of estimation based upon them.[56] (And might there be biases at this second level of corrective procedures?) A university education not only should teach (the techniques for acquiring) new ideas and worthy older ones but also should alert us to particular sources of informational and evaluative bias and impart techniques for compensating or correcting for such bias.

---

against his own personal materialist preconceptions, he had been forced to conclude that contemporary physics pointed to the lesson that the universe is at base spiritual. (To my knowledge, that has not yet occurred.)

Consider *Consumer Reports*, which guards against possibilities of bias, or suspicions of it, by refusing to accept advertising and sueing any company that quotes its favorable evaluations. Hence, it seems, readers and subscribers can trust its incentive to provide accurate and unbiased information and evaluations. But is its only incentive to serve readers, or does it also have an incentive to *please* those readers so that they will choose to resubscribe? The information will not be valuable to readers if it simply reconfirms what everyone already thinks. Hence *Consumer Reports* must frequently report that what is generally believed is *not* so, that what is generally thought to be the best product in fact is not, that the most expensive product is worse than another. So what is a reader to think when she reads such a story: that often enough popular beliefs are mistaken so that the magazine need not distort, slant, or shade anything in order to continue to please its readers, or that this is a case where the magazine is doing what it sometimes must in order to survive? I lean toward the first hypothesis, but it is illuminating to see the room for the second. In assessing print and broadcast journalism, we also must consider the incentives of their providers, how their careers are advanced by the pursuit and presentation of certain stories—for instance, about the personal lives of political candidates—and how this might bias which news is presented and what importance this news is given, and how this then might further bias the results of public decisions.

Political campaigns in the United States now make extensive use of focused interviews with carefully selected groups of people to discover which virtues of a candidate or drawbacks of an opponent have great emotional weight for these voters. See Elizabeth Kolbert, "Test-Marketing a President: How Focus Groups Pervade Campaign Politics," *New York Times Magazine*, August 30, 1992, pp. 18–21, 60, 68, 72. Political statements and advertising then selectively use this information to secure electoral victory—the actual performance in office of the victor seems to be affected very little. The themes emphasized are not a random or representative sample of the significant themes discovered. If such interviews on behalf of one candidate discover that he has one virtue and twenty flaws, while his opponent has twenty virtues and one flaw, his (emotionally powerful and appealing) advertizing then focuses upon his one virtue and upon his opponent's one flaw. Apparently, many voters do not discount for such unrepresentativeness, and the participants in the focus groups themselves do not seem averse to having their concerns so selectively exploited. This significant effect upon elections now constitutes a public problem.

A prospective buyer of a book, reading the quotations presented on the dust jacket or in an advertisement, can assume that the publisher is not presenting us with a random or representative sample of opinions about the book but instead is picking the *best* quo-

It is worth saying something about the general notion of bias. We can distinguish two kinds of bias. The first involves the uneven application of existing standards. Discrimination in the social arena, for instance, involves the uneven application of standards to different groups or individuals. There are many different standards, however, that might somehow be thought relevant to a decision or treatment of a case. What determines which of the possible standards will constitute the criteria for the choice, and what determines the weights these are given when the standards chosen are not a random sample from all the possible relevant ones?

There will be a bias in the selection of standards when the explanation of why *these* standards rather than others are chosen, or why these weights rather than others are given, in part involves the belief by some that these very standards and weights would work to the exclusion or detriment of particular groups and this motivated them to put forward these particular standards. These standards were chosen *in order* to exclude certain cases. Let us term such a case one of *second-level bias*.[57] When the standard is initiated as second-level bias but other reasons also can be produced for it, and the standard is continued in part for these other reasons, the definitional and normative situation becomes more complicated. (We also can ask why these other criteria and goals suddenly became salient, why they suddenly gained the weight they did? From among all the possible criteria, if these were thrust forward *in order to* justify the second-level discrimination, then

---

tations, with some attention also to selecting sources readers might be expected to know and respect. So the prospective buyer should correct for this bias in the sampling and think: since these are the best opinions selected from a distribution of all opinions of this book, my own is likely to be *less* favorable than the ones presented to me. (Do publishers of paperback editions print pages and pages of favorable but quite repetitive reviews from different sources to convince the reader that such opinions are so widespread that he can have reasonable confidence that his own opinion will match?)

I cannot resist, while speaking of books, to notice another phenomenon, one that indeed can be tied to our current theme. The popular press gives great prominence to prizes and awards carrying large financial benefit, but one literary prize of very modest amount gets very significant attention: the Pulitzer Prize, which is given in fiction, history, biography, poetry, and general nonfiction. One explanation of its prominence would be the age and distinction of this award, but I suggest another. The Pulitzer Prize also is awarded to journalists and newspapers, and so newspapers treat these awards as major news, meriting the front page. If someone were establishing a modest award for painters or choreographers, say, I would recommend that they tie it to awards for anchorpeople of TV news broadcasts and for the producers of such programs!

The promised connection is this: one cannot judge the importance of a story by the prominence of its treatment without considering the incentives of those treating the story. My own view is that *all* literary, scientific, artistic, and intellectual prizes should be given great prominence; but when evaluating that statement too, I expect my readers to consider its source.

this too constitutes a higher-level discrimination, but it is best to consider this too as at the second level.)

Very sophisticated observers sometimes can skillfully discuss the issue of first-level discrimination without noticing the attendant possibility of second-level discrimination. A study often cited by statisticians considers whether during a particular time period the graduate school of the University of California at Berkeley discriminated against women applicants in its admissions process.[58] Women applicants seemed to be as well qualified as male applicants by the standard criteria (undergraduate grades, number of courses taken in the subject, Graduate Record Examination scores, and so on), yet a far lower percentage of female applicants was being admitted to the graduate school. Mustn't this be a case of discrimination? No (answered the statisticians), for when we look at the admissions department by department, we find that each department admitted approximately the same percentage of female applicants as of male applicants. No department was discriminating. How then could the overall percentages admitted be so different? The applications of men and women were not concentrated in the same departments. Some departments admitted a lower percentage of their applicants than other departments did, and the women were applying more heavily to these departments. (To illustrate simply: if most of the women were applying to departments that admitted only 10 percent of their applicants, and most of the men were applying to departments that admitted 50 percent of their applicants, then different percentages of men and women applicants would be admitted to the whole graduate school, even though each department's record showed *it* admitting the same percentage of men and women applicants.) Case closed (said the statisticians): no discrimination.

A neat point. But all the study showed is that there was no first-level discrimination; the evidence showed none. We still can ask, though, why did different departments admit differing percentages of their applicants? Presumably because the ratio of applicants to possible admission places differed from department to department. Women just happened to apply to departments with a smaller number of admissions places per applicant. But did this "just happen"? Why aren't the sizes of graduate departments proportional to the number of well-qualified applicants? What determines how large a department is, how much of the university's resources go into teaching positions, graduate fellowships, and so forth in each department? Many factors might. *Suppose*, however, that some graduate departments are underfunded because they are more heavily populated by women graduate students. Suppose that for this reason certain subjects are not regarded as highly by university administrators or by the wider society as it allocates funding for graduate programs. Or suppose that other graduate programs

were better funded, able to admit a higher percentage of their applicants, because they were "male" subjects and hence thought of as socially more important. Some departments are kept smaller than they
otherwise would be *because* of their high percentage of women applicants; or other departments are kept larger because of their high percentage of men applicants. I am not claiming this is so but simply describing a not completely implausible possibility under which the
Berkeley statistics *would* fit a pattern of second-level discrimination.
The statistics alone would not demonstrate this; that would require
investigation of a structural question about the university's organization, namely, why the various departments differ in the percentage of
their total applicant pool that they are able to admit.[59]

In situations of second-level discrimination, the standards applied
(or the weights they are given) are not a random sample from the set
of possible relevant standards. Moreover, any criteria that purport to
justify these particular standards (or weights) are not a random sample (or objectively justified subset) of the possibly relevant evaluative
criteria. Here the sampling is intentionally biased. In other cases the
matter may be less clear. Consider the debate among literary theorists
about the nature of the literary canon and the membership conditions
for inclusion within it. There would be first-level discrimination
against women, minority writers, and writers from other cultures if
some or many of them were excluded from the canon even though
they now meet the very standards that heretofore have granted inclusion to majority male writers. Yet even if the existing standards are
evenly applied, we also can investigate the possibility of second-level
discrimination in the formation of the canon. Why is it precisely *these*
standards that are applied? Are there other virtues or criteria that
make works worthy of equally serious study by the same or by very
similar methods? Are there other interesting and fruitful methods that
could be devised to study and illuminate these differing works? That
does not mean one has to be able to state what those standards are
early in the process. The Greeks knew that the dramas of Aeschylus
and Sophocles were worthy of sustained attention before Aristotle
wrote his *Poetics* to enunciate explicitly the standards that such dramas
meet.[60] To ask about new standards does not require denigrating the
virtues captured by the existing ones.

It is within this domain of selection among many possible criteria
and standards, I think, that the sociology of knowledge gets its grip.
There are many possible kinds of reasons for and against any belief—
certainly any one concerning a controversial social or normative question—and there are many possible standards for evaluating such reasons. No one seeks out all possible reasons impartially and gives them
equal weight—including those of us who make some effort to examine

countervailing reasons—and the reasons that anyone accepts are not a random sampling of all the possible reasons. It seems reasonable to think that the factors studied by the classic sociologists of knowledge (in the tradition of Karl Mannheim)—such as class position, educational level, network of group ties, and so on—will affect which among the various possible rational reasons and evaluative standards a particular person pays heed to, which ones have saliency for him and are given some weight. (Recently, other writers have focused upon sex, race, and sexual preference.) When faced with a complicated societal situation, people in different social positions may notice and focus upon different aspects and therefore invoke different principles (suited for these aspects) that yield different conclusions. Each may be right: what each has noticed *is* a reason for their respective (opposed) conclusions. Each person also may be rational: believing things for reasons, reaching conclusions on the basis of evidence, invoking criteria for belief and evaluation that have much to be said for them. Yet each person is believing things for only some of the reasons, reaching conclusions on the basis of only some of the evidence, invoking only some of the criteria that have much to be said for them. The social factors (studied by the sociologists) act to narrow the range of possible relevant considerations that get considered. Within this range, our beliefs and actions may be rational. Even when not made relative to this range, they are not completely irrational—given that there is *some* reason for them, they are at least prima facie rational.

In the Preface we looked askance at the claim that rationality itself is biased. It might be claimed instead that, although rationality is not objectionably biased in its aim toward the goals it pursues—it corrects for that bias as best it can—it is biased in the very goals it pursues and in the manner of its pursuit. Doesn't rationality exclude emotion, passion, and spontaneity, and aren't these valuable components of a life? But rationality can pursue these. Even decision-theoretic rationality can recommend henceforth making many decisions without thought or calculation, if the process of doing this is more valuable than the losses that might be incurred by these less-reflective decisions, or if the process of calculation itself would interfere with the nature of other valued relationships, such as love and trust.[61] To be sure, if rationality were to recommend this, it would be doing so on the basis of reasons it considers and evaluates as good ones, so *that* recommendation would not be thoughtless. That is not the same as a *calculating* recommendation, however. Responsiveness to reasons does not require explicit consideration of them. Rationality can be modest and choose to step aside sometimes or even, in some types of circumstances, almost always.

IV

EVOLUTIONARY REASONS

THE RATIONALITY of a belief or action is a matter of its responsiveness to the reasons for and against, and of the process by which those reasons are generated. Why does rationality involve reasons? Here is one answer: beliefs and actions are to have certain properties (such as truth or satisfying desire), and it is more likely that they will if they are responsive to all the reasons for and against. (Might some other process that does not involve considering or weighing reasons at all be even more reliable in achieving that goal?) Whether or not considering reasons is the most effective or the most reliable method for achieving our cognitive goals, why is it effective at all? What connects reasons for and against to these goals? What makes something a reason? Among the welter of information there is, what constitutes something as a reason for or against a belief or an action?

We come to hold beliefs through some general process for arriving at, maintaining, and revising beliefs. For different kinds of beliefs, or even for the same kind on different occasions, we may employ different processes. Following a particular process upon a particular occasion may lead us to a belief that is true; using that process may (invariably or probabilisticly) cause us to believe the truth. The utilization of reasons can play a role in a process's being a probabilistic cause of believing the truth, and differences among reasoning procedures can affect the process's efficiency or effectiveness. It seems plausible to say that believing h for reason r will be conducive to reaching our cognitive goal of true belief only when there is some connection between the truth of r and the truth of h. It is this connection between reasons and the truth of what they are reasons for that explains the connection, such as it is, between believing for reasons and believing the truth. What, then, is the nature of the connection between reasons and what they are reasons for?

Reasons and Facts

Concerning reasons for a belief, the philosophical literature contains two views. One, the a priori view, holds that a reason r for an hypothesis h stands in some relation R to h, such that the faculty of reason can apprehend that this (structural?) relation constitutes one of support. Reasons are things the mind has the power to recognize.[1] The problem is this: why expect that h will actually be true when r is true and r stands in the relation R to h? If it is replied that we expect it because r is a reason for h, we still can ask what explanation we have of why h (often) actually is true when r is?[2]

The second view, the factual view, holds that r is evidence for h when it stands in a certain contingent factual relation to h. In *Philosophical Explanations*, I claimed that the evidential connection is a factual relation and presented an account of it in terms of the tracking relation between evidence and hypothesis (and in terms of probabilistic approximations of that relation).[3] I do not wish to insist, though, upon that particular account of the factual relation.

When that factual relation is appropriately specified, knowing that it holds, in combination with r, will constitute a reason for believing h. But without the knowledge that such a connection holds—although it does—and without any evident structural connection between r and h, will r constitute a reason for believing h? The factual view seems to leave out what most strikes the a priori view, namely, that in particular cases the reason connection appears (almost) self-evident. (Notice that the notion of *evidence* might fit a purely factual account even if *reason* does not.)

I suggest we combine the two views. A reason r for h is something that stands in a certain—let that be specified by a further bit of theory—factual connection to h, while the contents of r and h stand in a certain structural connection that appears to us strikingly to make h (more) believable given r. The reason relation is a factual connection that appears, apart from experience, to be one of support. (For the term *support*, you may substitute some favored description from proponents of the faculty of reason.)

There could be different bases for our acting in accordance with a factual connection: the action could be prewired (if the factual connection obtained in the past and there was evolutionary selection for that automatic fact-action sequence) or the action could result from operant conditioning. There is a third basis. Acting upon *reasons* involves *recognizing* a connection of structural relation among contents. Such recognition itself might have been useful and selected for. The attribute of a certain factual connection's *seeming* self-evidently evidential to us might have been selected for and favored because acting upon this factual connection, which does hold, in general enhances fitness. I am not suggesting that it is the capacity to recognize independently existing valid rational connections that is selected for. Rather, there is a factual connection, and there was selection among organisms for that kind of connection seeming valid, for noticing that kind of connection and for such noticing to lead to certain additional beliefs, inferences, and so on. There is selection for recognizing as valid certain kinds of connections that *are* factual, that is, for them coming to seem to us as *more* than just factual.[4]

If, frequently enough, samples of a certain sort resembled their populations, then generalizing from samples to population, or to the next encountered member, would frequently yield truths; and beings to whom such inferences seemed obvious and self-evident would frequently arrive at those truths. This example involves a general process of inductive inference. (Leda Cosmides and John Tooby have investigated the possibility of specialized inferential mechanisms effective for particular types of situations that were frequently encountered throughout our evolutionary history and hence selected for.[5]) Notice that this evolutionary selection might be an instance of the Baldwin effect.[6] In this particular case, those to whose "wiring" a connection seems closer to evident learn it faster, thereby gaining a selective advantage, and they leave offspring distributed around their own degree of finding it evident. Over generations, then, there can be movement toward finding that connection more and more self-evident.

Notice that this view leaves us—as before—with the problem of induction: a certain factual connection held in the past and selection led to our being organisms who see it as a valid basis of inference, but will this factual connection continue to hold now and in the future? The statement that this connection will continue to hold might itself stand in a seemingly valid connection to other facts we have known, but will *that* further connection (perhaps it is the one we began with) continue to hold? That it will is not guaranteed by its seeming evident to us, for that seeming was produced only by its having held in the past.

Moreover, that something seems self-evidently true to us does not, on this account, guarantee that it ever was, strictly, true. Consider, by analogy, what we now say of Euclidean geometry: it is true enough for almost all practical purposes; it is undetectably different, in the small, from spaces of small constant curvature; but, strictly, it is not true (of, as we say, "physical space"). If there had been selection for Euclidean geometry's seeming self-evidently true, that would have served our ancestors well. Nothing would have been gained by selection for some other geometry. Believing that alternative and making inferences automatically in accordance with *it* would not have bestowed any selective advantage (in *that* environment). For this alternative geometry to seem self-evident might have involved great costs in terms of the neurological resources devoted to it. And "intuiting" this alternative geometry might not have been within reach of what random mutation (in the

absence of stepwise selective pressures) might produce from the genetic endowment that existed then. This alternative geometry, literally
true, would not have been selected for as what seemed self-evidently
true to us. Given Euclidean geometry's close approximation to the
truth, and given the attendant advantages of its seeming self-evidently
true to us—advantages including quickness of inference, believing
serviceable (approximate) truths, and avoiding other more divergent
falsehoods—we can imagine Euclidean geometry's seeming self-evident as having been selected for; we can imagine selection for that geometry as our form of sensibility. Nevertheless, Euclidean geometry is,
we now believe, strictly speaking, false as a theory of physical space.
(And about what else, Hilary Putnam has asked, was geometry ever
supposed to be?) I do not claim that this evolutionary story *is* the true
account of why Euclidean geometry seems self-evident. It is an analogy to make the point—one we already know in general but tend to
forget in the arena of *reasons* and *inference* and *evidential support*—that
the apparent self-evidence of a connection's holding (by virtue of some
other manifest structural feature or relation) is no guarantee that it
does hold in fact.

Shall we make a similar claim about the "self-evidence" of deductive
rules of inference and of the principles of logic themselves? Are they
necessary, or is all of traditional a priori knowledge to be swept into
the evolutionary bin? Some writers have claimed that the principles of
logic are neither necessary nor knowable a priori; even if we now do
not have a formulated alternative, certain intractable phenomena—of
quantum mechanics or whatever—might drive us to revise even our
principles of logic.* My point is more modest. To explain why such

---

* See Hilary Putnam, "Three-Valued Logic" and "The Logic of Quantum Mechanics,"
reprinted in his *Philosophical Papers*, vol. 1: *Mathematics, Matter and Method* (Cambridge:
Cambridge Univ. Press, 1975), pp. 166–197, and W. V. Quine, *Philosophy of Logic* (Englewood Cliffs, N.J.: Prentice-Hall, 1970), pp. 85–86, 100. If logic and mathematics are continuous with and a part of empirical science, as Quine holds, then why do we not seek
for deeper scientific *explanations* of why these laws of logic or theories of mathematics
hold? Physicists continually seek even deeper explanations of the deepest currently
known laws, yet no comparable activity is carried on by logicians. It would be implausible to claim that this is because logicians already have discovered the most fundamental
laws. For why did this occur so early in the history of logic, while in physics it has not
occurred yet? In conversation, Quine points out that in *The Roots of Reference* (LaSalle, Ill.:
Open Court, 1973), pp. 76–78, he claims that some laws of logic are analytic; they are
learned to be true as we learn the meanings of the constituent words. (Yes, Quine!) But
this does not seem sufficient to account for why the explanatory search in logic for the
truths underlying the truths of the propositional calculus or of quantification theory
does not continue: iteration of these individually short, truth-preserving steps in long
chains of inference also preserves truth, and isn't that a mathematical (nonanalytic)
fact?

principles seem self-evident to us, one need not invoke their necessity. It might be enough that they are true, even if only contingently, even just "true enough"—recall the example of Euclidean geometry—and that they have held true durably for long enough to leave an imprint upon our evolutionary endowment.* This position is not open to W. V. Quine's cogent objection that all logical truths cannot owe their truth to convention, since the principles of logic themselves need to be invoked to derive the infinite consequences of the conventions.[7] We have suggested that the principles of logic do hold true—true enough anyway, and perhaps, for all we know, contingently—and that processes of evolution instill (not the truth of the principles of logic but) their seeming self-evidence. So there is no bar to assuming their truth in deriving the consequences of their being instilled as self-evident. The strength and depth of our intuitions about certain statements cannot be used as powerful evidence for their necessity if those statements are of a kind that, were they contingent facts, would have led to selection favoring strong intuitions of their self-evidence.[8]

Philosophers have faced the task of grounding Reason, grounding what we take to be evident. Hume's problem of induction was to find a *rational* argument to the conclusion that reason, or that portion of it embodied in inductive reasoning, (probably) works. Even if this problem could be solved,[9] there would remain the question of what grounds *that* rational argument, that is, why we should trust *any* rational argument. This was the problem Descartes faced—why must self-evident propositions, basking in the natural light of reason, correspond to reality?—and it has given rise to an extensive literature on the "Cartesian Circle."[10] (It is interesting to note that ultimately Descartes grounded his trust in rational argument in the trust in another being, namely, God.) Kant held that the rationalists could not show why our knowledge or intuition, our "reason" in my sense here, would conform to objects, and he suggested—this was his "Copernican Revolution"—that objects must conform to our knowledge, to the constitution of the faculty of our intuition.[11] (Hence our knowledge is not of things in themselves but only of empirical reality, for that is what is shaped by our constitution.)

If reason and the facts were independent factors, said Kant, then the rationalists could produce no convincing reason why the two should correspond. Why should those two independent variables be corre-

---

* But the discussion might continue: What explains why they are true and have held true for long enough to have such evolutionary effects upon our sense of self-evidence? If the contingent view has no plausible deeper explanatory hypothesis to propose, the proponent of necessity also must not simply claim that they held for so long because they are necessary, and he may be at a loss to explain why *they* are necessary.

lated? So he proposed that the (empirical) facts were not an independent variable; their dependence upon reason explains the correlation and correspondence between them. But there is a third alternative: that it is *reason* that is the dependent variable, shaped by the facts, and its dependence upon the facts explains the correlation and correspondence between them. It is just such an alternative that our evolutionary hypothesis presents. Reason tells us about reality because reality shapes reason, selecting for what seems "evident."

Such a view, we have said, can explain only the past correlation; it cannot guarantee that the future facts will fit the present reason. And the evolutionary explanation itself is something we arrive at, in part, by the use of reason to support evolutionary theory in general and also this particular application of it. Hence it does not provide a reason-independent justification of reason, and, although it grounds reason in facts independent of reason, this grounding is not accepted by us independently of our reason. Hence the account is not part of first philosophy; it is part of our current ongoing scientific view.[12] It is not meant to satisfy Kant's criterion that "everything which bears any manner of resemblance to an hypothesis is to be treated as contraband."[13]

We might best think of philosophy, I have said, as the love of reason—not the love of wisdom but the love of reasoning. Even the Greek skeptics and the British empiricists attend to and glory in their reasoning, though their reasoning tends to diminish or undercut the authority of reason and of reasoning itself—thus they skirt or face pragmatic paradox. The philosopher's attempt to ground reason is his effort to protect his love. (Or to ensure that his love will stay true to him?) Will accepting this evolutionary explanation of reason's power and beauty of appearance have the effect of diminishing that love? It is not clear that it must. Do our eyes and ears diminish in value when we learn that these perceptual organs have an evolutionary explanation? Still, some philosophers have heard reason's voice as heralding the necessary in contrast to the contingent, as providing access to more than actuality can encompass, and they may feel deprived of the special solace their love has brought.

The evolutionary account shows why something might come to seem evident to us on its face. Within the model of a network of components of varying weights that feed forward and are subject to an error-correction rule, reasons constitute a wider category than that; noticed factual connections are reflected in changing linkages and weights. So we are not limited to just the reasons that evolution has installed. This is fortunate. Evolution might instill as evident something that is only an approximation to the truth, and this might be

REASONS AND FACTS 113

inadequate for certain of our purposes later. Also, given that perfect accuracy is not to be had—at a reasonable cost, anyway—evolution may favor a proneness to some errors over others. Falsely believing there is no tiger present and standing still may have more deleterious effects upon fitness than falsely believing there is a tiger present and running unnecessarily. Hence, there might be evolutionary selection for mechanisms that are more prone to make that second kind of error.[14] In different circumstances, avoiding a given error may be less important. An adaptable processing system, with initial weights that can be modified, will be capable of achieving greater accuracy.

Recall our earlier distinction between (1) *p* being the rational thing to believe and (2) believing *p* being the rational thing to do. Natural selection works on the second, and only to the extent that there is a correlation between the two will it give us cognitive mechanisms geared to the first. Rather, natural selection will work first on: (3) action *A* is the most fitness-enhancing thing to do; or rather, *A* arises from capacities whose exercise in general have advanced inclusive fitness. Because what you do will be a product of your beliefs and your motivations and utilities, there is leeway in how predispositions to the behavior might be realized. Hence some dangers might be avoided, not by belief mechanisms that quickly treat ambiguous data as showing the presence of something dangerous, but by motivational mechanisms, for example, repulsions that lead one to avoid snakes.

Enhancement of inclusive fitness yields selection for approximate truth rather than strict truth. Knowing this, we can *sharpen* our goal and its procedures. If there is selection for the serviceability of a belief in action, and truth is that property that in general underlies serviceability, we can formulate procedures that focus upon the goal of truth and not just serviceability. Also, we can sharpen the notion of truth. Perhaps not *all* serviceability indicates truth or is underlain by it— evolutionary theorizing itself can tell us that different *types* of things can underlie serviceability—and we can say that truth is what underlies a subclass of serviceability. Once we become self-conscious about it, we can improve the accuracy of our given procedures.

Consider, again, the connection between the reliabiity with which a process for forming belief yields truths and the acquisition of beliefs on the basis of reasons. If evolution selects belief-forming mechanisms that are reliable, and if believing for reasons is a component of some such reliable mechanisms, then the organisms that result may care about and focus upon reasons rather than reliability. This focus is the way they are guided to reliability, but reliability itself is not their focus. Similarly, there was selection for psychological mechanisms that once statistically correlated with maximizing inclusive fitness, not for a concern with inclusive fitness itself. In situations where reliability and reasons actually conflict, and people become aware of this, they may lean with reasons rather than reliability; and when reliability occurs alone, that may seem an insufficient aim. Precisely that is what there was selection for their doing. A concern for reasons, present because of its past correlation with a reliable route to truth, now floats free.

Fitness and Function

Let us look more closely at the structure and contours of evolutionary explanation. Evolution, the literature tells us, involves heritable variation in fitness, transmission to offspring of parental characteristics that vary across organisms and play a role in nonrandom differential reproduction.[15] Fitness does not consist in actual reproductive success—lightning accidents can affect that—so Susan Mills and John Beatty have argued that it consists in an organism's (probabilistic) propensity to survive and reproduce.[16]

I suggest we see an attribution of greater fitness as an existentially quantified statement. To say an organism A is fitter than organism B in environment E is to say there exists some heritable phenotypic feature(s) F such that F explains (by causing) the greater reproductive success of A over B in E. Hence to say that A has greater reproductive success than B because A is fitter than B is *not* a tautology, even though it says that A has greater reproductive success than B in E because there exists some heritable phenotypic feature F that explains this greater reproductive success. There might be other explanations of this greater reproductive success, for instance, chance.

The existential quantification focuses attention upon the intermediate level of phenotypic traits and upon the activities and functions necessary to survival and reproduction of viable offspring that these traits carry out. The phenotypic trait F always works through one of these intermediate general functions G (such as evading predators, finding food, transforming energy, attracting a mate, getting sufficient moisture, maintaining heat, and so on) by enabling this function or activity to be done better, more efficiently, and so forth. A listing of *all* these intermediate functions would itself give more particular content to a theory of fitness; short of that, the more functions we can list, the more determinate content we have given the theory. A definition of fitness might incorporate reference to this intermediate level G of activity and function, intermediate between the phenotypic feature F and reproductive success itself, where each such activity and function Gi is such that, all other things being equal, the better the organism performs *Gi*, the greater the probability of its reproductive success. Thus, to say an organism *A* is fitter than organism *B* in environment *E* is to say there exists some heritable phenotypic feature(s) *F* and some intermediate-level function *Gi* such that *F* causes the enhanced performance of *Gi* and hence causes (perhaps probabilistically) the greater reproductive success of *A* over *B* in *E*.

There is an additional complication we must face. (No doubt, we would need to add further details to cope with further complications.) Since the more fit organism need not actually have greater reproductive success, due to chance mortality, chance mutation, or still other factors, perhaps we should instead say that the fitter organism's heritable phenotypic traits would explain greater reproductive success if that success occurred. In that case, *A* is fitter than *B* in *E* would be defined as follows. There is some heritable phenotypic trait *F* and some intermediate function *Gi* such that: (a) *A* is reproductively more successful than *B* in *E*, and *F* causes the enhanced performance of *Gi* and thus (perhaps probabilistically) explains this greater reproductive success of *A* over *B* in *E*; *or* (b) *B* has greater or equal reproductive success compared to *A* in *E*, and there is no heritable phenotypic trait *F'* such that *F'* explains the equal or greater reproductive success of *B* compared to *A* in *E*, and if *A* *were* reproductively more successful than *B* in *E*, then this would be explained by *A*'s possession of the heritable trait *F*.

It might be better, however, to avoid these counterfactual complications and definitional clauses, since such conditions are subject to complex counterexamples. Instead, we can hold that there is greater fitness only when there actually is greater reproductive success, though greater reproductive success can be caused by something other than greater fitness. This would be to say (roughly) that greater fitness is greater reproductive success that is (probabilistically) caused by heritable phenotypic traits (through the performance of some intermediate functions). Without the greater actual reproductive success, there is no greater fitness. Yet the other organisms that *do* show greater reproductive success are not automatically counted as more fit, because their greater reproductive successes need not be (probabilistically) caused by some heritable phenotypic trait. (Although this construction would make the survival of the fittest tautological, the fitness of the survivors would not be. The empirical claim then might be added that, for the preponderant part, the survivors *are* more fit.)

The notion of fitness we have described is a comparative one ("more fit than ____ in environment *E*"). For various purposes one wants a stronger measure of fitness than just a comparison, but that measure need not be a single real number as opposed to some more complicated mathematical entity—an ordered n-tuple, a vector, a matrix, a tree structure of matrices, or whatever. Which probabilities an organism has of leaving exactly n offspring in the next generation, John Beatty and Susan Finsen point out, is itself a reproductive strategy of that organism, and there can be selection among such strategies.[17] I suggest that we instead consider a vector $[p0, p1, p2, \ldots, pn]$, where pi is the probability of leaving exactly n offspring in the next generation (and this probability is zero for all i greater than n). Why throw away any of this information?[18] In addition to the 0th generation vector, we want to consider the longer-term fitness of an organism, its various probabilities of leaving exactly i organisms in the second generation, which will be a function of its previous one-generation vector along with the one-generation vectors of each of its (potential) offspring; and so on for succeeding generations. There is a puzzle, though. Particular specifications of these mathematical structures will be life-history characteristics, among which there will be selection. In terms of *which* notion of fitness, then, can we explain the greater fitness of one such specification over another in environment E? If one array of vectors dominates another, matters will be simple; but in the absence of dominance, complications abound. The actual course of history might turn out to be an *unlikely* path through the matrix, and even the notion of the *probable* survival of the fittest (as explained by our first account) may not be given a clear sense. Is this general puzzle avoided because the particular notion of fitness to be used depends upon the particular phenomena to be explained?

The evolution that we know of involves not simply heritable variation in fitness but also imperfect replication of genetic material in offspring. Most mutations are deleterious, and organisms (of a certain complexity) contain mechanisms for editing and correcting mistakes in replication; but such mechanisms are imperfect. Even if such perfection were possible, it might well have been selected against. We all are descended from mutations that fared well in competition with their more accurately replicated kin. Yet a *too* faulty error-correction mechanism governing replication would not preserve the mutation it allows and would not preserve *itself*—it is an inherited device—across the generations. Hence the degree of accuracy of the genetic error-correcting mechanism is itself something that is subject to selection, and the leeway our actual common mechanism allows should not be considered a defect—those with more perfect error-correcting mechanisms are still protozoa.*

---

* It might be useful to compare the genetic error-correcting mechanism to a Turing machine, with a scanner moving square by square, making changes as needed, adding

I also believe there is room for a concept of fitness more general than the one that compares the differential success of reproducing organisms. Consider the question of why there are reproducing entities (or organisms) at all. Once reproductive organisms exist, they spread. Shouldn't there be a more general notion of fitness to encompass the advantage that reproducing living things may have in comparison to nonliving things? Perhaps the measure should speak of the competition for atoms or molecules: are living organisms successful in incorporating them into living things? Hence one might arrive at a ratio of biomass to nonbiomass in the local (closed) material environment. (I am told by Richard Lewontin that in botany the *number* of organisms is not always clear or relevant, so a notion of fitness that focuses upon other material measures might be useful there as well.) Is there a theoretical limit to how much of the universe's matter can be incorporated into biomass? Locally on earth, are we still on the rising curve? What shape has that curve taken over time? New and interesting questions may arise when we formulate a more general concept that illuminates why reproductive life survives and spreads, one that includes the usual biological notion of fitness as a particular specification.

We have considered rationality as a biological adaptation with a function. What is a function? How does the notion of function fit within a biological and evolutionary framework? Ernest Nagel offers an illuminating analysis of a homeostatic system, such as the temperature regulatory system of our bodies. Such a system maintains the value of one of its state variables V within a certain range in a certain environment, so that when V is caused to deviate some distance (but not any arbitrarily large distance) outside that range, the values of the other variables compensate for this, being modified so as to bring V back within the specified range.[19] Nagel presented this as an analysis of a teleological or goal-directed system, the goal or function of the system being to maintain the variable V within that range. According to this account, any other variable V' universally associated with V also would constitute the goal-state of such a homeostatic system, a counterintuitive consequence that might be avoided by looking to the *explanation* of why the system maintains V within that range. Not everything with a function, however, is a homeostatic system. The function of a dining room chair might be to support a person at a table,

---

new squares to the tape from the surrounding material as needed. Might some of the formal structure and results of computation theory illuminate this portion of biology? Perhaps we need a theory of a slightly imperfect Turing machine that sometimes is subject to miscomputation. Notice the analog of self-reference in the phenomenon of an error-correcting mechanism repairing, among other material, that which is causally responsible for the (next) reproduction of *that* error-correcting mechanism.

but if it performs its function poorly it does not modify the values of some of its state variables so as better to provide bodily support.

To handle this case and others, Larry Wright proposes that something's function helps to explain why it exists: the function of X is Z when Z is a consequence or result of X's being there, and X is there because it does Z.[20] Christopher Boorse objects that if a scientist makes a hose with a break in it and is killed by escaping gas before he can repair the break, still it is not a function of the break to release gas, even though the break results in the release and continues to exist because of it.[21]

Let us take a fresh look. Z is a function of X when Z is an effect of X and X was designed or shaped (or maintained) to have this effect Z. Such designing or shaping can be done either by a human designer or by the evolutionary process. In either case, the designing itself seems to be a homeostatic process whose goal is that X produce Z. A human designer shapes a chair so that it will support a person, altering features of it—in the planning or in the making—so that this function can be performed effectively. Over generations, evolution shapes organisms and bodily organs so as to have certain effects more effectively; it selects for organisms for which this is so. (Of course, processes in addition to adaptive selection—for instance, genetic drift—are at work in evolution. And viewing evolution as, in significant part, a homeostatic mechanism does not entail that it is an optimizing mechanism.) The Nagel and Wright views can be combined, I suggest, to present a more complete picture of function. Z is a function of X when Z is a consequence (effect, result, property) of X, *and* X's producing Z is itself the goal-state of some homeostatic mechanism M satisfying the Nagel analysis, and X was produced or is maintained by this homeostatic mechanism M (through its pursuit of the goal: X's producing Z). (One might drop the first clause requiring that X actually have the effect Z: not all functions are carried out.)

This account explains why biologists do not say the function of junk DNA is to do nothing or to be more expensive to get rid of than to retain, or that the function of a segregation distorter is to disrupt meiosis.[22] Although these *are* effects, the junk DNA and segregation distorters were not shaped by a homeostatic process to have these effects. No homeostatic process aimed at these effects or selected for them. Notice that the view proposed here does not automatically make the goal-state of a homeostatic system its function. A thermostat created by an accidental combination of elements would not have the *function* of regulating temperature even though it had this effect. In my account, the homeostatic mechanism is the designer, not the designed object, and *its* goal is that some other thing X produces effect Z, some other thing X that it creates or maintains, and it is X to which a function is attributed. Which effects of X are its function? The ones X was produced or designed for (or maintained because of) by some homeostatic mechanism. (Since some side effects will be coextensive with the effects that were selected for, either an attribution of function will have to be tied to an *explanation* of why an effect was selected for, where explanation is not an extensional notion, or the account presented here will be a necessary but not a sufficient condition for an effect's being a function.)

The processes of evolution produce entities with functions, but evolution itself would have a function—for example, of producing such entities with functions—only if there were some *other* homeostatic process that produced or maintained evolution to have that effect. Notice that it is not a consequence of this view that things (morally) *should* perform their functions; beings created and shaped by a homeostatic mechanism to be slaves and work hard would (on this account) have that function, yet nevertheless they should rebel. Notice also that some existing thing that was not shaped by a homeostatic process might at some time start to be *used* for a purpose—for instance, a large flat stone as a picnic table. Here we might say that it has been *given* a function; we do the same thing with it as with something that does have a function through a homeostatic mechanism. It *functions as* a table, though that is not its function. But if we now shape or maintain the object so as to keep it within the range of characteristics whereby it can be so used to that effect, such as cleaning moss and fallen branches off that particular rock, then its continued condition directed toward having that effect—usability as a picnic table—*is* the result of a homeostatic mechanism and so now may have *become* its function.

Rationality's Function

Reasons themselves are evidence* for what they are reasons for. But why do we believe and act for reasons? What is *their* function? The answer may seem evident. Reasons are connected to the truth of what they are reasons for—that is the factual connection—and so believing for reasons is a route to believing the truth. Still, it is worth probing further. According to our analysis of function, the function of "believing or acting for reasons" will be some feature or effect this has that some underlying homeostatic mechanism "aims at" its having. Since

---

* This consists, I have suggested, in a double connection: a factual connection that also is structural and seems self-evident.

rationality is taking account of (and acting upon) reasons, what rationality is, what function it has, will depend upon a fact about the world, namely, what homeostatic mechanism(s) actually operated, and toward what goal, in shaping us to act and believe on the basis of reasons.

The first homeostatic mechanism to consider is the evolutionary process operating through natural selection. Was believing or acting for reasons a trait that was selected for, and if so, why? Notice that there could have been selection for traits that yield believing or acting for reasons as a *by-product* without that having been directly selected for. In that case, believing or acting for reasons would not have an evolutionary function; there would not be any property P such that an evolutionary homeostatic mechanism had as its goal-state (maintaining) the fact that believing or acting for a reason has that property P. It is because the world changes in nonregular ways, we have said, that organisms need adaptive mechanisms to respond to local circumstances; the whole job cannot be done effectively by permanent structure and prewired responses, along with operant conditioning. Reasons and reasoning all would be useful to an organism facing new situations and trying to avoid future difficulties. Such a capacity for rationality, whether directly selected for or riding piggyback upon other capacities, might well serve an organism in its life tasks and increase its inclusive fitness. This would give to explicit rationality the task of coping with changing facts and needs, and perhaps of modifying our phylogenetic behavior patterns when we learn of current changes that make them unsuitable.

Evolution may have instilled in us phylogenetically information about, and patterns of behavior suitable to, stable facts of our evolutionary past. We do not have to think explicitly about (or even know about) the regular alternation of day and night; our bodily rhythms do that job for us, as jet-lagged travelers discover. Some facts are stable enough so that each organism need not arrive at a knowledge of them itself; evolution will have wired that in. Rationality may have the evolutionary function of enabling organisms to better cope with new and changing current situations or future ones that are presaged in some, possibly complex, current indications. That rationality *can* do this is itself one of the stable facts, not a fact we need explictly to know. All we need is to have it built into us, as the presence of gravity is. Evolution employs and builds mechanisms around constant and stable environmental features. It is not just that gravity is a constraint upon some characteristics—for instance, size—but that gravitational force is utilized in the working of some processes. The physiology of astronauts is seriously disrupted by prolonged weightlessness because their physiological mechanisms evolved in an environment of steady gravity and were designed to utilize and function in tandem with that. Those processes do not duplicate what gravity already does (and the attempt to duplicate it, in the presence also of gravity, would only produce excessive force and harmful results.)

We might try out the following hypothesis. The list of philosophical problems that thinkers, without evident success, have long struggled with—the problems of induction, of other minds, of the existence of the external world, of justifying rationality—all mark assumptions that evolution has built into us. There are other, less familiar problems too.

But why think it is necessary for us to solve these problems? If all human beings heretofore have been born in environments surrounded by other people, there is no need for them to learn or infer for themselves that these are people with minds similar to their own. Every human would have to know this to function effectively; those cousins of our ancestors who could not manage to learn this left no similarly uncomprehending decendants. Those who learned it most quickly had some advantage, and so, via the Baldwin effect, evolution would instill easier and easier learnability of this until eventually that knowledge was built in. Similarly, those cousins of our ancestors who could not manage to learn that there was an independently existing "external world," one whose objects continued on trajectories or in place even when unobserved, did not fare as well as those who quickly recognized obdurate realities. Those who could not learn to generalize from past experience (in a way that was appropriate then) succumbed to dangers that left them fewer decendants. It was never the function of rationality to *justify* these assumptions that embodied stabilities of our evolutionary past but to utilize these assumptions in order to cope with changing conditions and problems *within* the stable framework they established. It should not be surprising that our rational instruments could not provide conclusive reasons or "justification" for these assumptions. They were not designed for that purpose or for the purpose of providing conclusive reasons for their *own* use.[28]

"Probability is the guide of life," Bishop Butler said, but we are unable to establish the rationality of acting, in particular situations, on the basis of what is most probable. Indeed, until recently, on most extant theories of probability, it made no sense to ascribe a probability to a particular event, and reasons would be needed to show, for instance, why what would occur in a hypothetical infinite sequence of events should guide us in one particular very finite case. Recently, propensity interpretations of probability have been formulated that do attribute probabilities to particular events. But still, on these theories and also on the view that construes probability as a *theoretical* term within science to account for certain phenomena, we are left with the unanswered question of why we should act this next time upon the most probable. The rationality of acting on probability is expressed within utility theory by the Von Neumann–Morgenstern condition that if a person prefers x to y, then the person prefers that probability mixture giving the higher probability of x, among two probability mixtures that yield (only) x and y with differing probabilities. If x is preferred to y, then $[px,(1-p)y$ is preferred to $qx,(1-q)y$ if and only if p is greater than q]. This last sentence has exactly the form of a Carnapian reduction sentence[23] and so suggests the project of implicitly defining probability in its terms. Instead of worrying over justifying why we should act on probabilities, instead define probabilities in terms of how we should act. This project was carried out by L. J. Savage, who laid down a set of normative (and structural) conditions on behavior, on preference among actions, sufficient to *define* a notion of personal probability.[24] For instance, if a person who prefers x to y chooses act A rather than act B, where A yields x if state S obtains and y if state T obtains, while B is the reverse, yielding y if state S obtains and x if state T obtains, then we might take his choosing A as showing that he holds, as *defining* his holding, S to be more probable than T. But defining probability in terms of this *one* preference among acts can run into trouble. Suppose that same person also prefers z to w and chooses act C over D, when C yields z if state T obtains and w if S does, while D yields the reverse, w if T obtains and z if S does. This would indicate the person holds T more probable than S. But his earlier preference of A over B indicated that he holds S more probable than T. If one is going to define personal probabilities in terms of preferences among acts, this conflict must be avoided. Hence, Savage imposes a condition: if the person prefers A to B as above for particular outcomes x and y, where x is preferred to y, then for *every* z and *every* w such that the person prefers z to w, she will prefer D to C above. However, there is no independent rationale for this as a normative requirement, unless that rationale recognizes some independent notion of probability, other than the personal, and takes the person's choices as indicating that she acts on a probability that she believes to be greater.[25] (She might instead be acting upon some principle that does not involve probability, or involves it in a different way.) Thus, the condition assumes that the person always should have some clearly specified probability beliefs and always should be acting upon them (in the manner specified by the Von Neumann–Morgenstern axiom). But this is the very question at issue—why is it rational to act on the more probable—and that question is not circumvented by Savage's attempt to define probability in terms of action.[26] And to this issue so central to the notion of instrumental rationality and the rationality of belief—why in a particular in-

stance we should act on the most probable or believe the most probable will occur—the resources of rationality have thus far not provided
a satisfactory answer.[27]

Consider Kant's attempt to make principled behavior the sole ultimate standard of conduct, apart from any particular desires an individual might have. Principles, however, are devices—I do not say they
are an evolutionary adaptation—formed to function in tandem with
already existing desires, some of which were biologically instilled.
Thus principles are partial devices. Yet Kant truncates the context in
which principles are able to function by eliminating the cofactors they
are designed to function with; principles alone are to do all the work,
the very idea of principle. Our earlier discussion of principles gave
them no such disembodied scope or task. It is not just our rationality
and our principles that are partial, designed to work in tandem with
external things. We human beings are partial creatures, not wholly autonomous. We are part of the natural world, designed to work in tandem with other parts and facts, dependent upon them. Human memory uses information stored in (arranged) objects in the external
world;[29] we too are physical creatures who occupy ecological niches.
The evolutionary account of rationality and its limitations fits one
theme in the writings of Ludwig Wittgenstein, John Dewey, Martin
Heidegger, and Michael Polanyi, who also, for different reasons, see
rationality as embedded within a context and playing a role as one
component along with others, rather than as an external, self-sufficient
point that judges everything.[30]

The evolutionary explanation of why we cannot rationally justify
certain assumption—our rationality was designed to work in tandem
with those facts, performing other functions—is not itself a justification of these assumptions. Just as Euclidean geometry need only have
been "true enough," so too the belief in other minds and in an independently existing external world could become fixed (via the Baldwin
effect) *without* being strictly speaking true—all these beliefs need to
have been is "true enough." So perhaps we cannot be sure exactly
what truths we are working in tandem with.

Further, that a regularity has held in the past, Hume taught us, does
not guarantee that it (probably) will hold in the future. That past facts
led to assumptions being built into us that fit them does not mean that
those facts will continue to hold and those assumptions will continue
to serve us. And even if *some* regularity that held in the past will continue, Nelson Goodman points out that there are many such regularities that fit the past yet will diverge in the future. Which one is it that
will continue?[31] Evolution only selects traits that have been useful thus
far. Traits equally useful until now are equally favored, however much

the usefulness of these traits might diverge in the future. Evolution does not especially favor usefulness in the future, though afterward it will come to favor what turned out to be useful in that now past-time that previously was future. From this perspective, when it is claimed that evolution encapsulates past stable regularities in our phylogenetic inheritance, the question is not simply whether the regularities of the past will continue to hold so that our inheritance will continue usefully to serve us, but whether evolution has picked out the "right" regularity or given us "green" in a "grue" world. (Can Goodman's rules of projection be interpreted as standards of comparative fitness?)

Still, the fact that rationality was not designed to justify itself or its framework assumptions does not entail that it is *impossible* for rationality to do so. (Yet the fact that philosphers have failed until now lends weight to the view that it would not have been efficient to have left such justification, or even such an inference, up to every single person individually.) Nor does it mean that we cannot find reasons *against* the unrestricted truth of the framework assumptions, even if they were evolutionarily instilled. Recall the example of Euclidean geometry, which, even if selected for as "self-evident," can be discovered to be not strictly accurate. To be sure, we may discover this by application of other reason relations that were evolutionarily instilled or, more to the point, by modifications of those reason relations (where we were led to the modifications on the basis of still other reason relations). It was not necessary that we ever started with reason relations that were perfectly accurate mirrors of obtaining facts. A group of *roughly* accurate reason relations can shape itself into a more accurate group. One roughly accurate tool can detect and correct flaws in another; this second, now improved tool can do the same for a third; and this third then can examine the first tool and detect and correct some flaws in it. All can be improved to a point where each becomes more accurate than any one of them initially was. Over time, the character of each initial tool might be changed significantly, and all three tools together might be used to devise some new fourth tool.[32]

There is a second homeostatic shaping mechanism to consider: the processes by which societies mold their members. The capacities that underlie believing or acting for reasons may have been the subject of natural selection (for whatever reason); but once these capacities existed, *society* might have seized the opportunity to produce (somewhat) rational members. When social scientists speak of rational choice, their aim usually is to explain features of social institutions and to show how rational individuals make and maintain society.[33] This work is illuminating, but we also need to investigate how and why society makes and maintains rational members. People are not born rational. To whatever extent some rational processes *are* a product of innately controlled developmental patterns, these processes are shaped and overlain by socially instilled processes, norms, and procedures. What social processes do this shaping, and why do those social processes exist? (Is it solely because of the *causal* effects of acting or believing on the basis of reasons that society inculcates these traits?)

Social institutions and social structures are maintained by people's actions and choices within the constraints and incentive structures they face, which themselves are set up by other institutions and the behavior of other people within them. Like a large jigsaw puzzle, where each piece fits only in the space left by all of the other pieces, each person's actions are performed within the space of constraints and incentives left open by the actions of all the others. Institutions will have continuity when they are able to *reproduce* themselves, when in conjunction with the other institutions in the society they are able to recruit, train, and provide incentives to new members and functionaries. Part of this training may involve norms and habits of rationality, modes of choice and belief formation.[34] The institution would be creating somewhat rational individuals who are responsive to certain kinds of incentives, who learn and take account of certain kinds of constraints, in order to reproduce these institutions themselves, perhaps somewhat altered, in the next time period. We need not conceive of institutions as trying to reproduce themselves. The process is a selective one: those institutions that (even in conjunction with others) do not propogate, reproduce, or replicate themselves do not survive. That is why we find that almost all existing institutions employ means to recruit and train new persons to take over those functions necessary for the institutions' continuance.*

* In addition to the social functions of rationality, there also is the topic of its social character, the ways in which rationality is interpersonal. Jürgen Habermas has argued that rationality is impossible without an open willingness to listen to opinions from every source and without the liberty and resources such potential sources of opinion would need in order to participate in reasoned discussion. But rationality does not require the most extensive sifting of evidence, computational exertion, and so on. That process itself has its costs, and some (rough) decision would be made about the amount of time and energy to be put into any particular decision or formation of belief. Notice that such costs are personal costs, not peculiarly epistemic ones. If such limits do not necessarily make any particular individual's beliefs and actions irrational—indeed, it might be irrational for them not to impose any such limits—then it is not clear why social limitations, lack of full democratic participation in opinion formation, and so on must prevent the views of the individuals within the society (or of the society itself, if one has a notion of social rationality) from being rational. It might be claimed that the nature of the process by which such cost limitations are decided upon is what makes the difference. However, in parallel to the individual deciding for himself how much investigation to undertake, the rulers of a nondemocratic society could decide how wide-

Hence, a significant function of rationality may be to propogate institutions into temporally later institution stages, not to serve the interests of the individuals who are trained and shaped into rationality. (The precise nature of the institution will affect whether this shaping strengthens or weakens the connection between reasons and reliably arriving at the truth.) In *The Selfish Gene*, Richard Dawkins saw organisms and their behavior as devices selected to serve the reproduction of genes.[35] ("A chicken is an egg's way to make another egg.") Our reflections here raise another possibility, that rationality is shaped, selected, and maintained not to serve a level below that of organisms but to serve a level *above*: the level of institutions.* This does not mean we can ignore the interplay between individuals and institutions: each shapes the other in a way that affects the future shaping of itself.

Sometimes there will be competing hypotheses about the level at which selection has operated. Consider the economist's (standardly made) assumption of wealth-maximization. This assumption, more specific than utility-maximization, gives detailed content to his theories. Maximization is invoked for its mathematical tractability and power, so let us consider the weaker and more plausible assumption that people are seriously concerned with wealth (even if they do not maximize this and even if it does not come lexicographically first). This might be given a social explanation in terms of the institutions that shape people's psychological concerns and motivations and the way particular motivations aid the functioning and propagation of those institutions. There is another possibility, though. It has been reported as a widespread phenomenon across societies (though not holding in the last 150 years within Western industrialized societies) that wealthy people tend to have more children. In polygamous societies, wealthy people (usually males) tend to have larger numbers of mates (wives),

---

spread their own sources of information and countervailing opinion would be; so it is not clear why their beliefs and decisions could not be rational. To be sure, they also should consider possible *biases* in the limited sources of information they employ, but this, too, they could learn of by a limited *sampling* of wider opinions. So it does not seem that democratic and open discussion and opinion formation throughout a society are *necessary* conditions for the rationality of its members', or of its own, decisions and beliefs. The ancient Greeks were not barred from having rational beliefs by the fact that their society included slaves. Democratic rights have a different basis.

* There has been much discussion among biologists and philosophers of biology about the unit of selection or the level at which selection takes place. One spur to this discussion has been the issue of group selection. A phenomenon often cited as supporting group or interdemic selection, and apparently not explainable via individual selection, is the limitation in the virulence in the myxoma virus among rabbits. It is worth noting that this phenomenon would fall under *individual* selection if there were modifier action by the genes for less virulent strains, with the phenotypic effect of reducing segregation distortion.

and in all societies wealthy individuals may have been better able to provide their offspring against material vissicitudes.[36] There also is evidence that within hunter-gatherer societies in the twentieth century—apparently the closest contemporary match to a significant portion of our evolutionary past—chiefs and wealthier individuals tended to leave more offspring. Let us suppose that, all other things being equal, people with a strong desire for wealth tend to amass more than those with a less strong desire; that is, it is more likely that they will. If there had been a genetically based heritable psychological predisposition to be (more) concerned with wealth—I do not claim this as anything more than a possibility—then individuals possessing this predisposition would have tended to produce more offspring surviving to reproductive age, and these offspring too would have tended to possess the heritable disposition, hence to amass more wealth, hence to have more children. A heritable disposition to desire and strive for wealth would have been selected for. The percentage of those with that heritable desire would increase over the generations. (Since not more than 50 percent of the individuals can be wealthier than average, how will this affect the resulting equilibrium of the percentage of wealth-maximizers in the population, in combination with such various factors as the degree of mobility in the society?) Thus, one might have an evolutionary explanation of the economist's assumption, if not of wealth-maximization, then of a strong desire for wealth. Are so few of us concerned with the higher things of life because those of our ancestors' contemporaries who did care left fewer offspring and *we* are descended from those who tended to care about material possessions instead? Of course, the biological and institutional hypotheses are not exclusive; both factors may interact in producing a phenomenon.*

Rationality, I stated previously, is self-conscious in that it aims to

---

* Biological factors also may interact with other kinds of social factors, such as parents intentionally shaping the psychology of their children—surely a widespread phenomenon. Perhaps parents do this for the well-being of their children, or for their own convenience in interaction, or because larger institutions have shaped them into doing that. But there is one other possibility worth mentioning, namely, that parents themselves have an inherited predisposition to shape their children's psychology to be more like their own, to reinforce in their children those psychological traits the parent has. Such a predisposition would amplify the inherited psychological predispositions of the children with regard to those traits the parents shared with them, and so this predisposition to reinforce and shape might also have been selected for, at least when it was in combination with other heritable psychological traits that served inclusive fitness. (If a heritable predisposition to mold one's children's psychology to match one's own did exist, would we expect its genetic basis to be closely linked chromosomally to the bases of some other important psychological predispositions?) It would not be surprising, then, for nature-nurture influences to turn out to be very difficult to disentangle, if their nature leads parents to nurture so as to amplify those psychological traits their children share with, and sometimes have inherited from, them.

correct biases in the information coming to it and in its procedures of reasoning. Earlier, we wondered whether rationality's function is not a limited one within a framework of evolutionarily instilled assumptions, some of which mark philosophical problems we are unable to solve. Should we see escaping from intellectual bias too as having only a delimited function, working within the framework of the fundamental biases of a society as it presents and weights reasons and information? I find that a troubling thought. How wide is our scope for correcting bias? Should we rest content with the range of options about belief and action that our society presents to us and with the range of values it has instilled to further truncate these options, and then employ reasons only to choose among the options *within* this range? Or should we start with all the reasons for and against, conceiving these as broadly as we can, correcting for any biases we can detect due to the social transmission of information and the social weighting and evaluation of reasons, and then do our best to make our decision on this unbiased basis? (If this process leaves a tie among options, we can then allow the inherited values and assumptions of the society to be determinative.)

The first course seems unduly sanguine if not dogmatic; the second seems the course of rationality. The second is the one I want to endorse. Yet to consider each and every option is inefficient. If the bias in society's presentation of reasons represented a weighting these reasons should have, one that a person would arrive at after careful and lengthy consideration, then it would be efficient to follow society's guidance. Are societal biases comparable to a Bayesian assignment of prior probabilities?

Different kinds of adaptation fit different tempos of change. It is inefficient for each person to have to learn everything from scratch and to construct every bit of knowledge all by himself. Our genetic heritage, evolutionarily instilled, was shaped over very long time periods to match or respond to constancies over those time periods. That there are enduring middle-sized physical objects that move continuously, that gravity exerts a continuous strong pull coming from the center of the earth—these constancies have held over long stretches of our evolutionary past. (One of the long-term constancies is that other things frequently change, so we also were shaped to have as part of our permanent genetic endowment mechanisms to respond to such changes.) What our genes respond to undergoes change—thus far—over eons.

What is adapted to factors that change more quickly, over many generations rather than eons, is, some have said, social traditions, institutions, and rules of behavior.[37] Other factors change from lifetime to lifetime—for instance, what occupational skills are most needed in modern (nontraditional) societies. (This tempo can increase so that needed occupations change significantly during one person's lifetime, contrary to expectations.) There are other adaptations to factors that change slowly within a lifetime; these include behavioral habits and enduring personal ties. Then there are factors that change frequently, every day or from moment to moment; our perceptual apparatus is geared to notice changes happening about us, and social information mechanisms too are geared to bring us news of more distant changes. There are different "sets of adaptations keyed to environmental changes of different durations."[38]

Sometimes it will be rational to accept something because others in your society do. Consider the belief mechanism that brings you to accept what (you can see) most other people believe. We all are fallible, so the consensus of many other fallible people is likely to be more accurate than my own particular view when it concerns a matter to which we all have equal access. For a wide range of situations, the mean of a larger sample of observations is likely to be more accurate than one randomly selected individual observation. (Suppose the observations are normally distributed around the true value or are determined by the true value plus random error factors.) About such matters, then, you should correct yourself to move closer to the consensus view, unless you have some special reason to think others have been misled and that you are different—for instance, they have been misled in a way that you are not as subject to.* If the majority's views are formed by myth and superstition, while mine are based upon the scientific literature (or reports of it), wherein views are formed more carefully and reliably, then I may have reason to think the minority view is correct. The Marxist tradition held that other people's views were shaped by ideological mechanisms of obfuscation and hence exhibited "false consciousness"; those who knew more of such mechanisms, or who had read the theories that unmasked them, could thereby feel justified in dismissing the consensus as unreliable.

Our question now is whether bias itself can have a function due to some social homeostatic mechanism that produces it. That would depend upon the nature of social processes. In the case of evolutionarily instilled assumptions—supposing there are such—they sufficiently matched facts to give an advantage to people reaching them easily. Does societal bias in the weighting of information and reasons result from some selective mechanism attuned to important facts or serve widespread purposes in the society? If so, this would support the con-

---

* Should we therefore reinterpret Solomon Asch's famous experiment on social conformity?

servative view that existing institutions, traditions, and biases have some strong presumption in their favor. But I am skeptical. Only if this selective process was severe and the criterion that guided its selecting was desirable could we grant legitimate weight to whatever bias the process produced.[39]

A conservative presumption in favor of institutions, traditions, and biases that have existed for a long time is extremely implausible on its face, unless it is severely restricted. Slavery existed for a long time, and so has—these continue—the subordination of women in society, racial intolerance, child abuse, incest, warfare, and the Sicilian Mafia. How much weight we should give to the fact that something has long endured depends upon why it has continued to exist, upon the nature of the selective test it has passed, and upon the criterion embodied in that test. (And the nature of the environment in which that selection took place may have changed relevantly, so that what once was adaptive no longer is so.) It is possible to overestimate the severity of a test, but it also is possible to underestimate it. Marxists thought the only test capitalist society and its institutions had passed recently—since the time it completed the task of overturning feudalism—was to serve the interests of the ruling class, and so they set out to break what they didn't understand. (Viewing the resurgence of Marxism in humanistic and cultural academic studies, one might say that Marxism repeats itself, the first time as tragedy, the second time as farce.)

Even when there is a known reason for something's survival, and even when some of the functions it performs are worthwhile, that does not settle the question of whether its continuance is desirable. That will depend upon whether we can devise and institute an alternative that it is rational to believe will be better and be worth its attendant risks. A society will choose sweeping institutional change, though, only if it is driven to make some change or other. So a society's decisionmaking *will* tend to be conservative, though not as a result of assessing that what exists resulted from some stringent selective process with a laudable criterion.

Capitalism arose from feudalism through a series of gradual transformations, each of which produced visible positive benefits along the way (increases in productivity, in the size of the population that could be sustained, and so forth) and thus provided reasons and incentives to take further steps. Capitalism arose by a "hill-climbing" method. (A complex and interconnected mechanism such as the eye can evolve if the way to each component produces some beneficial improvement, if each increase in sensitivity to light produces some benefits, even though less than the full benefits given by the completed eye.[40]) Such a route is only guaranteed to produce a local optimum, but even if capitalism were only that, it would be stable (in the face of a movement advocating what that movement takes to be a global optimum) if no sequence of small steps, ever improving, led from it to the different (purported) global optimum. If this were the case, there would be a problem for society in reaching the global optimum.[41] Of course, we are intelligent and rational; we can look ahead and decide to cross a valley. The more numerous and great the changes needed to reach a destination, though, the more distant it is. How strong are the reasons for thinking things will be better there? When things are reasonably good at the local position, this voyage into the unknown will seem too fraught with serious dangers, however well supported it seems by theoretical argument. (For how good are our theories, how good our understanding of society?)

Hence it is not surprising that bold and thoroughgoing social "experiments" (that involve and require concerted changes of many factors) are more likely to be undertaken where the general situation is desperate and where there are few independent centers able to resist such change. (The Marxist revolution took place in Russia and not, as Marxists had expected, in the advanced capitalist countries, and it was followed as a model in parts of the economically undeveloped world.)

Two kinds of reason can be given for confidence in a societal trip. First, it can be undertaken in small steps, each of which can be seen to be beneficial and hence will build confidence in proceeding further. But this is to say that we are not at a local optimum yet, and so this reason does not help with the problem of reaching a distant global optimum. (The theoretical description of capitalist society in Adam Smith's *Wealth of Nations* came only after the trip already had been undertaken, with some positive results. Not only the past steps but this theory too encouraged further steps. The theory, moreover, had convincing authority because it explained the successful results of the past steps—it wasn't "only theory.")

A second kind of reason for making a societal trip is that small-scale experiments along those same lines already are successful (in the existing society). Yet if the global optimum could work well only if instituted at the level of a whole society—or internationally?—but not when embedded within a society having a different character, then it will not be possible to find such local encouraging successes. Even if such small-scale experiments do work, there will be the question of whether their results can be extrapolated. Will they work in the large? Will they work with everyone and not just a specially selected population of participants or monitors?

A society doing reasonably well by its own lights will not, on its own, reach a global optimum unconnected to it by local improvements; global experiments will not be tried out for the first time there. They may be tried elsewhere, though, and demonstrate their viability and effectiveness there. Also, with international economic ties and competition, an external example may operate to lead people to support a great modification in their own society.[42]

In addition to the biological and social mechanisms that shape our acting for reasons, there is the shaping we each personally do ourselves, the ways in which we modify and direct our conception and utilization of reasons toward purposes that *we* choose—to be sure, using biologically and socially shaped capacities (and also the results of previous personal shaping) in this process. Whatever the initial functions of reasons were, we can use our ability to employ reasons to formulate new properties of reasons and to shape our utilization of reasons to exhibit these properties. We can, that is, modify and alter the functions of reasons, and hence of rationality.

V

INSTRUMENTAL RATIONALITY

AND ITS LIMITS

Is Instrumental Rationality Enough?

ENOUGH for what?" counters the instrumentalist, pleased that we seem to grant his view in asking our question. But the issue is whether instrumental rationality is the *whole* of rationality.

The instrumental notion of rationality can be formulated in decision-theoretic terms within the framework of *causal* decision theory, whose notion of (probabilistic) causal connection captures the central notion of instrumental rationality: the means-ends connection. We (and causal decision theory, too) must construe this connection broadly, though, so as to include the relation of an action to broader actions that it specifies and is a *way* of doing—as flying to Chicago is a way of traveling to Chicago. Among the goals to be achieved may be the performance of an action, and one way to achieve this is to do it one particular way; instrumental rationality, as the efficient and effective achieving of goals, will include this. So instrumental rationality does not always involve bringing about something *else*, something completely distinct. And instrumental rationality can acknowledge that doing an action (or having done it) might itself have some value, a value that (with some stretching, perhaps) can be included in what the act produces. (In what follows, when I speak of "causal" and of "instrumental," I mean to include the instantiation aspect and the utility of doing the act itself.)

The notion of instrumental rationality is a powerful and natural one. Although broader descriptions of rationality have been offered, every such description that purports to be complete includes instrumental rationality within it. Instrumental rationality is within the intersection of all theories of rationality (and perhaps nothing else is). In this sense, instrumental rationality is the default theory, the theory that all discussants of rationality can take for granted, whatever else they think. There is something more, I think. The instrumental theory of rationality does not seem to stand in need of justification, whereas every other theory does. Every other theory must produce reasons for holding that what it demarcates is indeed rationality. Instrumental rationality is the base state. The question is whether it is the *whole* of rationality.

Some will object that any extension of instrumental rationality is unjustified and that to justify such an extension by procedures that are not themselves purely instrumental begs the question. (If noninstrumental procedures are justified by instrumental ones, do they always bear the instrumentality of their origins?) So let us ask why we should be *instrumentally* rational. Why should anyone pursue their desires or goals in the most efficient and effective way? Because then it is most likely that they will achieve their goals or satisfy their desires, at the least cost (and so be able to achieve the greatest overall goal and desire satisfaction). But why should they achieve their goals and satisfy their desires? Because that is what they want to do. But why should they satisfy *that* desire? Is there any noncircular answer, any answer that does not beg the question of justifying instrumental rationality?

If other modes of rationality cannot justify themselves without circularity, the same can be said of instrumental rationality.* So that is not, by itself, a conclusive criticism of the other modes. In any case, it is not clear what instrumental rationality's rejection of circularity is based upon. Is there empirical evidence that circular justifications, as wielded by us in the situations in which we actually are pushed to use them, lead to a lower degree of desire achievement (or of reaching the truth) than some other (particular) procedure would?

I have not raised this question of why desires should be satisfied in order to claim that instrumental rationality could not (in principle) be the sole content of rationality. The instrumentalist may take the goal of satisfying desires to be given, rather than rational, and a critic who demands that satisfying desire itself be shown to be rational is importing a standard the instrumentalist would reject. Nor have I raised the issue of justifying instrumental rationality in order to question its legitimacy. (I have no doubts about that, at least in the case of instrumental rationality directed toward rational goals.) I shall claim, though, that there also are other legitimate modes of rationality, and hence that the concept of rationality is not exhausted by the instrumental. I raise the issue of justifying instrumental rationality to parry early the instrumentalist's charge that other modes of rationality cannot be justified without circularity. All are in the same boat.

On a causal-instrumental account of rationality, our standards of rationality must depend upon our view of the character of this world and upon our view of what we are like, with our capacities, powers,

---

* Arguments for instrumental rationality presumably will adhere to standards effective in achieving cognitive goals. The thoroughgoing instrumentalist, however, does not think there is a rational requirement to accept or pursue those particular goals; so, if he is right, his arguments will *at best* (rationally) convince only people who happen to share those goals.

disabilities, and weaknesses. (On a broader account, not simply instrumental, there still will be a similar, though partial, dependence.) Certainly, if rationality is fixed by effects, then what will actually (or generally) have certain effects is an empirical question. Some standards will be causally most efficacious in reaching a goal in one kind of world involving one kind of person, but not in another, where different standards will be most efficacious. Clearly, there is an interplay. We use our standards at one time to discover the world's character and our own, and on the basis of this new understanding we modify or alter our standards so as to make them, as wielded by us, (most likely to be) most efficacious in that kind of world (as we newly understand ours to be). The process continues, for those new standards lead to still further modifications in our view of the world and of ourselves, and hence to still newer standards, and so forth. Our view of the world and of ourselves, and our notion of what counts as rational, are in continual interplay.

We might think of the *pure* theory of rationality as the theory of what standards are to be adhered to by any kind of being in any kind of world, that is, by every kind of being in every kind of world. But it seems unlikely that, if there *are* any such standards, they will be very contentful or get us very far. Still, they might provide a starting point for the project, within one world, of using these pure standards to form a view of that world and oneself, then modifying the standards accordingly, forming a new view on the basis of these modified standards, and so on. There is no reason, however, to believe that any such pure standards lie back in the actual history of our own more contentful ones. Our standards were born with impurities, and philosophy's attempt to redeem us from this original sin has thus far been unsuccessful.

There is a further interplay to mention. Our principles of decision and principles of reasoning are intertwined. We reason about which principles of decision to follow—our second chapter was an instance. And we also can decide which principles of reasoning to follow. The policy of following a particular group of principles of reasoning is a course of action. Two such courses involving different groups of principles of reasoning can then be evaluated by a principle of decision to determine which course of action is best. Which principles of reasoning are deemed best might depend upon which principle of decision is employed.

This point clearly applies to those who would justify principles of reasoning by their reliability in arriving at truths, the most reliable mode of reasoning being the most justified. We also would want to consider how we fare when things go *wrong* with the principle of reasoning, in those cases when it does not lead to the truth. If one principle is most reliable but disastrous when wrong, while another is somewhat less reliable but also not so very bad when wrong, we may well favor the latter, forgoing some reliability for other benefits. And some kinds of truths may be more valuable to us than others, for intellectual or personal reasons, so we may favor a method that does well at reaching *these*, even if that method's overall reliability is less than another's. So a method of reasoning itself may be subject to decision-theoretic considerations of expected utility, not simply probability. Other considerations might enter to make the simple maximization of expected utility seem inappropriate for the choice of principles of reasoning, and so a different principle of decision would then be used.

A principle of decision is established (tentatively) by a method of reasoning, a method of reasoning by a principle of decision. It would be too ambitious a project to investigate all possible pairings of principles of decision and principles of reasoning, to see which ones, and under what conditions, are mutually supportive. But we should hope that in our own situation there is significant mutual support between whatever set of principles of decision we most favor and whatever set of principles of reasoning we find most convincing. A discrepancy here should be a spur to change. What we want is a convergence over time that we can rationally term self-correction.

Even if rationality were understood and explained only as instrumental rationality, that rationality can come to be valued in part for itself—see John Dewey on means becoming ends—and so come to have *intrinsic* value. The *nature* of that rationality would be, let us suppose, wholly instrumental, but its *value* would not be. We value a person's believing and deciding rationally in a way that is responsive to the net balance of reasons, and we think that is good and admirable in itself, perhaps because so deciding and believing uses our high and intricate capacities and expresses them, or perhaps because that embodies an admirable and principled integrity in guiding beliefs and actions by reasons, not by the whims or desires of the moment. Moreover, there is the theme emphasized by Heidegger: instrumental tools, used often enough, can become extensions of ourselves; our boundaries can extend through them to *their* ends as we interact with the world. Thus rationality—and also principles, the topic of our first chapter—originally wholly instrumental, can with sufficient utilization become an extension of ourselves and be assimilated within ourselves as an important part of our identity and being.

We also might see rationality as our route to *understanding*, not simply as a means to it but as a constituent or component of understanding. Some complex systems can be understood—by us at least—only by means of an articulated theory, one whose interconnections with other theories and whose supporting reasons we know, whose ability to withstand objections (and whose contouring to meet these objections) we can trace. Notice that rationality is not simply instrumental in finding such a theory but also is a defining component of what it is to understand that theory and the phenomenon it describes. If understanding is something we now value in part for its own sake—whyever we originally began to value this—and if rationality enters into the nature of such understanding as a constituent, then rationality too may be valued, in part, for its own sake.

In formulating a decision theory that incorporates symbolic and evidentially expected utility in addition to causally expected utility, however, we have widened the notion of rationality beyond the simply instrumental. Rationality is not just a matter of what (probably) will be led to or produced. In Chapter 2 we concluded that causal decision theory is not, all by itself, a fully adequate theory of rational decision. A rational decision, we said, will maximize an action's decision-value, which is a weighted sum of its causal, evidential, and symbolic utility. But instrumental rationality is wholly captured and exhausted by the notion of causally expected utility. Since causally expected utility is just *one* aspect of rationality, there must be more to rationality than instrumentality. People have always thought this, of course. Evidential and symbolic factors have functioned with *very* significant social consequences in human history (recall again the literature on the role played in the development of capitalism by the Calvinist view of *signs* of election).

We already have included these noninstrumental factors in our two-stage theory of rational belief. The first stage eliminates as candidates for belief statements whose credibility value is less than that of competing statements. These credibility values themselves will be determined by a network's linkages that are in accordance with (probabilistic) factual connections, and hence whose weighted transferrings are instrumental in achieving true belief or other cognitive values. But the second stage, deciding whether to believe a statement whose credibility value is not topped by that of any competing statement, is explicitly noninstrumental. What is assessed then is the decision-value of believing the candidate statement, that is, its weighted evidential, symbolic, and causal utilities. (The instrumentalist would use Rule 2 as interpreted by causal decision theory, rather than Rule 5.)

I have been assuming that when decision-value is involved, and not simply causally expected utility, then that calculation is not wholly instrumental. For we then care not just about the results produced, about their probabilities of being produced, but also about what is indicated and symbolized. Could the instrumentalist claim, however, that this too is a solely instrumental calculation? If we let the goal be maximum decision-value, and let the relevant utility function be linear with this, won't the person be choosing that action which is causally most effective in producing maximum decision-value, and hence once again be acting instrumentally? It seems that here the relevant probabilities will not all be causal ones; the relation of the action to its symbolic or evidential utility will not be causal. However, our already widened description of instrumental rationality includes the way that one action is a way of doing another. So why not also include within instrumentality these relations that an action stands in to its evidential and symbolic utility? This might make the question of instrumentality trivial, but an interesting point still would hold, though now redescribed. The goal of some actions would now be maximum decision-value, which is not only a noninstrumental goal—we always knew that the goals of instrumental actions could themselves be noninstrumental—but also a goal that describes and mandates an action standing in noninstrumental relation to a goal. The broader notion thus "saves" instrumentality only by seeing the goal of an "instrumental" action as that action's standing in noninstrumental relations to other goals. And for our purposes, that is what constitutes *non*instrumentality.

But what about the credibility value of a statement, as that is determined within a processing network of reasons for and against? Is credibility value wholly instrumental, in that the resultant weights in the network will be determined solely by how effective those weights are in causally achieving various cognitive goals, such as true belief, explanatory power, and simplicity? That will depend upon the nature of the feedback rule, the learning rule within the network of the processing system that fixes the credibility values. What is it that feeds back, and according to what rules of revision does it do so? Will there be room here too for evidential and symbolic factors?[1]

My argument that instrumental rationality is not the whole of our rationality has not been disinterested. If human beings are simply Humean beings, that seems to diminish our stature. Man is the only animal not content to be simply an animal. (Since my argument is motivated, you—and I too—should be alert to correct for any biases in its treatment of reasons.) It is symbolically important to us that not all of our activities are aimed at satisfying our given desires. Principles, we have seen, provide one means to control and reshape our desires. (Kant asked too much of them, however, when he divorced them from their connection to desire and expected them to generate actions solely from respect for principle itself.)

One way we are not simply instrumentally rational is in caring about symbolic meanings, apart from what they cause or produce. The proponent of instrumental rationality cannot easily claim that such caring is irrational, for he has no relevant criterion of rationality—why then should this caring be any more irrational than any other? Symbolic meanings are a way of rising above the usual causal nexus of desires, and it is symbolically important to us that we do this. Does this mean that acting on symbolic meanings, taking symbolic utilities into account, is a *means* to rise above this Humean nexus?—the instrumentalist asks with a smile. Perhaps, but even if it doesn't accomplish that, it can *symbolize* it.* Even with the processes of forming and maintaining our beliefs, then, we can care not simply about what those processes causally produce but also about what they symbolize. Our discussion of principles in the first chapter was, for the most part, instrumental; we considered the functions that principles could serve. Here we see a possible meta-function—to rise above the serving of other functions—and so following principles too may have a symbolic utility.

I have claimed that there are legitimate modes of rationality in addition to the instrumental—these include the evidential and the symbolic—yet the question remains open of the priority among these different legitimate modes. And what priorites we will choose to establish.

Rational Preferences

There is, of course, a familiar criticism of the notion of instrumental rationality as purporting to exhaust the whole domain of rationality. Something is instrumentally rational with respect to given goals, ends, desires, and utilities when it is causally effective in realizing or satisfying these. But the notion of instrumental rationality gives us no way to evaluate the rationality of these goals, ends, and desires themselves, except as instrumentally effective in achieving further goals taken as given. Even for cognitive goals such as believing the truth, we seem to have only an instrumental justification. At present, we have no ade-

---

* Since an orientation toward symbolic meaning itself has a symbolic meaning for us, apart from its actual consequences, symbolic utility can support itself. The act of following the principle of taking account of symbolic utility itself has symbolic utility, and so falls under that principle as an instance. Instrumental rationality too can support and subsume itself. On self-subsumption, see my *Philosophical Explanations* (Cambridge, Mass.: Harvard Univ. Press, 1981), pp. 119–121, 131–140.

quate theory of the substantive rationality of goals and desires, to put to rest Hume's statement, "It is not contrary to reason to prefer the destruction of the whole world to the scratching of my finger."[2]

I want to take a few tentative steps toward a theory of the substantive rationality of desires and goals. Let me emphasize that my purpose is not to endorse the *particular* conditions I shall put forward or to defend their particular details. Rather, I hope to show what promising room there is for conditions of the sort that I discuss, and what directions there are for moving beyond Hume.

As a philosopher, true to form, I begin a discussion of content by looking at form. One tiny step beyond Hume, not something he need resist, I think, are the constraints on how preferences hang together that are formulated in the standard Von Neumann–Morgenstern conditions or their variants that decision theory presents—for instance, that preferences be transitive, that when two options both incorporate the same two possible consequences but differ in the probabilities they give these, the option that gives the more preferred consequence the higher probability is preferred.[3] Some of these conditions are justified by instrumental considerations, such as the "money pump" argument that preferences be transitive,* while others are presented as normatively appealing on their face. (Unless these latter can be given an instrumental justification also, isn't this already a step beyond instrumental rationality?) Contemporary decision theory takes this one step beyond Hume: although it does not say that any individual preference is irrational, it does say that a group of them together can be. Let us suppose that there are normative principles specifying the structure of several preferences together and that these principles are conditions of rationality. (The literature contains putative counterexamples and objections to some of the Von Neumann–Morgenstern conditions; the

---

* The idea is that with nontransitive preferences, for example preferring x to y, y to z, and z to x, a person who starts with z can be led to pay a small amount to improve his situation to the y which he prefers to it, another small amount to improve his situation to the x which he prefers to y, and then another small amount to improve his situation to z—the very z he started with—which he prefers to x, thus ending up a net loser. See Donald Davidson, J. McKinsey, and Patrick Suppes, "Outlines of a Formal Theory of Value," *Philosophy of Science* 22 (1955): 140–160, who attribute the argument to Norman Dalkey. The argument assumes that a person is always willing to act on each individual preference, considered in isolation, and willing to act on each one *repeatedly*, no matter what he may knows about how all of them hang together, no matter how he may foresee his sequential action on individual preferences leading him into just this sort of trouble. This certainly is an implausible assumption. Since the money pump argument is meant to justify the normative condition that preferences be transitive, it would be interesting to formulate exactly what normative condition *it* depends upon and presupposes.

point here is not to use those particular ones but some such appropriate set of conditions.[4])

I. The person satisfies the Von Neumann–Morgenstern or some other specified appropriate set of conditions upon preferences and their relations to probabilities.

This suggests at least one further condition that a person's preferences must satisfy in order to be rational, namely, that she must prefer satisfying the normative conditions to not satisfying them. Indeed, for any valid structural condition C of rationality, whether rationality of preference, of action, or of belief:

II. The person prefers satisfying the rationality condition C to not satisfying C.[5]

(This condition should be stated as a prima facie one or with a ceteris paribus clause, as should many of the ones below. The person who knows that he will be killed if he always satisfies the condition that indifference be transitive, or the condition that he not believe any statement whose credibility is less than that of an incompatible statement, may well prefer not to.) Since the person is, let us assume, instrumentally rational,

III. The person will, all other things being equal, desire the means and preconditions to satisfying rationality conditions C.

These rationality conditions C not only concern the structure of preferences but also include whatever the appropriate structural conditions are on the rationality of belief. Hence the person will desire the means and preconditions of rational belief, she will desire the means and preconditions for the effective assignment of credibility values (and for deciding about the utility of holding a particular belief).

A person lacks rational integration when he prefers some alternative x to another alternative y, yet prefers that he did not have this preference, that is, when he also prefers not preferring x to y to preferring x to y. When such a second-order preference conflicts with a first-order one, it is an open question which of these preferences should be changed. What *is* clear is that they do not hang together well, and a rational person would *prefer* that this not (continue to) be the case.[6] We thus have a requirement that a person have a particular third-order preference, namely, preferring that the conflict of preferences not obtain. Let S stand for this conflict situation, where the person prefers x to y yet prefers not having this preference, that is, let S stand for: xPy & [not-(xPy) P (xPy)]. Then

IV. For every x and y, the person prefers not-S to S, all other things being equal.

This does not mean the person must choose not-S over S no matter what. An addict who desires not to desire heroin may know that he cannot feasibly obliterate his first-order desire for heroin, and thus know that the only way to resolve the conflict of preferences is to drop his second-order desire not to have that first-order desire. Still, he may prefer to keep the conflict among desires because, with it, the addiction will be less completely pursued or his addictive desire less of a flaw.[7]

Hume claims that all preferences are equally rational. But an understanding of what a preference is, and what preferences are for, might make further conditions appropriate. In recent theories, a preference has been understood as a disposition to choose one thing over another.[8] The function of preferences, the reason evolution instilled the capacity for them within us, is to eventuate in preferential choice. But one can make preferential choices only in some situations: being alive, having the capacity to know of alternatives, having the capacity to make a choice, being able to effectuate an action toward a chosen alternative, facing no interference with these capacities that makes it impossible to exercise them. These are preconditions (means) for preferential choice. Now, one does not have to prefer that these conditions continue; some people might have reason to prefer being dead. But they need a reason, I think; the mere preference for being dead, for no reason at all, is irrational. There is a *presumption* that the person will prefer that the necessary conditions for preferential choice, for making any preferential choice at all, be satisfied; she need not actually have the preference, but she needs a reason for not having it.

V. The person prefers that each of the preconditions (means) for her making any preferential choices be satisfied, in the absence of any particular reason for not preferring this.

So a person prefers being alive and not dying, having a capacity to know of alternatives and not having this capacity removed, having the capacity to effectuate a choice and not having this capacity destroyed, and so on.[9] Again, we might add

VI. The person prefers, all other things being equal, that the capacities that are the preconditions for preferential choice not be interfered with by a penalty (= a much unpreferred alternative) that makes him prefer never to exercise these capacities in other situations.

There is something more to be said about reasons, I think. (I propose this very tentatively; more work is needed to get this matter right.)

Suppose I simply prefer x to y for no reason at all. Then I will be willing, and should be willing, to reverse my preference to gain something else that I prefer having. I should be willing, were it in my power, to reverse my preference, to now start preferring y to x, in order to receive 25 cents. I then would move from a situation of preferring x to y to one of preferring y to x *and* having 25 additional cents. And won't I prefer the latter to the former?* Perhaps not, perhaps I *strongly* prefer x to y, and do so for no reason at all. Having a strong preference for no reason at all is, I think, anomalous. Given that I have it, I will act upon it; but it is irrational to be wedded to it, paying the cost of pursuing it or keeping it when I have no reason to hold it. Or perhaps I prefer preferring x to y to not having this preference, and I prefer that strongly enough to outweigh 25 cents. So this second-order preference for preferring x to y might make me unwilling to give up that preference. But why do I have this second-order preference? I want to say that, unlike any arbitrary first-order preference, a second-order preference requires a reason behind it. A second-order preference for preferring x to y is irrational unless the person has some reason for preferring x to y. That is, he must have a reason for preferring to have that first-order preference—perhaps his mother told him to, or perhaps that preference now has become part of his *identity* and hence something he would not wish to change[10]—or have a direct reason for preferring x to y, a reason concerning the attributes of x and y. But what is a direct reason? Must a reason in this context be anything more than another preference? It must at least be another preference that functions like a reason, that is, one that is *general*, though defeasible. To have a reason for preferring x to y is standardly thought to involve knowing some feature F of x such that, in general, all other things being equal, you prefer things with F to things without them, among things of the type that x is.** (Preferring cold drinks to warm does not require preferring cold rooms to warm ones.)

> **VII.** If the person prefers x to y, either: (a) the person is willing to switch to preferring y to x for a small gain, *or* (b) the person has some reason to prefer x to y, *or* (c) the person has some reason to prefer preferring x to y to not doing that.

I don't say that *all* of a person's preferences require reasons for them—it is unclear what to say about ones that are topmost; perhaps they are anchored by ones under them—but first-level ones do require reasons

---

* Let us leave aside the consideration that if someone else offers me the 25 cents, I might prefer not having my preferences determined by that external source.

** The reader can supply the emendation when it is a negative feature of y that is most important.

when the person is not willing to shift them. Once we are launched within the domain of reasons for preferences, we can consider how more general reasons relate to less general ones, we can impose consistency conditions among the reasons, and so forth. The way becomes open for further normative conditions upon preferences, at least for those preferences a person is not willing to switch at the drop of a hat. Especially in the case of preferences that go against the preconditions for preferential choice mentioned above, a person will need not just any reasons but reasons of a certain weight, where this means at least that the reasons must intertwine with many of the person's other preferences, perhaps at various levels.[11]

We also might want to add that the desires and preferences are in equilibrium, in that knowing the causes of your having them does not lead you to (want to) stop having them. The desires and preferences withstand a knowledge of their causes.[12]

> **VIII.** The person's desires and preferences are in equilibrium (with his beliefs about their causes).

Since preferences and desires are to be realized or satisfied, a person whose preferences were so structured that he always wanted to be in the other situation—preferring y to x when he has x and preferring x to y when he has y—would be doomed to dissatisfaction, to more dissatisfaction than is inherent in the human condition. The grass shouldn't always be greener in the other place. So

> **IX.** For no x and y does the person always prefer x to y when y is the case and y to x when x is the case. (His conditional preferences are not such that for some x and y he prefers x to y/given that y is the case, and prefers y to x/given that x is the case.)

Desires are not simply preferences. A level of filtering or processing takes place in the step from preferences to desires—as (we shall see) another does in the step from desires to goals. We might say that rational desires are those it is possible to fulfill, or at least those you believe it is possible to fulfill, or at least those you don't believe it is impossible to fulfill. Let us be most cautious and say

> **X.** The person does not have desires that she knows are impossible to fulfill.

Perhaps it is all right to prefer to fly unaided, but it is not rational for a person to *desire* this. (It might be rational, though, to wish it were possible.) Desires, unlike mere preferences, will feed into some decision process. They must pass some feasibility tests, and not simply in isolation: your desires must be jointly copossible to satisfy. And when it is discovered they are not, the desires must get changed, although a desire that is altered or dropped may remain as a preference.*

Goals, in turn, are different from preferences or desires.[13] To have or accept goals is to use them to filter from consideration in choice situations those actions that don't serve these goals well enough or at all. For beings of limited capacity who cannot at each moment consider and evaluate every possible action available to them—try to list all of the actions available to you now—such a filtering device is crucial. Moreover, we can use goals to generate actions for serious consideration, actions that *do* serve these goals.[14] And the goals provide salient dimensions of the outcomes, dimensions that will get weight in assessing the utility of these outcomes. Given these multiple and important functions of goals, one would expect that for an important goal that is stable over time we would devote one of our few channels of alertness to it, to noticing promising routes to its achievement, monitoring how we currently are doing, and so on.[15]

How do our goals arise? How are they selected? It seems plausible to think that they arise out of a matrix of preferences, desires, and beliefs about probabilities, possibilities, and feasibilities. (And then goals reorganize our desires and preferences, giving more prominence to some and reversing others because that reversed preference fits or advances the goal.[16]) One possibility is that goals arise in an application of expected utility theory. For each goal G_i, treat pursuing goal G_i as an action with its own probability distribution over outcomes, and compute the expected utility of this "action." Adopt that goal with the maximum expected utility, and then use it to generate options, exclude others, and so forth.

There is an objection to this easy way of fitting goals within an expected utility framework. The effect of making something G_i a goal is a large one. Now G_i functions as an exclusionary device and has a status very different from another possible goal G_j that came very close but just missed having maximum expected utility. A marginal difference now makes a very great difference.[17] It seems that large differences, such as one thing setting the framework whereby other things are excluded, should be based upon pre-existing differences that are significant.** Consider the descriptive theory of decision proposed by

---

* I am not concerned about the word *desire* or about which phenomenon that word actually gets applied to. Perhaps it is the term *goals* that marks those things that we must not know to be impossible jointly to realize. What is important is the conceptual distinctions involving increasing constraints, not the labels.

** At least, when there is no practical necessity to deviate from this norm, as with the difference between the last person admitted and the first rejected to a program with a fixed number of admission places, and no necessity of placing many marginally varying entities into a smaller number of classificatory categories.

Henry Montgomery. There, an individual seeks to justify a choice by finding a dominant structure, and she uses mechanisms such as combining and altering attributes and collapsing alternatives in order to get one action weakly dominating all others on all (considered) attributes. Thereby, conflict is avoided, for one action clearly is best; there is no reason for doing another.[18] Will such dominance always set up a *gulf* between actions that is significant enough to make a qualitative difference with large effects and so be applicable to the formation of goals? Yet one action can weakly dominate another when there are six dimensions, the two actions tying on five of these while the first action is (only) slightly better on the sixth. Even in this framework, we seem to need more than simply weak dominance; perhaps we need *strong* winning on one dimension or winning on many of them.

Returning to the expected utility framework, we might say that goal G_i is to be chosen not simply when it has maximum expected utility but when it beats the other candidate goals *decisively*. For each j, $EU(G_i) - EU(G_j)$ is greater than or equal to some fixed positive specified quantity q. (There remains a similar but smaller problem, though. G_i beats the other goals decisively, yet there is no decisive difference between beating decisively and not doing so; the difference $EU(G_i) - EU(G_j)$ might barely reach, or just fail to reach, q.)

To make something a goal is, in part, to adopt a desire to find a feasible route from where you are to the achievement of that goal.[19] Therefore,

> **XI.** A person will not have a goal for which he knows that there is no feasible route, however long, from his current situation to the achievement of that goal.

Moreover, we might say that a rational person will have some *goals* toward which she will search for feasible routes and not just have merely preferences and desires. She will filter out actions that cannot reach these goals, generate for consideration actions that might reach them, and so on. And some of these goals will have some stability, so that they can be pursued over time with some prospect of success.

> **XII.** A person will have some stable goals.

A rational person will consider not only particular (external) outcomes but also what he himself is like, and he will have some preferences among the different ways he might be. Let Wp be the way the person believes he will be when p is the case; let Wq be the way he believes he will be when q is the case. (These include the ways that p, or q, will cause or shape or prompt him to be.) There is a presumption, which can be overriden by reasons, that preferences among ways of being will take precedence over lower-level preferences that are personal ones. (Personal preferences are ones derived solely from estimates of benefits to himself.)

XIII. If the person prefers Wp to Wq, then (all things being equal) he does not hold the (personal) preference of q to p.[20]

Condition XIII holds that the way the person is, what kind of person he is, will have greater weight in his preferences than (what otherwise would be) his personal preferences. (Is this condition culture-bound and plausible only to people in certain kinds of cultures?)

The dutch book argument that someone's probability beliefs should satisfy the axioms of probability theory says that if they do not, and if she is willing always to bet upon such probability beliefs, then someone can so arrange things so that she is sure to lose money and hence reach a less preferred alternative. This argument says that if her (probabilistic) beliefs are irrational, she can be guaranteed to end up worse off on her utility scale. We might try the dual of this argument, imposing as a condition:

XIV. A person's desires are not such that acting upon them guarantees that she will end up with irrational beliefs or probabilities.[21]

Various things might come under the ban of this condition: desiring to believe something no matter what the evidence; desiring to spend time with a known liar without any safeguards; desiring to place oneself in a state—through alcohol, drugs, or whatever—that will have *continuing* effects on the rationality of one's beliefs. But this requirement is too strong as stated; perhaps acting upon the desire will bring her something she (legitimately) values more than avoiding some particular irrational beliefs or probabilities.[22] Similarly, the dutch book requirement is too strong as usually stated, for perhaps some situation holds in the world so that having incoherent probabilities will bring a far greater benefit—someone will bestow a large prize upon you for those incoherent probabilities—than the loss to be incurred in the bets. The dutch book argument points out that loss can be guaranteed, but still it might be counterbalanced; so too the irrational beliefs or probabilities you have through violating condition XIV might be counterbalanced. To avoid this, the moral of the dutch book argument must not be put too strongly, and similarly for condition XIV.

These fourteen conditions can take us some considerable distance past Hume toward substantive constraints upon preferences and desires. Empirical information about the actual preconditions of satisfying the conditions of rationality, and of making preferential choices—mandated by conditions III, V, and VI—might require quite specific substantive content to one's preferences and desires, the more so when combined with the constraints of the other conditions.

Can we proceed further to specific content? One intriguing route is to attempt to parallel with desire what we want to say about the rationality of belief. For example, people have held that a belief is rational if it is formed by a reliable process whose operation yields a high percentage of true beliefs. To be sure, the details are more complicated, but we might hope to parallel these complications also. A rational desire, then, would be one formed by a process that reliably yields a high percentage of ___ desires. But how are we to fill in that blank? What, for desires, corresponds to truth in the case of beliefs? For now, I have no independent substantive criterion to propose.

We can, however, use our previous conditions, and any additional similar ones, to specify the goal of that process: a desire or preference is rational only if it was formed by a process that reliably yields desires and preferences that satisfy the previous conditions on how preferences are to be structured, namely, conditions I–XIV. This says more than just that these fourteen conditions are to be satisfied, for any process (we can follow) that reliably yields the satisfaction of these conditions may also further constrain a person's desires and preferences.

> **XV.** A particular preference or desire is rational only if there is a process P for arriving at desires and preferences, and
>   **(a)** that preference or desire was arrived at through that process P, and
>   **(b)** that process P reliably yields desires and preferences that satisfy the above normative structural conditions I–XIV, and
>   **(c)** there is no narrower process P' such that the desire or preference was arrived at through P', and P' tends to produce desires and preferences that fail to satisfy conditions I–XIV.*

If we say that preferences and desires are *rationally coherent* when they satisfy conditions I–XIV (and similar conditions), then condition XV says that a preference or desire is rational only if (it is rationally coherent and) it is arrived at *by a process* that yields rationally coherent preferences and desires.

Not only can that process P reliably yield rationally coherent preferences and desires, it can *aim* at such preferences and desires, it can shape and guide preferences and desires into rational coherence. The

---

* Clause c is a condition meant to handle the reference class problem and to exclude desires also formed through a subprocess that reliably yields violations of the above normative conditions. No weight should be placed on the particular details of clause c as formulated here; it simply is an acknowledgment of the problem and a placeholder for an adequate condition to handle it.

process P can be a homeostatic mechanism, one of whose goal-states is that preferences and desires be rationally coherent. In that case, a *function* of preferences and desires is to be rationally coherent. (Similarly, if the belief-forming mechanism B aims at beliefs being approximately true, then one function of beliefs is to be approximately true.)

We therefore might add the following condition.

XVI. The process P that yields preferences and desires aims at their being rationally coherent; it is a homeostatic mechanism, one of whose goal-states is that preferences and desires be rationally coherent.

And similarly,

XVII. The cognitive mechanism B that yields beliefs aims at these beliefs satisfying particular cognitive goals, such as these beliefs being (approximately) true, having explanatory power, and so on. B is a homeostatic mechanism, one of whose goal-states is that the beliefs meet the cognitive goals.

A *function* of preferences and desires is to be rationally coherent; a *function* of beliefs is to meet the cognitive goals. That follows from our earlier account of function, if these mechanisms P and B are indeed such homeostatic mechanisms. Suppose these homeostatic mechanisms do produce beliefs and desires with these functions. Is it *their* function to do so? That depends upon what other mechanisms and processes produce and maintain those desire- and belief-forming mechanisms. If those preference and cognitive mechanisms P and B were themselves designed, produced, or altered and maintained by homeostatic devices whose goals included *aiming P and B at being devices that produced rationally coherent preferences and approximately true beliefs*, then we have a double functionality. It is a function of the preferences and beliefs to be rationally coherent and approximately true, and it also is a function of the mechanisms that produce such beliefs and preferences to produce things like that, with those functions.

XVIII. There is a homeostatic mechanism $M1$ whose goal-state is that the preference mechanism P yield rationally coherent preferences, and P is produced or maintained by $M1$ (through $M1$'s pursuit of this goal-state).

XIX. There is a homeostatic mechanism $M2$, whose goal-state is that the belief mechanism B yield beliefs that fulfill cognitive goals, and B is produced or maintained by $M2$ (through $M2$'s pursuit of this goal-state).

It is plausible to think that our desire- and belief-forming mechanisms have undergone evolutionary and social shaping that in some significant part aimed at their having these functions. There is more. Once people become self-conscious about their preferences and beliefs, they can guide them, monitor them for deviations from rational coherence and truth, and make appropriate corrections. Conscious awareness becomes a *part* of the processes P and B, and consciously aims them at the goals of rational coherence and truth.

XX. One component of the homeostatic preference- and desire-forming process P is the person's consciously aiming at rationally coherent preferences and desires.

XXI. One component of the homeostatic belief-forming process B is the person's consciously aiming at beliefs that fulfill cognitive goals.

This self-awareness and monitoring gives us a fuller rationality. (Some might suggest that only when these conditions are satisfied do we have any ratior.ality at all.)

Self-conscious awareness can monitor not just preferences and beliefs but also the processes by which these are formed, P and B themselves. It can alter and improve these processes; it can reshape them. Conscious awareness thus becomes a part of the mechanisms $M1$ and $M2$ and so comes to play a role in determining the functions of the preference- and belief-forming mechanisms themselves.

XXII. One component of the homeostatic mechanism $M1$ that maintains P is the person's consciously aiming at P's yielding rationally coherent preferences.

XXIII. One component of the homeostatic mechanism $M2$ that maintains B is the person's consciously aiming at B's yielding beliefs that satisfy cognitive goals.

Rationality thus comes to shape and control its own function. (And does self-aware rationality also come to consider the processes that produce and maintain $M1$ and $M2$, and then play a role in those processes too?)

Another possibility is an historical theory. A rational desire would be one that was (or could be) derived from an initial set of (biologically) given desires by a certain kind of (presumably rational) process. Rationality of desire then would be relative to the biological starting point (and the process of derivation or transformation); the Alpha Centaurians might start with very different innate desires and reinforcers. But should it be true by definition that our biologically given desires are rational? Perhaps this marks a limit to our rationality, the fact that we are *creatures*. We start with certain desires and predispositions; although we are not forever stuck with exactly these—we can modify and transform them in various ways—we always will be at a place reachable from *there*.

Let me emphasize, again, that my purpose in discussing the twenty-three conditions is not to endorse these *particular* ones or to defend their specific details but to show what room there is for rationality conditions of this sort and to show how the Humean picture is changed when all these conditions are brought to bear together.

Testability, Interpretation, and Conditionalization

Two other proposed routes whereby more content is ascribed to rational desires and preferences leave me skeptical. The first asks what must hold true if decision theory is to be an empirical theory with testable content, a theory someone can (be discovered to) violate.[23] Any actual pattern of already chosen alternatives can be construed to conform to the normative conditions if the outcomes are parsed, divided, and described in sufficient detail, for instance, "receiving x on a Tuesday at 5 P.M. when given it by someone born on such and such a date." If holding these specific descriptions constant yields a violation of the conditions, then produce further detailed descriptions of the alternatives—this can always be done—to resolve the discrepancy. The way to firm up testability, the argument continues, is to introduce an exhaustive list of aspects of alternatives that a rational person would consider or let affect her choices. We then can test whether her choices satisfy the normative conditions over alternatives fixed by *those* aspects it is rational to consider. Hence, if decision theory is to be an empirical and testable theory, it presupposes rational preferences or, at least, further (rational) content to preferences.

This argument proceeds too quickly, I think. *Any* specification of the alternatives, of the aspects that can be used to distinguish alternatives, will specify the decision theory so that it is a testable empirical theory. The specification need not list aspects that are held to be *rational* to consider. Nevertheless, it can be discovered that a person has been violating the conditions over *those* particular alternatives. To be sure, (a defender) of the person might claim that he *is* satisfying the normative conditions over some other set of alternatives. Now consider the existentially quantified hypothesis that there is *some* set of alternatives, specified by some set of aspects, over which the person is satisfying the normative conditions. Merely as a description of his past choices, this will hold true; some specification or other will fit his past choices. But this does not mean that specification has been *guiding* his choices. If preference is, at least, a disposition to choose, then the claim that he has those preferences over those specified alternatives commits one to further consequences, not only about his actual future choices but also that particular other choices *would* be made—all the while assuming that his preferences are not changing. There are subjunctive consequences of the hypothesis. It is not a trivial truth or a logical one—it is an empirical claim—that there is some set of aspects specifying alternatives so that a person does and would make choices in accordance with the normative conditions over such alternatives. There may be no such set of aspects.[24]

But how shall we discover whether there is or not? Does the burden of specifying the particular aspects, of stating the existential instantiation of the existentially quantified hypothesis, rest upon the denier of the claim that a particular person's choices satisfy the conditions or upon the proponent? Given the burdens of establishing the negative of such an existentially quantified statement, compared to the relative ease of specifying *one* instantiation of it, one would think that the burden of specification rested upon he who claims that the normative conditions are satisfied, especially if they seem not to be on the usual and obvious specifications. With regard to the argument we are considering, though, all we need note is that any specification of the alternatives gives rise to an hypothesis that is testable in principle. The alternatives need not be specified in a way that especially recommends itself to reason. Consider the situation that would arise if a person is *not* satisfying the conditions over any alternatives fitting the proposed rational listing of aspects, yet there is some *other* (nonrational) listing of aspects over which the person is satisfying the conditions. (That is, the person has satisfied the conditions over *those* alternatives in his past choices, the specification already has been offered; we now check future choices of the person and discover that indeed he continues to satisfy the conditions over those specified alternatives, which now have been specified in a way that is not an ad hoc description of already observed data but a specification offered in advance and borne out by the correctness of its predictions.) Would the proponents of the argument we are considering really want to say that this person is not acting in accordance with decision theory, simply because his specification of alternatives does not have what they (perhaps correctly) deem to be rational content?

The second argument to more content is an interpretative one. We cannot interpret persons as performing intentional actions, having preferences and desires at all, unless we ascribe some content to their desires and goals, circumscribing them in some way so that they are something like ours, similar to what we would have in their situation.

This is the thrust, at any rate, of various and variant recently fashionable principles of charitable interpretation, applied first to the content of statements and belief, and then more generally to their combination with preferences.[25] Because I find these guiding principles for interpretation inadequate even as applied to statements and beliefs, I shall discuss them in this, their strongest context rather than in their further application to preferences and desires. (This view is worth discussing at some length, if only because of its great prominence currently in application to other topics within philosophy.)

The root of my dissatisfaction is that these positions seem imperialistic, giving an undue weight to the position we happen to occupy, to our own beliefs and preferences. One might try to avoid this by assuming that we all have a common evolutionary background. This would limit the generality of the claim, which heretofore has been put forward as one about (the beliefs and preferences of) all rational agents on earth or elsewhere in the universe. Because no single desire is necessary to serve inclusive fitness in all environments, there does not seem to be an illuminating level of generality so that one can predict that *every* evolved organism will share *some* desires. If our own beliefs or preferences lack authority for us, it seems implausible that they can gain authority by this interpretation argument, which makes them the benchmark for all beliefs and desires. So much for the general grounds for skepticism; now for the details.

It will not do to interpret (or translate) someone's sayings or writings to make these as *true* as possible, for we may know that person was in no position to have learned what we have about the truth; he has not done the experiments, gathered the data, and so on. More reasonable might be to

1. Interpret or translate what the person says and does so as to make the person as *rational* as possible.[26]

This proposal involves the assumption that the person uses the same standards of rationality that we do. Yet there is strong prima facie evidence that some people do not reason or draw inferences in accordance with (what we take to be) correct standards.[27] There also is evidence that certain drugs make people's processes of belief formation less rational. And some people explicitly announce they follow different principles of rationality.[28] It would seem to distort these cases if our standards of rationality were imputed to them. Moreover, a society's standards of rationality can change and develop over time. It has been argued that literacy brings with it an attentiveness to consistency and reasoned support—written statements can be repeatedly examined and compared to others—and hence leads to the formulation of new standards of reasoning and criticism.[29] An anthropologist might therefore be wary of ascribing certain standards of rational belief to preliterate societies, and hence of interpreting individuals there so that they satisfy those standards.

A fall-back position could hold that adults might well instantiate and exhibit different standards of rationality as a result of cultural inculcation and of their own individual life experiences, but that all infants start with the same initial modes of belief formation, the same capacities and predispositions to form beliefs. All adult beliefs are the rational result of those initial processes of belief and desire formation as they operate upon the experiences and data that an individual's life and culture send her way. Even if there are no initial differences among individuals in their dispositions to form beliefs or to acquire new dispositions, their differences in life experiences may lead not just to later differences in specific beliefs and desires but also to differences in their modes and procedures of acquiring beliefs and desires and their ways of acting upon these. And some of these different procedures might be *instilled* by the different experiences, not simply concluded from them in accordance with the prior procedures. One scientific theory might explain all of these resultant differences (and whatever initial ones there might be), yet this is not to say that some one theory of rationality will apply at each stage or at any one. (The term *rational* may have no application to the common initial infant stage of piling up beliefs.)

Donald Davidson has argued that we cannot make coherent sense of the notion of radically different conceptual schemes. His criterion of radical difference is the surprising one of nontranslatability—not in accord with the way I normally would use the notion of "different conceptual scheme"—but nevertheless, the argument may seem to imply that some common strand of rationality must be at work in every linguistic culture.[30] Yet Davidson himself offers a counterexample to his own view: translatability may not be transitive among conceptual schemes. We might be able to translate the Saturnians, who are able to translate the Plutonians; yet we cannot translate the Plutonians, whose conceptual scheme is not understandable by us. Davidson's attempt to deflect this example is weak: he asks how we know the Saturnians are *translating* Plutonian. Here's how. They are then doing the same thing, that is, using the same procedure (and meta-procedure) they use when they translate English into Saturnian, and this procedure maps each sentence Ei of English onto the same sentence Si of Saturnian that *we* map (when we translate) onto Ei. We have as good reason to think they are translating as we do to think we are.

Yet cannot we translate Plutonian by translating into English the Saturnian sentences that the Saturnians have translated Plutonian into? In that case, won't we understand the Plutonians after all? And it might be argued that even if the intermediate Saturnians do not actually exist, the possibility of their existence is enough to show that it is possible for us to understand and intelligibly translate the Plutonians, which is all the Davidsonian thesis may need.[31] The notion "directly translatable by" is nontransitive. But when two groups or individuals, not directly translatable, stand in a chain of direct translations through intermediaries, isn't that enough to constitute indirect translation and so translation *simpliciter*? I think not.

The reason "directly translatable by" is nontransitive is that it (only) requires sufficiently great but not exact overlap between the conditions of application of concepts or statements, and a chain of sufficient overlaps may lead to insufficient overlap between the endpoints. Hence we can imagine two distinct intermediate chains of direct translation through different planetary civilizations; each link of these chains shows sufficient overlap. Through one chain of gradual shifts with large overlap that begins with an original source S, we translate our nearest chain—neighbor Y's statement y as z; through another chain of gradual shifts with large overlap that begins with that same original source S, we translate our nearest neighbor X's statement p as q. Yet z and q may be as different as you please, as different as our concepts "cow" and "entropy."* Hence, one cannot demonstrate mutual intelligibility by imagining the existence of *some* intermediate chain of translations. One must show that there cannot be two such chains that are distinct enough to lead to radically different translations. Yet, clearly, such distinct chains might exist; and if we knew of them, wouldn't we say that we could not understand the civilization at that endpoint at all?**

* Here is an analogy. In a parallel distributed processing system, some space representing the activated vectors of the intermediate units as subregions can have a sequence of overlapping regions, each region being close enough to act as an attractor on any particular vector in the other region, yet the first and the last can be quite distinct and different, not nearly close enough to attract a vector in a region at the other end of the chain. Two such chains leading in different directions would lead to very different regions as endpoints. That region which begins each of the two distinct chains might have no statable conceptual description in our own vocabulary (other than a vocabulary that speaks explicitly of weights and activation vectors), even if the two regions that end the chains do have such conceptual descriptions, which differ enormously from each other.

** Perhaps we could have some reason to think one of these long chains is more circuitous and wandering than another, so suppose that is not the case here: in the large conceptual space, each path is equally serpentine. The discussion might continue by asking how we know that each link along the chain, even far distant from us, involves a

We also might have ways of catapulting ourselves into radically different conceptual schemes, which we then could use though not translate, for example, into the mystic's through the use of certain drugs or procedures to produce mystical experiences. Alasdair MacIntyre suggests we can go to another society and learn its ways and language from the beginning, as a child there does, and then discover that we cannot translate their talk into English.[32] We thus might be able to use other conceptual schemes that are not, by our standards or by any others we are able to state, rational.

Ronald Dworkin has proposed another guiding principle of interpretation:

> **2.** Interpret (and translate) so as to make what the person says and does as good as possible, as justified, principled, and correct as possible.[33]

Dworkin proposes this primarily as a principle of interpreting rules in an institutional context, and he also thinks it plausible as a principle of literary interpretation. Under this mode of interpretation, something is seen "in its best light," in its best possible light. We might call this principle of putting the best possible gloss on everything the Panglossian Principle. Dworkin would formulate the principle so that this attitude need not be taken toward genocidal or enslaving institutions. But isn't it misleading also in the case of institutions that (we know) represent *compromises* among competing interests or that were shaped by the willy-nilly results of attempts to gain or maintain power? Won't we understand such an institution better when we see it as the result of the processes that actually produced it, rather than through the prism of an attempted rationalization?

Let us examine another guiding principle,

> **3.** Interpret (and translate) to make what the person says as intelligible as possible.

This gives a place to the other guiding principles as well, for truth, rationality, and goodness are *ways* of being intelligible. But they are not the only ways, and deviations from these ways also can be intelligible. Yet we do not always want to translate so as to make the content of what is said as intelligible as possible. The person may have taken a drug that we know tends to produce unintelligible nonsense in people's speech.

Principle 3 therefore must be modified:

---

translation? Must that concept translate sufficiently closely to ours directly, or is it enough that it translates indirectly?

4. Translate "p" so as to make as intelligible as possible the fact that in that context that person said "p."

It is this whole fact that is to be made intelligible, the fact that in that context that person said "p." Principle 4 offers guidance about how to translate "p," and it also allows leeway to include what historians and anthropologists do in considering the historical and cultural context, as well as the person's aims and motives, his fears and superstitions.

We can take a wider purview. The person said not only "p" but also "q," "r," and "s." Shouldn't we translate so as to make as intelligible as possible the fact that in those various contexts he said all those particular things? His contemporaries and forerunners said other things too. Shouldn't we translate so as to make as intelligible as possible the facts of all of their sayings, and might this overturn or modify what would make most intelligible the fact (when treated in isolation) of his saying "p"?

The previous principles—translating so as to maximize truth, or rationality, or goodness—were exciting but inadequate. Principle 4, on the other hand, seems boringly obvious and unilluminating. "*Of course* we are to translate and interpret so as to make it—that is, its being said—as intelligible as possible."

To whom are we to make the fact of his saying that as intelligible as possible? To ourselves, the translators and interpreters. Therefore, our standards of intelligibility will enter—along with our theories of speech, action, life, and society—as we judge what interpretation makes that fact most intelligible. Our standards, however, are not imported *into* his views or attributed *to* him—although the principles of making his views as rational or as good as possible would have done precisely that. "Speaking in tongues" can be made intelligible without making what is spoken intelligible. Make intelligible the saying, not (necessarily) the said.

One way to make as intelligible as possible the fact of his saying what he did is to *explain* as well as possible his saying that. This will draw upon our theories of human behavior and our common sense about it, and will fit his speaking into these. The more detailed our explanatory network, and the more details of his speaking and of his speech that fit within it, the more intelligible we have made these. To show his purpose in saying what he did, to identify what illocutionary act he performed in saying it—all this can add to the intelligibility of his saying that.

Can we also help make the fact of his saying that as intelligible as possible by showing that what he said is as true or rational or good as possible, in other words, by following the previously discussed guiding principles? Only if we have reason to think he was being accurate or rational or good right then.* If we have reason to think he *wasn't*, reading what he said as accurate or rational or good will produce puzzlement, not intelligibility.

Suppose, however, that someone proposes to make *what he says—not the fact of his saying it*—as intelligible as possible. Can this be another goal of interpretation, and will it involve making the statement true, correct, justified, or rational? Yet falsehoods, evil directives, and insulting statements all are quite intelligible—that is, their *content* is completely intelligible. What we may not understand is why someone would say these things or promulgate them, but this leads us back to explaining their being said.

Nonetheless, don't we understand something better when we see the best rationale it can be given—whether or not the person who said it could or would have offered this rationale—when we see what *could* be said for it? I would not deny this, just as we also understand a statement better when we see what could be said against it. In discovering its strengths and weaknesses, in uncovering its connections with other theories and other problems, we more thoroughly explore its nature. The most charitable interpretation presents only one facet of something's nature.

Notice the analogy between the issues we have discussed and recent discussion about evolutionary theory, between those who would offer adaptational explanations for a vast range of features—seeing them as having been selected *for*—and those who would explain many features as not having direct adaptive value but arising in other evolutionary ways, for example, as side effects of other traits that *were* selected for

---

* Some years ago, in objecting to C. G. Hempel's (deductive or statistical) nomological model of explanation as a necessary condition for historical explanation, William Dray held there was another mode of historical explanation, rational explanation, that did not use laws but explained an action by showing it was the (or a) rational thing to do in those circumstances. (See William Dray, *Laws and Explanation in History* [London: Oxford Univ. Press, 1957].) Hempel replied that in this type of explanation we need to add that the agent had the disposition to be rational and exercised it then, that is, this was a situation in which he *would* do the rational thing. Hence, Dray's explanations involve an implicit law: for that agent and for a range of circumstances or situations of type S, he would do the rational thing in a type-S situation. And the explanation would continue: the person was in situation si; si was a type-S situation; in si, action A was the rational thing to do; therefore, he did A. (See C. G. Hempel, "Rational Action," *Proceedings and Addresses of the American Philosophical Association* 35 [1961–62]: 5–23.) For *some* individual, what might most need explaining is why he acted rationally that time. Since he almost always acts irrationally, it is not enough simply to say of an act he performed that it was the rational thing to do. Was it done by accident? Does he have a tendency to act rationally in a narrow range of specified situations of which this was one? Did he have a fit of temporary rationality?

or as the results of satisfying various structural constraints or of genetic drift, and so on. To think that the *only* way to understand an intellectual product is to make it as rational or as good as possible is akin to thinking that the only way to explain a feature of an organism is to show that it is optimal or maximally adaptive. Our principle of making the generation of that intellectual product as intelligible as possible corresponds to the view that recognizes many different modes of evolutionary explanation and leaves it an empirical matter which ones will apply in a given (type of) case.[34] Although the issues are structurally parallel, one still might pursue different explanatory strategies in these two areas, perhaps because one believes the selective pressures are stronger in the biological realm.

Let me mention one other possible route to further contentful conditions on preference. Bayesian conditions for the revision of probabilities over time have been proposed, so-called Bayesian conditionalizing, and one might try to parallel these with intertemporal conditions upon utility. Just as yesterday's conditional probability of hypothesis h on evidence e is supposed, when evidence e comes to be known, to yield a new probability today of h that is equal to that previous conditional probability, so too one might develop a notion of conditional utility and propose an analogous condition of intertemporal conditionalizing.[35]

However, if yesterday's particular probabilities or preferences have no special authority—all they are required to do is satisfy the axioms of probability theory or the Von Neumann–Morgenstern normative structural conditions on preference—then why should they exert any authority on today's particular probabilities and preferences? The structural conditions on preferences at any one time say they must hang together in a certain way; if they do not, it is left open which ones may be revised. From the normative condition that preferences be transitive, conjoined with the premises that a person prefers x to y and prefers y to z, one *cannot* derive the conclusion that she should prefer x to z. Perhaps she should not prefer x to y or y to z. The requirement that preferences be transitive should *not* be read to state that if a person prefers x to y and prefers y to z, then that person should prefer x to z. Rather, the requirement of transitivity should be read to state: it should not be the case that a person prefers x to y, prefers y to z, and does not prefer x to z. From this condition, no detachable conclusion can be derived about what particular preference a person should have.[36]

Consider this (putative) intertemporal version of the structural condition that preferences be transitive: if on Monday a person prefers x to y and prefers y to z and has no preference between x and z, then on

Tuesday that person should prefer x to z. That would be an objectionable condition. Perhaps on Tuesday the person instead should stop preferring x to y or y to z. Of course, on Tuesday the person cannot alter the fact that on Monday he preferred x to y and y to z. Can one argue as follows: although it is true that the correctly interpreted condition at *one* time merely says that preferences should not be discordant in a certain way, leaving it open which particular ones should be revised to reach concordance, nevertheless, an intertemporal condition, combined with the fact that the past is unalterable, now yields the conclusion that the person *should* have a particular preference today? That argument, too, would be objectionable. Suppose the person on Tuesday comes to prefer z to x and wishes that on Monday he either had not preferred x to y or had not preferred y to z. Because there is nothing he can do to change those past facts, does that mean he must now institute a present fact, preferring x to z, that he also would object to? Surely not.

Yet there is the well-known money pump argument: a person with intransitive preferences who is willing to make small payments to realize his more preferred alternative can be brought by a sequence of such payments to go around a circle, ending up where he started, but poorer. (And that cycle can be repeated.) Intertemporally also, the person who on Monday prefers x to y and y to z, yet on Tuesday prefers z to x, if he starts with z on Monday, can be led to pay money to end up where he started. (He pays on Monday to shift from z to y, and then pays again to shift from y to x, and then he pays on Tuesday to shift from x to z.) Yet that fact cannot show that he should prefer x to z on Tuesday, or should act as if he does; for he does not, and need not. His preferences can *change*, and not merely develop as implications of his previous ones. It would be absurd to have an intertemporal normative condition that says someone can never reverse a preference, even though someone who does might pay on successive days to end up right where he began. Such a normative condition is made no more plausible by its being an intertemporal analog of the condition that preference be asymmetric.

Similar objections apply to the use of a notion of conditional utility for a further intertemporal requirement of conditionalizing—no one actually has proposed that, after all—and they also apply to the much-approved criterion that probabilities should evolve over time in accordance with the principle of Bayesian conditionalization.[37] According to the doctrine of strict Bayesians, to whom the only admissible notion of probability is one measuring a person's degree of belief, these personal probabilities need only satisfy the axioms of probability theory. Any particular probability assignments, any combination of degrees of belief, that satisfy these will do equally well.[38] Hence, the particular probabilities on Monday have no special authority. The Bayesian does have an argument for why the probabilities at any one time should satisfy the axioms of probability theory. Corresponding to the money pump argument for preferences is the dutch book argument for probabilities: a person whose probabilities, whose degrees of belief, do not satisfy the axioms of probability theory, and who is willing always to bet at the odds indicated by her degrees of belief, can be offered a series of bets that she would be willing to accept, such that from the results of all the bets together she cannot win any money and (depending upon which axioms we are considering) either she can lose some money or she must lose some money.*

There also is an intertemporal version of this dutch book argument: a person whose probabilities do not evolve over time in accordance with the principle of conditionalization can be offered a sequence of bets through which she cannot win any money and must end up losing money.[39] But consider a person who decides, for whatever reason, to hold probabilities today that do not stand in the desired conditional relation to her probabilities yesterday. Such a person may want her probabilities to hang together over time, and so she may wish her probabilities had been different yesterday, but unfortunately it is too late to change that. Should she now be bound by the dead weight of the past, by probabilities that, after all, may have had little to be said for them other than that together they then satisfied the (atemporal) axioms of probability theory? But that would require her to have a degree of belief today that she does not wish to have and to bet on odds today that she does not wish to bet upon. (Shouldn't she treat yesterday's probabilities as a sunk cost?) Surely, she may act upon today's probabilities and count herself fortunate that no one actually placed certain bets with her yesterday. Even if she had placed certain bets yesterday, that does not mean that today she must bet on the implication of her yesterday-beliefs that she now rejects, throwing good money after bad. (Suppose she thinks that yesterday's probabilities were the result of a fevered state or of the belief—delusional, she now

---

* The fact $F1$ that a bet is *offered* on p, when it is not generally true that a bet is offered on every proposition q, may alter the personal probability of p from what it previously was. The betting behavior now indicates the personal probability of p, given fact $F1$. Suppose that the bet is not offered by another person, but there exists a situation with an act A available whose payoffs actually correspond to that of some bet on the truth of p. What doing this act indicates is the personal probability of p given fact $F2$, where $F2$ is the fact that such a "betting" act is available about p when it is not available about every proposition q. Under what conditions can we get at the probability as it was before, without contaminating and altering it?

realizes—that God was speaking directly to her then. Would the Bayesian maintain that today she must conditionalize upon those probabilities? Or would the Bayesian say that yesterday's were not conditionalized upon those of the day before, so that they now can be ignored? On Tuesday, the person does not conditionalize upon her probabilities of Monday; when Wednesday comes, is she to conditionalize upon these faultily derived Tuesday probabilities, or should she conditionalize upon Monday's with all the new evidence she has gained since then?) She also may reject her previous probabilities because she has thought up new hypotheses that are alternatives to a given one; giving more structure to that category of "alternative," and seeing what the detailed content of some alternatives are, leads her to reconceptualize a domain and so to reallocate probabilities in a way that is not the conditionalization of previous ones upon new information but more like a new assignment of initial probabilities.[40]

Even if she actually made bets yesterday based upon her probabilities then, nevertheless she might want to bet on her probability judgments of today. True, that will guarantee that she must lose *some* money, but she may prefer a small loss that is certain to a large one that is likely, where the latter is what would occur, according to her view today, if she bets today upon what she now considers to be bad odds, the ones based upon yesterday's probabilities conditionalized.

But our position on preferences is not that of the strict Bayesians on personal probabilities; they impose no conditions on the probabilities at any one time beyond their satisfying the axioms of the probability calculus. In the previous section, I proposed conditions on preferences that go beyond the usual structural normative conditions. If the person's preferences and utilities yesterday satisfied those further conditions, isn't that enough to block the remark, "Perhaps he should have had different preferences yesterday," and so to justify conditionalizing upon the preferences and utilities he actually did have then? Yet there are other preferences, too, that would have satisfied those further conditions along with the structural ones. All that seems required is that today he arrive at some set of satisfactory preferences, that is, at preferences satisfying all of the imposed conditions that also could have arisen by conditionalization out of some set or other of satisfactory preferences yesterday. But this latter set need not be the particular set he actually had yesterday. And it does not seem that this very weak intertemporal condition imposes any additional content to the earlier requirement that a person's preferences be satisfactory at a time, that is, currently satisfy the structural and additional conditions upon preference proposed earlier.

None of the avenues we have explored in this section have, in my view, yielded adequate further contentful conditions on preference. I do believe that we should go beyond the stringent Humean view, and in the previous section I very tentatively proposed some contentful conditions. I myself would welcome a more powerful contentful theory of the rationality of preferences and desires, one to further constrain and restrict them beyond anything said here, although not to fix them completely.

Kant tried to derive goals from the notion of rationality itself, in its guise as adherence to principle. We claimed earlier that principles are devices with specific functions, designed to work in tandem with (and to modify) goals that are given. The Kantian attempt to divorce principles from *any* given goals and then to derive goals or specific constraints upon maxims of conduct from the bare notion of adherence to principle fails. If our rational procedures were designed to work in tandem with given biological goals (or with desires and goals whose pursuit was statistically correlated in our evolutionary past with the enhancement of inclusive fitness), then it is not surprising that an attempt rationally to derive goals *de novo*, starting without *any* goals or desires, fails. This does not mean we are stuck with the desires and goals we start with. Our rational procedures enable us to modify these to some significant extent, by steps that make individually small changes but that can, when iterated, produce a large cumulative change.

Suppose that someone does succeed in devising a completely adequate theory of the substantive rationality of desires. Given such a theory, we then would be in a position to say that an action or procedure for forming beliefs is rational when it is *instrumentally* effective in achieving (not any arbitrarily given goal but) *rational* goals. To be sure, that is a great improvement. Instrumental rationality no longer would exhaust the whole domain of rationality; there also would be the substantive rationality of the goals to contend with. Still, even with this modification, rationality would remain largely instrumental.[41] It is the step to decision-value that decisively transcends this broadly instrumental structure.

Philosophical Heuristics

What scientists and philosophers do in constructing theories is rational thinking: they formulate intellectual problems, think up possible solutions to those problems, test and evaluate the solutions, and so forth. This thinking may be instrumental, but it is not, in the first instance, directed toward belief, not even a belief about what is the best solution to the problem. Hence the type of reasons for and against that we discussed earlier do not stand in the forefront. Nevertheless, a theory of rationality should be able to encompass and illuminate that kind of theoretical activity.

Philosophers who write about reasoning tend to concentrate upon an exceedingly narrow range of thinking as the sole legitimate mode of reasoning. (And sometimes writers on rationality treat it mainly as an exclusionary device, whose main purpose is to disparage something as "irrational," rather than as positively marking an efficient and effective vehicle.) If the very best reasoning that philosophers and scientists do in originating their own theories fails to fit the narrow area they have marked as legitimate, then clearly that characterization of rational thought needs to be expanded.

Thinking up a new theory might be seen as solving an intellectual problem, perhaps after first noticing or finding it. There are two interrelated areas to investigate then: problem setting and problem solving. The study of problem setting explores how fruitful problems are found and sharpened, what features characterize a problem situation, and what factors set or shape these. The study of problem solving looks at what a person does and accomplishes *within* that problem situation: the pattern of her attempts to solve the problem or transform it, the progress and stumbling blocks, the way the final product seems to her to advance the problem or to fall short of her goals. (We also can study the extent to which she did advance or solve the problem, importing standards and knowledge other than her own.)

What is an intellectual problem? A useful characterization of the general structure of a problem is offered in the literature of artificial intelligence and formal heuristics. A *well-defined problem* is one in which each of the following features is explicitly specified and delimited.

1. A *goal*, an evaluative criterion for judging outcomes and states.
2. An *initial state*, consisting of a (starting) situation and the resources that are available to be used.
3. *Admissible operations* that can be used to transform states and resources. These admissible operations are stated in the form of rules that may be applied to transform the initial state and then to transform again and again the resulting transformed states.
4. *Constraints* on what intermediate states can be passed along the way, what final states may be reached, what operations may be done when, how many times, in what order, and so forth.
5. An *outcome*, a final state.

A *solution* to the problem is a sequence of admissible operations that transforms the initial state into an outcome that meets the goal, without violating any constraints at any time along the way.[42] Examples of well-defined problems are formal puzzles such as "missionaries and cannibals"—today we would find another description—and tasks of formal proof ("starting with these axioms and using only these rules of inference, prove this theorem").

This list of components is illuminating, even though most problems people face cannot be specified with such exactness.* And often people do not simply *face* given problems; their task is to *make* a problem, to *find* one in the inchoate situations they are in. The task of formulating a well-defined problem to capture what you (will) take to be the important aspects of your situation may not be a task that itself is best treated (or approached) as a well-defined problem. Nevertheless, the problem model's listing of four problem components (goals, initial state, admissible operations, and constraints—the outcome is the product that will solve the problem, not a component that constitutes it) is

---

* In the problem model, a goal is an evaluative criterion such that, given any outcome, there is a clear, determinate, and feasibly reached answer to the question of whether that outcome satisfies that criterion. Yet in life it may be unclear whether and to what extent an outcome satifies a goal. The goal may be a long-term one, with the more immediate outcome making the achievement of the goal more or less likely. An evaluation may be comparative and in the hands of others, as when architectual plans are submitted in a competition. Hence, surrogate evaluations, interim ones, may be used as estimates of a final evaluation. There also may be more than one relevant goal, perhaps with a ranking or weighting of them, but often the priorities will be vaguer; the goals will be unordered, and the list of goals itself may be open-ended. (In developing a project, someone might see how it can take a direction that effectively achieves a certain goal that was not salient to him beforehand; this thereupon *becomes* a goal or purpose of the work.) Goals too may not be predetermined; a person may select his goals or alter the ones he has been given.

Resources may have differing degrees of availability, with some being easier to acquire and use than others, some having more costs than others. The situation in which a person starts also may be unclear to him or her. The admissible operations too may not constitute a list as well defined as the permissible means of proof in mathematics—and even here could not someone formulate a *new* acceptable means of proof that doesn't fit a previously known rule? Sometimes the problem is to devise, create, or construct means to get to a goal, rather than to employ already existing means. (Since the person will have to use other means in devising these, might that be said to be the better-defined problem she faces?) Some means of transformation may be more costly than others, or be suspected of drawbacks if repeated too often. A person even may be doubtful whether an operation is admissible or not. In arguing against a position a person has put forth, can one point out that he does not adhere to it in his own life? Can one use *reductio ad absurdum* arguments in mathematics? Can one tell a white (or gray or black) lie in order to achieve a valuable goal? Constraints too need not be very well defined, and their boundaries may be unclear. Thinking might devise a new way to avoid a given constraint altogether, undermining or circumventing the reasons why it seemed to hold. Constraints might be a matter of degree, more or less difficult or costly to violate. We might better construe a constraint as a *gradient*. (How *difficult* is it to move in that direction, how much energy does it take to move or stay there, how costly is it in term of time or resources, how much resistance must be overcome?)

an illuminating one, even though we would like to loosen the specificity of these for application to real-life situations, and even though we think an important part of intellectual activity consists not in solving such problems but in arriving at them. A model need not illuminate every stage of intellectual activity in order to illuminate one.

The problem model describes how the situation appears to the person with the problem, and we can use it to understand his attempts at solution. He may be wrong about some features of his "problem space," however; he may have more resources than he knows, fewer constraints than he thinks. Still, it is how he thinks of the situation that shapes what he does. In retrospect, we can try to explain why he was wrong about a particular aspect of the problem space; and if he is stuck, he himself can check to see if he is wrong about some aspect.

How is an intellectual problem *found*, how is it noticed, isolated, and formulated? And once the problem is formulated, how does the thinker manage to produce a *solution* (or at least an attempted solution) to it? We do not have any very precise theory of *methods* of intellectual work, of principles, rules of thumb, maxims, and ways of constructing such intellectual works. Tools that may help in reaching a result or solution, the literature terms *heuristics*, and it distinguishes these from algorithms, which are guaranteed to produce a solution (if one exists) in a finite number of steps. The formal literature of heuristics tries to formulate rules that can be programmed on a computer and mechanically applied. Our purpose is different: to find nonmechanical rules and principles that will be helpful to an intelligent person, even if it takes some understanding, intelligence, and skill to apply them.

My interest here is to examine rules of thumb for the construction of philosophical and other intellectual theories, for the fruitful formulation and solution of intellectual problems. But the framework discussed here, of problem structures and heuristic rules, also may be useful in understanding how (some) intellectual work of the past proceeded. To discuss the "problem structure" as a major organizing focus for intellectual history would divert us from our major concern here; for the interested reader, I add an extensive note.[43]

Karl Popper sees intellectual problem solving as proceeding by a process that tries out tentative solutions and criticizes them, modifies the problem in the light of this, proposes new tentative solutions, and so on, until the problem is solved. What we usually see, except in those rare cases where we possess detailed notebooks in which the thinker mapped and developed his thoughts,[44] is the *finished product*, which usually consists of a stated problem (which may not be the original one), a solution offered to that problem, and perhaps some replies to possible criticisms of this solution. It is no easy task to reconstruct from this final product the whole process, perhaps consisting of many iterated steps, that led to it. Heuristic principles enter at each and every stage. We can try to identify principles or rules for formulating and selecting a problem, principles and rules for formulating a tentative solution to a problem, principles for criticizing possible solutions to a problem, and principles for reformulating a problem and modifying it in the face of criticisms and difficulties with earlier proposed solutions. Popper's outline of these stages alerts us to different types of heuristic procedures that might enter into the construction of an intellectual product.

A matter of some current discussion is the extent to which intellectual products result from the use of *general* heuristics that might be applied in a wide range of areas and subjects, and the extent to which they result from specific heuristics that embody much information about structures, patterns, and procedures that are specific to one intellectual domain or subdomain.[45] We also might characterize subjects by the type of general and specific heuristics they use, just as we might, in part, characterize the intellectual *style* of particular thinkers by their favored heuristics.

Here are some examples of heuristic principles and procedures, a grab-bag sample, almost all directed at the very first stage of generating a first tentative solution to an intellectual problem. (I have in mind here *theoretical* problems; other kinds of heuristics would be employed for other kinds of intellectual problems.) These *particular* rules of thumb are of interest in themselves. We also should notice how much broader the domain of rationality is than just principles of evaluating evidence for and against. Remember, these are heuristic rules—there is no guarantee that in any particular application they will succeed.

1. When a conflict between intellectual positions has gone on for a long time without any resolution or large movement, look for an assumption or presupposition that is common to *all* the contending positions.[46] Try denying that assumption and, within the new space this opens up, try constructing a new position.

One possible explanation for the previous lack of intellectual resolution is that all of the contending positions and parties have been locked within an intellectual framework that precludes adequate solution of the problem. (Another is that the current framework is adequate but no one has yet been smart enough to resolve the issue within it.) After the solution *is* formulated, some assumption that everyone was taking for granted will look somewhat arbitrary.

But how is one to identify an assumption that everyone, including oneself, is taking for granted? Consider the problem of connecting the nine dots by four straight lines without taking the pen off the page.* How is one to identify the assumption that is excluding the solution? Perhaps by making everything boringly explicit—"Each line drawn must end at a dot"—and then checking to see whether that explicit statement is indeed in the original conditions of the problem. (Or is it helpful simply to say, for other problems, "Remember, you are allowed to go outside the dots"?)

Here is one example of an assumption that (I think) is currently framing a problem. With regard to the Einstein-Podolsky-Rosen paradox and Bell's inequality, when it is said that the correlation between the separated particles violates locality, it is assumed that the topology and metric of the space have stayed fixed. If the production of the two particles alters the topology and metric of the space, producing a lengthening wormhole between them as they separate, for instance, then the effects from one to the other may be (in that newly metricized space) quite local. By dropping this assumption of fixed topology and metric, one can investigate alternative theories within differential geometry that yield an appropriately changing topological structure, and search for and check its testable consequences.

2. More often than not, I suspect, an underlying assumption is explicitly identified only after a radically new possibility is considered. (So the usual route to this new possibility is not, first, to identify the underlying assumption, second, to deny it or suppose it does not hold, and, third, to see what new possibilities then come to the fore.) Still, we can use such a radically new possibility, once it is thought of, to ask what is the deepest assumption that it violates, what other possibilities also violate it, what new framework is appropriate when this assumption is dropped, and so forth.

3. Pay special attention to explaining unexpected symmetries or unexpected asymmetries, ones that there is no special reason to think should hold or some reason to think should not hold. (Einstein begins his paper on special relativity by speaking of Maxwell's electrodynamics, as usually understood, as leading to "asymmetries that do not appear to be inherent in the phenomena."[47]) If there is an asymmetry in a property, yet all the relevant factors in a context bear symmetrically upon that property, consider a wider context in order to find a relevant factor with asymmetrical import.

4. Apply an operation or process that has been fruitful elsewhere to a new case that is similar in appropriate respects, making appropriate

*

modifications for the differences between the cases. (For example, take the production viewpoint applied by Emil Post to generating the set of theorem strings in logic and apply it to linguistics, so that its goal becomes that of generating the set of grammatical strings of a language— a route by which Noam Chomsky could have arrived at his initial restructuring of linguistics.) This is an instance of a more general maxim:

5. Try models or analogies from other well-developed areas to structure the inchoate material you are dealing with.

But how is one to find a *fruitful* analogy to help solve a problem in the *target* area you are trying to structure? Assuming that you already have a problem stated that has the standard structure already described—goal, initial state and resources, admissible operations, and constraints—here are three suggestions from a work on induction.[48]

a. Start with the initial state of the target and systematically modify it until you arrive at an intellectual structure you already command. Use the admissible operations of *that* structure to formulate corresponding ones for your target system and apply them to the initial state to see if they lead to the goal. (If they bring you close to it, consider how these corresponding operations might be adjusted or modified to lead to the goal exactly.)

b. Start with the goals G of the target. Find structurally similar goals G' in some other realm. Look to operations O' that led to G' in that other realm. Formulate corresponding operations O in the target realm. Check to see if these operations yield the goals G in the target realm.

c. Start with the target goals G and the target initial state. Formulate a hunch about what features $F1, \ldots, Fn$ of the initial state will be relevant to reaching the goals, that is, will eventually feed into operations that will yield the goals. Then formulate a description D of the target system's initial state using *only* those features. Search for another realm with structurally similar features $F1', \ldots, Fn'$. Translate the target goals G into that realm as G'. In that realm, see what operations O' lead from the initial state (with features $F1', \ldots, Fn'$) to G'. Translate that operation O' into the corresponding operation O in the target realm. Check to see if O in that target realm yields the goals G.

These are *specific procedures* for forming a possibly fruitful analogy, ones we might use to reconstruct the thought processes that a thinker went through (or might have gone through). Other procedures are less specific and would present problems for an historian's attempt to reconstruct how the intellectual product actually was made. For example: immerse yourself in a problem and then roam, search, and be alert for clues that suggest fruitful analogs. (Following this advice, a person might browse over the titles of books on her bookshelf, leaf through pages, walk the streets, or whatever.) The assumption here is that, when you have immersed yourself in a problem, external aids can strike sparks about fruitful arenas in which to search for analogies. Notice that just as working on a problem helps prepare the mind for noticing solutions, so too might going through the above three explicit procedures for searching for analogies. Even if they fail, they give one a better idea of what *kind* of analog is needed, and hence help guide the (partly unconscious) search.

One will be better able to find fruitful analogies to a problem the larger one's stock of different intellectual structures and theories that can be drawn upon. (For a difficult problem that has resisted attempts by others, such a kit bag of structures and solved problems should include examples from very different areas and arenas. Other people already will have tried unsuccessfully to use the equipment close by. Thus, formulators of new approaches often possess a history in which they acquired unusually varied resources.[49]) Most thinkers tend to live off the intellectual capital they acquired early; it seems desirable, at some point, to add difficult new structures and tools that, in addition to their direct uses, can serve as sources of analogies and stimulate the structural imagination.

6. Work backward from the goal and forward from the initial state to see if you can get this transcontinental railway to meet.[50]

7. Reduce one hard problem to a set of easier problems, and use other heuristics to solve these.[51]

8. Examine *extreme* cases, consider what will result if some parameters are set at zero or at infinite value, and then reconsider your intermediate case in the light of this extremal behavior.

9. Investigate and list the general features that a correct answer to the problem must have. Look for something that has these features. If you find exactly one and cannot find any others, try to prove that this object uniquely satisfies the conditions and hence is the solution. If you cannot find any, try to prove that nothing can satisfy all those conditions; if successful in this, you will have an impossibility result, such as we sometimes find in social choice theory or in the theory of decision under uncertainty.[52] Simply dropping one condition may restore consistency but leave the remaining conditions too easily satisfied by too many different objects. Relaxing a condition slightly might restore consistency while still leaving a tight set of conditions with a unique solution—a desired result. The task is to consider which of the proposed conditions on a solution should be modified, or which dropped and what then substituted in its place, and then to investigate whether anything satisfies the newly formulated set of conditions.

10. With a new particular idea, formulate a little formal structure or model to embed this idea and then explore its properties and implications.[53]

11. Find a more *abstract* description of a process, notion, or phenomenon and investigate its properties to get a more general and powerful result; increase the abstractness of the description until the results become less powerful.

12. In investigating a relation R (for instance, 'explains' or 'justifies'), consider also the structure of the whole domain that is induced by R. What special problems are raised by this global structure, and what modifications in R would produce a different and better global structure?

13. Transform known phenomenon to discover new ones.[54] When it is known that a stands in the relation R to b: (1) Investigate the *scope* of the phenomenon: what is the list of things that can be substituted for a and yet stand in the relation R to something or other; what is the list of things that can be substituted for b and yet be stood in that relation R? (2) *Characterize* the extent of the phenomenon by describing the properties demarcating each scope. (3) Investigate how things are changed if some other apparently similar relation R' is substituted for R. (4) Investigate what new phenomenon results if one component is substituted for by another in a particular process.

14. If you try to force a decision or description in an unclear case by presenting a parallel case where the decision or description is clear, state the difference between the two cases that makes them differ in clarity and show why this difference does not also make it appropriate to decide the cases differently, even oppositely.[55]

15. There recently has emerged a new procedure for generating questions, sharpening puzzles, and stimulating detailed ideas: build a computer simulation of the phenomenon or process.

16. It also would be useful to formulate some principles about the generation of fruitful *thought experiments* in science and in philosophy. (Recall W. V. Quine on the anthropologist doing radical translation, Hilary Putnam on twin earth, Ludwig Wittgenstein on the builders, and the example of the experience machine.)[56]

These particular heuristic principles are worth trying, I think. By describing them here I also hope to spur others—not only philosophers—to formulate fruitful heuristic principles for the various stages of intellectual inquiry. Not "mechanical" ones—their use may involve considerable knowledge and a "feel" for the material. It is somewhat surprising that in training philosophy students, teachers have made no serious effort to formulate such rules of thumb for intellectual endeavor. Instead, the students are presented with finished products (books and articles) and the example of their teachers examining these, and then left to figure out for themselves how those things are made. Some explicit hints might be helpful.

Rationality's Imagination

The instrumental procedures and patterns of rational theoretical thinking are varied. Aiming at things other than belief—for instance, at novel and fruitful intellectual products—they do not always focus upon the marshaling and assessment of reasons for and against (the heuristic principles are an instance). Rationality of belief, too, is not simply a matter of applying (mechanical) rules to weigh given reasons. Imagination plays an important role. By imagination I mean simply the ability to think up new and fruitful possibilities. The list of heuristic rules, then, might be the beginnings of a theory specifying what such imagination is and how it works.

The credibility of a statement is determined by the reasons for and against it and by other statements that undercut or enhance these reasons. Detecting alternate possibilities that might undercut a statement is not a mechanical matter, however. Evidence is presented for an hypothesis, but were all relevant variables controlled for? Each relevant variable marks an alternative hypothesis that might account for the data. That is why each must be controlled for—otherwise the weight of support the existing data provides for the hypothesis will be less. Yet imagination and ingenuity are needed to detect what unconsidered variables might plausibly play a role in generating the data. In applying Rule 1 for belief, imagination also enters. Does any competing, incompatible statement have higher credibility? It is not a mechanical matter to formulate the alternative statement most worth considering—relativity theory is an alternative to Newtonian mechanics, but only Einstein managed to formulate it—or sometimes even to know that it is an alternative, a conflicting and incompatible statement.

The generation of new alternatives plays an important role in action as well as in belief. A choice of action is made among alternatives. Better choosing among the existing alternatives is one way to improve the results. Another way is to widen the range of alternatives to include promising new ones. An imaginative construction of a new alternative, heretofore not thought of, might be what makes the greatest improvement possible. There might be helpful rules about when to seek such new alternatives, but the results will depend upon actually finding them. There is no mechanical (algorithmic) procedure for generating the most promising alternatives—none that we know of, anyway. Heuristic maxims could help.

Do these considerations make imagination a component part of rationality? Some might insist that rationality consists only in making the best choice among *given* alternatives—actions or beliefs. This seems a needless and arbitrary truncation. But even if imagination were not a component, it still would be a partner in rationality, important as a means in achieving rationality's goals. In some situations, much more might be gained by generating new alternatives and choosing among them roughly than by choosing finely and with perfect discrimination among the existing alternatives only. The second best among the new alternatives might be far superior to the very best among the old ones. It is as important to cultivate the relevant imaginative powers as to sharpen the discriminative ones.

Without the exploration and testing of other imaginative possibilities, the procedures of rationality, by focusing only upon the *given* alternatives, will be myopic. Even when they do well for us, they may restrict us to a local optimum. The well-known analogy used in the literature on maximization concerns getting to the highest point in a geographical terrain. A nearsighted person with a range of vision of ten feet might follow this procedure: look around completely, and then move to the highest point he can see (which will be within ten feet); repeat the procedure again and again until every point he can see is no higher than the point he is standing upon; then stop. If he starts on the side of a hill, this procedure will get him to its top; but it will not get him to the top of the higher next hill, whose side he did not begin upon. This procedure will get him to a local highest point, a local optimum, but not to an overall highest point, not to a global optimum.

Without the imaginative generation and testing of new possibilities, rationality alone will get us only to a local optimum, to the best of the already given alternatives. It is a nice feature of rationality that it *will* get us to that. We have to be careful, though, that rationality does not operate to *restrict* us to that. It is too easy, and tempting, for rationality to become a device that views the imaginative generation and testing of new possibilities as irrational and so excludes it. The process of exploring new possibilities will be imperfect and apparently wasteful; many of the possibilities explored will turn out to be useless. Yet rationality must be tolerant of this and not demand guarantees of success in advance.

The contexts of discovery and of justification—thinking up hypotheses and assessing their credibility—cannot be separated completely. To assess an hypothesis's credibility, we have to think up and consider its best incompatible alternative. (We could make the assessment of an hypothesis explicitly be relative to a given incompatible one, but this would not give us any detachable conclusion about the first hypothesis.)

The question "What alternative novel possibilities are there?" is the first step in human progress, in generating new theories, new inventions, new ways of making, acting, cooperating, thinking, and living. To ask this question requires a willingness to break with tradition, to venture out into unknown territory. To answer requires the ability to think up new and fruitful possibilities; that is, it requires imagination.

Not everyone will want to explore possibilities in all areas, and it would be inefficient for everyone to try. We benefit from the activities of others and from the differences among us that lead others to do, and think of, what we ourselves would not. Philosophers of science have tried to formulate a mechanical procedure that would lead all scientists to make exactly the same decision about whether to accept a particular scientific theory (in a situation where particular evidence is available, particular alternative theories have been formulated, and so on). But differences of opinion have an important function in the ongoing progress of science, Thomas Kuhn has noticed. Things work well when some scientists vigorously explore and champion new theories while others equally vigorously defend and modify the existing theory to handle new phenomena. It is the development along these diverse avenues that eventually produces the detailed knowledge of different theories' abilities and limitations and so brings about whatever general agreement the scientists show.[57]

Frederick Hayek has emphasized how in social life, too, we benefit from the explorations of individuals who try out new methods of production, who develop new products, who experiment with new behavior patterns and different modes of life, and so we gain advantage from the general liberty to explore in this way, even when we ourselves do not take advantage of that liberty. After some results of their explorations are in, other people may choose to emulate them, and eventually we too may do so. Even if we do not, we can benefit from the activities of those others who do, and hence from the activities of the original explorers and innovators. Perhaps most of such exploration and innovation is fruitless, but the costs will be borne mainly by those who have chosen to explore; and when the (relatively) few fruitful innovations spread their effects, we all will benefit.[58] The social nature of our economic, intellectual, and political lives enables us all to benefit from imaginations we do not ourselves possess—and no one can be equally imaginative in all areas, if only because this requires an alert attention we are limited in.[59]

Rationality has two sides. What is exciting about rationality is its sharp cutting edge, its bold venturesomeness. Exacting standards of credibility and full consideration of counter-reasons and of undercutting factors make Rule 1 a potent weapon: don't believe something when some incompatible statement is more credible. Young readers thrill now, as young auditors did then, to Socrates' exactitude and courage in puncturing pompous belief. The boldness of rationality consists in its willingness to formulate what before was not even within the purview of thought and to countenance a belief previously dismissed as outrageous—provided that when all the reasons are considered, it *is* indeed more credible than any competitor. With decisions also, rationality is no respecter of arbitrary constraints: the question is which action *does* maximize all the relevant functions, and if that action is heretofore unheard-of, that is no matter. This glory of rationality is shown most clearly in the amazing, striking, startling, and sometimes disconcerting theories that emerge in scientific investigation, but it is shown in more ordinary contexts too. The first side is rationality's romantic side, depicted in Karl Popper's exciting story of science as the sharp criticism and testing of ever bolder theories, always walking the precarious tightrope over the chasm of refutation. Even when we know its oversimplifications and lacunae, this story can inspire.

But rationality's power does not reside only in its striking individual triumphs. Rationality has a cumulative force. A given rational decision may not be very much better than a less rational one, yet it leads to a new decision situation somewhat different from that the other would have produced; and in this new decision situation a further rational action produces its results and leads to still another decision situation. Over extended time, small differences in rationality compound to produce very different results. A given belief may not be very much more credible than an incompatible one, but these two beliefs support different further statements, and the compounding of differences in credibilities along these routes can lead to vastly different bodies of belief. In chess, some players wear down an opponent through an accumulation of small advantages; other players make daring yet pointed attacks and sacrifices. Like the very greatest chess champions, rationality does both.

Our explorations have led us to new principles of rationality. A principle of rational decision mandates the maximization of decision-value, which takes us beyond the simply instrumental structure of rationality. Two principles govern rational (even apparently purely theoretical) belief, dissolving the dualism between the theoretical and the practical: do not believe any statement less credible than some incompatible alternative—the intellectual component—but then believe a statement only if the expected utility of doing so is greater than that of not believing it—the practical component. And rationality of belief involves two aspects: support by reasons that make the belief credible, and generation by a process that reliably produces true beliefs. Our evolutionary account of reasons explains the puzzling connection between these aspects but reverses the direction of Kant's "Copernican Revolution."

This evolutionary perspective also yields a new picture of the nature and status of rationality, a characteristic traditionally deemed to play a most important role in fixing humanity's specialness. Rationality is an evolutionary adaptation with a delimited purpose and function. It was selected for and designed to work in tandem with enduring facts that held during the period of human evolution, whether or not people could rationally demonstrate these facts. Many of philosophy's traditional intractable problems, resistant to rational resolution, may result from attempts to extend rationality beyond this delimited function. These include the problems of induction, of other minds, of the external world, and of justifying goals—the Kantian attempt to make principled behavior the sole ultimate standard of conduct is another extension of rationality beyond its bounds. It would be an exceedingly lucky accident—though not impossible—if our rationality that was shaped for other delimited purposes itself sufficed to demonstrate the truth of *all* of the very conditions it evolved alongside of in order to work in tandem with.

We have explored the limits of instrumental rationality, but these should not be overemphasized. Instrumental rationality is a powerful disciplined tool, included as a significant part of and infusing every other conception of rationality that purports to be complete. Our conditions on the rationality of goals suggest a broadened notion of instrumental rationality as the effective and efficient pursuit of rational goals. These conditions, however, do not fully specify the substantive rationality of goals or desires, and for that perhaps we should be thankful. A fully specified theory of substantive rationality opens the door to despotic requirements, externally imposed. To be sure, the lack of such a theory allows some objectionable desires, including some unethical ones, but it is a substantive theory of ethics that should deal with these—despite philosophers' persistent attempts to subsume ethics within rationality. Instrumental rationality leaves us the room to pursue our *own* goals autonomously.

Moreover, we have developed a notion of rationality that goes beyond even the widened notion of the instrumental (as the effective pursuit of rational goals) to include the symbolic and the evidential.

To be sure, our taking account of symbolic and evidential factors also may have an evolutionary origin, just as the causally instrumental does. Whatever the evolutionary function of our capacity for symbolization—whether to strengthen other desires, or to maintain them through periods of deprivation in reinforcement by their actual objects, or to enable people to coordinate their actions in prisoner's dilemma situations where cooperation otherwise would not occur—this function need not be our current goal, any more than maximizing inclusive fitness is. Once we possess the capacity, for whatever reason, we can utilize it for our own reasons and purposes. We should no more limit this capacity to serving its original function than we should our mathematical capacities.

The evolutionary basis of rationality does not doom us to continuing on any previously marked evolutionary track. (But neither does knowing the evolutionary function of a trait and realizing that it no longer serves that function guarantee that we will choose to alter the trait, even if we are able. We may retain that trait because it was the impulse to a mode of life that we now value independently, and thus we give it a new function.) We have used our rational capacities to reach knowledge of this evolutionary basis, although those capacities were not selected for that precise effect. Goals instilled because they served inclusive fitness can now be pursued even when they conflict with such fitness—pursued by individuals or (for some time at least) by groups. We can use our imagination to formulate new possibilities, whether goals or theories or adventurous plans, all unrooted in specific previous evolutionary functions. Even if imagination itself, the ability to think up new possibilities, has an evolutionary function, we now can use this capacity for whatever purposes we choose.

The beliefs and actions of a rational person are ones generated (and maintained) by a process that reliably achieves certain goals, where reasons play some appropriate role in guiding this process. What counts as a reason, originally, may have a basis in evolutionary selection, but the guidance reasons provide is not mechanical or blind. We take cognizance of reasons, weigh them, consider objections to them and ways they might be undercut, and we conform our conduct and beliefs accordingly.

Becoming self-conscious about reasons and reasoning adds another dimension of control and development. Philosophy was the first discipline to carry this self-consciousness beyond that usual to reflective people in general by making reasoning itself the subject matter. (Hegel and Fichte later made self-consciousness their subject matter.) Purposes and principles were formulated, criticized, reformulated, developed further, and systematically interconnected. (Others have since joined philosophers in the task, generating a large literature in theoretical statistics, decision theory, and cognitive science.)

This developed body of theoretical principles—arrived at in part by using the principles that evolution has instilled, but going beyond these—can be used to guide our thought and behavior. This process gets self-conscious also. The group of principles of rationality that people explicitly develop can be applied to those principles themselves—some of them to others, perhaps some to themselves—leading to new modifications and developments. That trajectory can take us far from our evolutionary origins.*

Rationality evolved as an adaptation against a background of stable facts that it was selected to work in tandem with. One such fact is the presence of other creatures with a similarly evolving rationality. Descartes depicts an individual alone in his study determining which of his beliefs could not be false or the product of a skilled deception. His meditations present a procedure that each of his readers is to follow also, alone in his or her own study. However, there is no reason to think that evolution would shape our rationality to conform to such Cartesian individualism. If rationality evolved alongside the concurrent rationality of others, then each person's rationality may have a character that fits it to work in tandem with that similar rationality of others.[60] We would not then expect rationality to set out to prove that others are rational or to be able to do so; this is something it assumes and works with in order to get on to other business.

In what ways does our rationality use the rationality of others? We are predisposed to learn language from others and also to learn facts that elders show and tell us. We are predisposed to accept what they say and to accept their corrections of what we say, at least until we have amassed enough language and information to be able to ground doubts and raise questions. "But why is it rational ever to trust anything another person tells you?" Our rationality is not built to answer that question; rather, it builds upon such trust, and gets further built upon it. If trust it is—it may be more like unthinkingly taking for granted that others (of the group we first learn from) will teach us.

Once we have acquired some basis in language and factual beliefs, we can use this to question and modify the beliefs of others. The conjoint evolution of rationality does not condemn anyone to intellectual conformity. If there is a presumption that others are to be believed, this

---

* There is a possibility, though, that an initial defect in rationality can get magnified rather than corrected when rationality is used to modify itself: that defect itself, in application, causes larger ones. Care can be taken to avoid this, including external tests of a sort whose verdict is not automatically guaranteed to be positive, even though it comes from the changed system of (purportedly) rational principles that is being tested.

can be overcome. Were they in a position rationally to believe a particular statement or to have learned it from someone who was in such a position? Is that person a member of a group, an appropriate reference class, such that there are statistics about the group's beliefs on a topic that undercut our presumption of belief? Is there any special reason to think this person is motivated to mislead you or not to take due care in being accurate? Have you thought of possibilities the other person has not that are relevant to assessing the belief? In this interpersonal realm too there is room for the formulation, discussion, and development of further principles of rational belief.[61]

Language is a manifestation and vehicle of rationality, and its social nature has been emphasized by many writers: Wittgenstein speaks of the role of agreement in judgments; Quine writes of language as a social art; and Hilary Putnam depicts the division of linguistic labor whereby the reference of some of our terms is determined by the way we lean upon the knowledge of experts.[62] Because our linguistic abilities evolved in tandem with those of others, all of whom were born in an environment of adult speakers—we can leave aside speculations about the origins of language—it would be surprising if the phenomena of language and meaning were independent of such social surroundings.

Evolution in an environment of other people makes possible specialization in traits designed to work well in the presence of other traits. The native "propensity to truck, barter, and exchange one thing for another" of which Adam Smith spoke[63] would be of little use if it were possessed by only one person. A propensity to exchange needs other partners with similar propensities. And just as there is a division of labor and specialization of skills in society, might there also be a division of biological characteristics within a group, with some people more bellicose and martial, some swifter, some cannier, and some stronger because it is not biologically feasible for humans to have every one of these traits and because many or all benefit by living with others who have complementary traits? (I would prefer to find a basis for such variety in individual selection rather than in group selection.)

That seems plausible, but another thought is more unsettling. Could rationality itself be (underlain by) a set of traits that shows some natural variety among the members of a group? In Pleistocene hunter-gatherer societies was there evolutionary selection for some people being more intensely rational in belief and calculation, just as there was for some being stronger and some swifter? Did almost all benefit from the cooperative activities and exchanges this mixture of traits made possible? Perhaps all such variation in exhibited rationality is due instead solely to nonbiological differences. Whatever the cause, one suspects that the more rational have long laid claim to some enhanced status, if only because they were better at articulating and verbally defending such claims. Others, no doubt, paid little attention to this self-preening of the intensely rational.

What has happened, though, is that rationality has reshaped the world. This is the great theme of Max Weber's writing: economic and monetary calculation, bureaucratic rationalization, general rules and procedures came to replace action based upon personal ties, and market relations were extended to new arenas.[64] Rationality, together with related institutional changes that explicitly utilize and depend upon rationality, has brought many benefits and thus enabled rationality to extend its domain further.

Yet this has made the world, in various ways, inhospitable to lesser degrees of rationality. Those cultures whose traditions are unreceptive to Weberian rationality have fared less well. Within Western societies, the balance has shifted in the division of traits that served in hunter-gatherer societies. Rationality first was able to extend its sway by bringing benefits to other traits too, but the other traits became more dependent upon rationality and rationality became more powerful and subject to fewer constraints. Rationality is proceeding now to remake the world to suit itself, altering not only its own environment but also that in which all other traits find themselves, extending the environment in which only it can fully flourish. In that environment, the marginal product of rationality increases, that of other traits diminishes; traits that once were of coordinate importance are placed in an inferior position. This presents a challenge to rationality's compassion and to its imagination and ingenuity: can it devise a system in which those with other traits can live comfortably and flourish—with the opportunity to develop their rationality if they choose—and will it?

Plato spoke of apprehending eternal forms, Aristotle of the intellectual intuition of first principles and of mind cognizing essences, Descartes of clear and distinct ideas and truths bathed in the natural light of reason, and Spinoza of the intuitive cognition of the essence of things. The reader of our evolutionary account may well wonder what has become of the Dignity of Reason. Deflationary accounts of reason are not new, of course; Hume and Kant too consigned reason to more limited functions. (Kant deprived "speculative reason . . . of its pretensions to transcendent insight," he said, "in order to make room for faith.") Yet a knowledge of reason's origins and original functions need not rob reason of all nobility. (We do well to remember that the nobility too, despite their frequent claims, had no special origins.) Consider curiosity. Even if some degree of curiosity was selected for because of its role in yielding new truths with practical usefulness, once such a capacity exists it can be turned to investigate the origins of the universe, the nature of infinity, the origins and development of life on earth, and the scope and limits of human reason, all for the sake of satisfying intellectual curiosity itself and for the knowledge that brings, with no further motivating purpose. And if reason is not an infallible cognizer of an independent reality, perhaps that makes its triumphs all the more astonishing and impressive. Whatever the practical origins of aesthetic discernment may have been, it has been used to produce great works of art. When the very loftiest human creations are seen to derive from humble origins and functions, what needs revision is not our esteem for these creations but our notion of nobility. And how very humble *was* a starting point that could propel us to the loftiest human accomplishments, how mean was an origin of such potentiality and potency?

Rationality gives us greater knowledge and greater control over our own actions and emotions and over the world. Although our rationality is, initially, an evolved quality—the nature of rationality includes the Nature in it—it enables us to transform ourselves and hence transcend our status as mere animals, actually and also symbolically. Rationality comes to shape and control its own function.

Our principles fix what our life stands for, our aims create the light our life is bathed in, and our rationality, both individual and coordinate, defines and symbolizes the distance we have come from mere animality. It is by these means that our lives can come to mean more than what they instrumentally yield. And by meaning more, our lives yield more.

NOTES

I. HOW TO DO THINGS WITH PRINCIPLES

1. A weaker assumption would maintain, not that *every* correct judgment is yielded by an acceptable principle, but that some or most are. Still, finding an acceptable general principle that yields a particular judgment would (tend to) show that judgment was correct. Failure to find one, however, would not be a conclusive reason for abandoning the judgment, for it might be one of those that stands alone, no consequence of any acceptable principle.

2. Mark Tushnet has argued that in the legal arena the requirement of principled decision constitutes no constraint upon the result a judge can reach; if the previous cases fit a principle (even an established one) whose result the judge wishes to avoid in the present case, this case always can be distinguished from the others by some feature or other. See Tushnet, "Following the Rules Laid Down: A Critique of Interpretavism and Neutral Principles," *Harvard Law Review* 96 (1983): 781–827. However, merely to distinguish the case (at best) allows the new judgment; it does not *support* it. To support it, the judge would have to formulate a new principle, plausible on its face, that fits (most of) the old cases, this new one, and some obvious hypothetical ones as well; that is, she would need a principled rationale for the distinction she wishes to make and for why that distinction should make a difference. It is no easy matter to formulate acceptable principles, much less to do this as frequently as one's desires about new cases would mandate.

3. See C. G. Hempel, *Aspects of Scientific Explanation* (New York: Free Press, 1965), pp. 264–272, and Ernest Nagel, *The Structure of Science* (New York: Harcourt, Brace and World, 1961), pp. 47–78.

4. Abstract principled reasoning lends support to a particular position by recruiting other accepted judgments as support. Some writers have suggested that this abstract and impersonal mode is only one particular mode of justification.

5. I have not checked to see what empirical studies of people's decisions exist to support this *empirical* claim by the legal theorists, what alternative legal structure functioned as the control, and so on.

6. All of the small number of data points we possess seem to fall on a straight line, but for all related phenomena we have found that a linear relationship does not hold. Perhaps here it is an accident of the particular data we happen to have.

7. See the list of factors in Thomas Kuhn, "Objectivity, Value Judgment and Theory Choice," in his *The Essential Tension* (Chicago: Univ. of Chicago Press, 1977), pp. 320–339, and W. V. Quine and Joseph Ullian, *The Web of Belief*, 2d ed. (New York: Random House, 1978), pp. 64–82. The need for such additional criteria may result not just from the finiteness of our data. Quine has claimed that the totality of all possible observations does not uniquely select an explanatory theory. (See his "On the Reasons for Indeterminacy of Translation," *Jour-*

nal of Philosophy 67 [1970]: 178–183, and "On Empirically Equivalent Systems of the World," *Erkenntnis* 9 [1975]: 313–328.) It is difficult to determine the truth of this strong claim without an adequate theory of explanation and of what detailed structure the explanatory relation might involve.

8. See P. Atiyah and R. Summers, *Form and Substance in Anglo-American Law: A Comparative Study in Legal Reasoning, Legal Theory, and Legal Institutions* (Oxford: Oxford Univ. Press, 1987).

9. It would be interesting to investigate how far the parallel between the structural features of reasons and of causes extends, and to explain why this parallelism holds. Do reasons show parallels to phenomena of probabilistic causality?

10. See Herbert L.A. Hart, *The Concept of Law* (Oxford: Clarendon Press, 1961), pp. 155–159, and Chaim Perlman, *The Idea of Justice and the Problem of Argument* (London: Routledge and Kegan Paul, 1963).

11. That others can count upon our following certain principles also might deter them from some actions rather than induce them to cooperate. A nation or person with a principle to retaliate against particular offenses, notwithstanding immediate interests, might deter others from such offenses. Announcing such a principle increases the cost of making exceptions in order to ensure that none will be made.

12. The U.S. government wishes to issue debt and promises not to inflate its currency, but after the debt is taken up by others it will be to the advantage of the government to inflate—and the others realize this beforehand. Hence the government attempts to commit to rules for managing the currency, to be followed by an agency independent of Congress, rather than leaving itself absolute discretion. See Finn Kydland and Edward Prescott, "Rules Rather than Discretion," *Journal of Political Economy* 85 (1977): 473–491.

13. It would be useful to list and compare what bases, other than his accepting principles as objectively valid, there might be for reliance upon a person's actions. These might include the other (listed) functions of principles whose successful performance does not depend upon a belief in their objective validity.

14. See Carol Gilligan, *In a Different Voice* (Cambridge, Mass.: Harvard Univ. Press, 1982); see also Bill Puka, "The Liberation of Caring: A Different Voice for Gilligan's 'Different Voice,'" *Hypatia* 5 (1990): 58–82.

15. Following the philosophical tradition, I use the term *determine* to mean fix, cause, make happen—as in "determinism"—but notice too the term's estimate/evidential/epistemological side, as in "I haven't yet determined what he's trying to do."

16. George Ainslie, "Specious Reward: A Behavioral Theory of Impulsiveness and Impulse Control," *Psychological Bulletin* 82 (1975): 463–496; Ainslie, "Beyond Microeconomics," in *The Multiple Self*, ed. Jon Elster (Cambridge: Cambridge Univ. Press, 1986), pp. 133–175.

17. Can we use information about people's current degree of time preference to make a rough estimate about the harshness and riskiness of the environment and the life history of the organisms in whom this degree of

time preference first evolved? Might we use information about the general shape of the time preference curve to check theories about the domain within which selection operated (for example, how extensive a class of kin within kin selection)?

There might be features in addition to probabilistic discounting that time preference was selected, in part, to approximate. Susan Hurley (in conversation) mentions possible change of utility due to future changes of preference.

18. I first discussed the perils of double-discounting in "On Austrian Methodology," *Synthese* 36 (1977): 353–392.

19. This last shape is a consequence of the "matching law" equations. See Richard Herrnstein, "Relative and Absolute Strengths of Response as a Function of Frequency of Reinforcement," *Journal of the Experimental Analysis of Behavior* 4 (1961): 267–272.

20. I thank Amartya Sen for raising this question.

21. There also is the phenomenon of *regret*, a lowering of current utility due to looking back upon currently undesired past action. Having a tendency toward regret might help you somewhat to get over the temptation during B, since during B you can anticipate the lowered utility level during C and also afterward if you take the smaller, closer reward now. But will this anticipation feed back sufficiently into the overall utilities during B to affect the choice made then?

22. For a critical discussion of the single goal of maximizing the total utility over a lifetime, see my *The Examined Life* (New York: Simon and Schuster, 1989), pp. 100–102.

23. See also Jon Elster, *Ulysses and the Sirens* (Cambridge: Cambridge Univ. Press, 1979).

24. This focus upon a whole group of actions of a certain kind in the personal realm may remind some readers of rule utilitarianism in the public realm. But rather, our question is how the acceptance of a general principle affects the choice of a particular action that, in the absence of the principle, would not have maximal utility. The comparable question would be how someone with act utilitarian desires who (somehow) decides upon a rule utilitarian principle can manage to put it into effect in particular choice situations.

25. The promulgation of a principle also affects how third parties will carry it out; a designer of principles will take account of how others might distort or abuse them. For a related point about how social theorists such as Marx and Freud should have taken precautions against vulgarization, see my *The Examined Life*, p. 284.

26. An alternative explanation of principles incorporating "all" might propose that principles codify reasons and that reasons are universal (though defeasible); hence principles are too. But why is it that reasons are not "for the most part" but instead are "universal but defeasible," even though the percentages may be the same?

27. People frequently do not adhere to the doctrine of ignoring sunk costs, as indicated by their decisions when presented with hypothetical choices. On this, see H. R. Arkes and C. Blumer, "The Psychology of Sunk Cost," *Organiza-*

tional Behavior and Human Decision Processes 35 (1985): 124–140. Arkes and Blumer regard the people who deviate from the doctrine in the ticket example as being irrational.

Scott Brewer has wondered whether frequently the person anticipates that if he does not use this evening's particular ticket, he will worry that he will purchase another one, or make some additional other recreational purchase, in the future, and that (within his accounting scheme) he does not wish to spend that greater amount upon recreation; hence the costs may not all be past. Notice that the economist will condemn such partitioned accounting schemes as irrational.

28. See Bernard Williams's essay in J.J.C. Smart and Bernard Williams, *Utilitarianism: For and Against* (Cambridge: Cambridge Univ. Press, 1973); Williams, "Persons, Character and Morality," in *The Identities of Persons*, ed. Amelie Rorty (Berkeley: Univ. of California Press, 1976).

29. I owe this suggestion to Susan Hurley, who also asks, in reference to and in parallel to our earlier question about whether we can rely upon someone adhering to a principle when his only reasons for holding it are the benefits to him of our so relying, whether someone can expect to honor costs he has sunk if he will not think he earlier had some independent reason to sink them, a reason other than to get himself to honor them later.

30. See Thomas Schelling, "The Art of Commitment," in his *Arms and Influence* (New Haven: Yale Univ. Press, 1966), pp. 35–91. See also Schelling's discussion of "the rationality of irrationality."

31. It also might be a useful trait, especially for the young, to be optimistic about the chances of success of possible projects—otherwise no new and daring things would be tried—yet also to tend to stick to ongoing projects in which significant investment has been made—otherwise, at the first serious difficulty, one might turn to another untried project that one is still (overly) optimistic about.

32. Once an action or outcome comes to symbolize others, its presence may get taken as evidence for the others or as a cause of them, but this is a result of the symbolizing and not part of its original fabric (although this evidential or causal role may then reinforce the strength of the symbolic connection).

33. So a maximizing decision theory would assume. There are other forms of normative decision theory, such as Herbert Simon's "satisficing" theory, but this too would require the action that is done to have, or have imputed to it, a utility above the (shifting) level of aspiration.

34. Not that it need always be expressiveness that flows back along the symbolic connection. Other things may do so, and these will give rise to new characteristics of the action that themselves have high utility for the agent. The point is that utility is not what flows back.

35. So should we distinguish cases where the goal is x and someone acts symbolically to achieve x from cases where the goal is a symbolic connection to x and someone acts instrumentally to achieve that?

36. For a discussion of acts in equilibrium, see my *Philosophical Explanations* (Cambridge, Mass.: Harvard Univ. Press, 1981), pp. 348–352.

37. I thank Bernard Williams for mentioning this example. The parenthetical last clause, of course, precludes disconfirmation in the absence of an independent criterion of something's being sufficiently worked through. Williams also points out that some symbolic meanings involve a fantasy that is strictly impossible to realize; and it is unclear how utilities are to be assigned to impossible situations. I would not want to preclude, however, that even incoherent situations might have high utility for us.

38. See Charles Fried, *An Anatomy of Values* (Cambridge, Mass.: Harvard Univ. Press, 1970), pp. 207–218.

39. See Ronald Carson, "The Symbolic Significance of Giving to Eat and Drink," in *By No Extraordinary Means: The Choice to Forgo Life-Sustaining Food and Water*, ed. Joanne Lynn (Bloomington: Indiana Univ. Press, 1986), pp. 84–88.

40. See my *The Examined Life*, pp. 286–292.

41. For a discussion of how some product advertising employs this phenomenon, see my *The Examined Life*, pp.121–122.

42. See Raymond Firth, *Symbols: Public and Private* (Ithaca: Cornell Univ. Press, 1973); Clifford Geertz, "Deep Play: Notes on the Balinese Cock-fight," in his *The Interpretation of Cultures* (New York: Basic Books, 1973).

43. Indeed, given the extent to which symbolic meaning is socially created, maintained, and coordinated, as well as limited by social factors, we might find here a limit to methodological individualist explanations—an important one, given the effects and consequences of such meanings. For a symbolic utility might be social not only in being socially shaped and in being shared—that is, the same for many people in the society—but also in being viewed *as* shared—that trait being intrinsic to its having that symbolic utility. It is not clear how methodologically individualist explanations might cope with the intricacies involved. In any case, leaving aside symbolic meaning, it is not clear what a methodologically individualist account of language would look like.

44. Nelson Goodman, *Languages of Art* (Indianapolis: Bobbs-Merrill, 1968), pp. 45–95. On Goodman's theory of aesthetic merit, see my "Goodman, Nelson on Merit, Aesthetic," *Journal of Philosophy* 69 (1972): 783–785.

45. Catherine Elgin, *With Reference to Reference* (Indianapolis: Hackett, 1983), p. 143, discusses a particular chain with five links.

46. Can the symbolic utility of an action be viewed as an *interpretation* of that action, a way of seeing oneself or it a certain way, so that the various modes of interpretive linkage, and full theories of interpretation itself, might enter into the specification of symbolic utility?

47. In my *The Examined Life*, see the section on "The Ideal and the Actual." This also opens the possibility that people who do not want P to be followed to a certain result could arrange to have P followed to yet another monstrous result, thereby discrediting it.

48. For some critical reflections on the view that we are free when our actions are determined self-consciously by a law of reason, which is a principle constitutive of our essential nature, see my *Philosophical Explanations*, pp. 353–355.

II. DECISION-VALUE

1. For a selection of articles until 1985, and a bibliographical listing of others, see *Paradoxes of Rationality and Cooperation: Prisoner's Dilemma and Newcomb's Problem*, ed. Richmond Campbell and Lanning Sowden (Vancouver: University of British Columbia Press, 1985).

2. On causal decision theory, see Allan Gibbard and William Harper, "Counterfactuals and Two Kinds of Expected Utility," in *Foundations and Applications of Decision Theory*, ed. C. A. Hooker et al. (Dordrecht: Reidel, 1978), reprinted in *Paradoxes of Rationality and Cooperation*, ed. Campbell and Sowden; David Lewis, "Causal Decision Theory," *Australasian Journal of Philosophy* 59 (1981): 5–30; J. H. Sobel, "Circumstances and Dominance in a Causal Decision Theory," *Synthese* 63 (1985).

Nor did I notice the possibility of specific situations where the states were probabilistically independent of the actions yet causally influenced by them—Gibbard and Harper's Reoboam example—which should have marked a fourth row in the three-row chart on p. 132 of my original article.

3. On the maximization of conditionally expected utility, though not the term *evidential utility*, see my 1963 Princeton University doctoral dissertation, *The Normative Theory of Individual Choice* (rpt. New York: Garland Press 1990). See p. 232: "The probabilities that are to be used in determining the expected utility of an action must now be the conditional probabilities of the states given that the action is done. (This is true generally. However when the states are probability-independent of the actions, the conditional probability of each state given that one of the actions is done will be equal to the probability of the state, so the latter may be used." There also the formula for conditional expected utility was stated for the cases of the two particular actions being discussed then, though not the general formula for variable action. The general formula is presented in Richard Jeffrey, *The Logic of Decision* (New York: McGraw-Hill, 1965).

The issues that concern us in this book all arise when the probabilities, conditional or otherwise, subjective or objective, are sharply defined. Other issues have led some writers to formulate theories using probability intervals; see for example, Isaac Levi, *Hard Choices* (Cambridge: Cambridge Univ. Press, 1986). How exactly the views stated here might be restated within such frameworks is a question for investigation.

4. Attempts to reject the problem as ill formed, ill defined, or impossible in principle include Isaac Levi, "Newcomb's Many Problems," *Theory and Decision* 6 (1975): 161–175; J. L. Mackie, "Newcomb's Paradox and the Direction of Causation," *Canadian Journal of Philosophy* 7 (1977): 213–225; and William Talbott, "Standard and Non-standard Newcomb Problems," *Synthese* 70 (1987): 415–458. For a defense of the problem against many such criticisms, see Jordan Howard Sobel, "Newcomblike Problems," *Midwest Studies in Philosophy* 15 (1990): 224–255.

5. An exception is J. H. Sobel, who in "Infallible Predictors," *Philosophical Review* 97 (1988): 3–24, closes the paper by considering "a limit Newcomb Problem" in which the amount in the first box is increased from $1,000 to (al-

most) $1 million. Sobel does not, however, go on to consider the situation of reducing the $1,000 in the first box to almost nothing. In Kenneth MacCrimmon and Stig Larsson, "Utility Theory: Axioms versus 'Paradoxes,'" in *Expected Utility Hypothesis and the Allais Paradox*, ed. Maurice Allais and Ole Hagen (Dordrecht: Reidel, 1979), p. 393, the consequences of varying the amount in the second box, though not in the first, are considered.

6. If less than complete confidence in one principle leads a person to follow a combination of principles, what happens if he or she does not have complete confidence in this combination? If there is a determinate other principle that one has *some* confidence in, then, insofar as the argument depends only upon actual degrees of confidence, it seems that other principle should also be included in the weighting.

7. For a divergent view of evidentialist considerations, holding that these are appealing only when they match cooperative reasoning in interpersonal situations, see Susan Hurley, "Newcomb's Problem, Prisoners' Dilemma, and Collective Action," *Synthese* 86 (1991): 173–196.

8. "But what explains the disagreement between proponents of *CEU* and *EEU*? Is it a factual or a value disagreement?" This question assumes that both proponents share an *EU* formula and asks whether their disagreement resides within the probability or the utility component. Yet, if the *DV* formula is correct, then there are *other* things to disagree about, including the weights *Wc* and *We*, the nature of the formula, and also—to anticipate the next paragraphs—the inclusion of other factors. To ask "fact or value?"—allowing no other alternative—is to assume that what *must* be in common is the simple *EU* framework and that only *within* it can disagreement arise.

9. David Gauthier considers the question of what disposition of choice a person should choose to have in *Morals by Agreement* (Oxford: Oxford Univ. Press, 1985), ch. 6, secs. 2–3.

10. Nozick, "Newcomb's Problem," p. 125; Gibbard and Harper, "Counterfactuals." See also p. 000n2.

11. Rudolf Carnap maintained (*The Logical Foundations of Probability* [Chicago: Univ. of Chicago Press, 1950]) that sentences asserting that "the degree of confirmation of h on e is n" are, when true, analytic. Yet even he also held that *which* particular confirmation function is to be chosen (c^*, $c^\dagger$, or whatever from among the continuum of inductive methods), and therefore which one will specify this analytic relation, is a matter of pragmatic choice and will depend upon general facts about the universe.

12. See John Milnor, "Games against Nature," in *Decision Processes*, ed. R. M. Thrall, C. H. Coombs, and R. L. Davis (New York: John Wiley, 1954), pp. 49–59, and R. D. Luce and Howard Raiffa, *Games and Decisions* (New York: John Wiley, 1957), pp. 275–298. Earlier I said that symbolic meaning need not carry over proportionally into probabilistic contexts. Yet the *DV* formula includes symbolic utility as one of the weighted components. We might wonder whether symbolic utility will carry over into the weighted *DV* context. A shift to a probabilistic situation, however, is a shift to a *different* situation, while shifting to the *DV* formula does not shift the choice situation.

13. The one psychological study I know of that treats both causal and evi-

dential connections, and seeks to disentangle them, is G. A. Quattrone and Amos Tversky, "Causal versus Diagnostic Contingencies: On Self-Deception and the Voter's Illusion," *Journal of Personality and Social Psychology* 46 (1984): 237–248.

14. Not every mode of action involves a connection to a consequence to be placed within a formula alongside the causal, evidential, and symbolic connections. Consider acting without motive, a mode whose variants are spoken of in the literature of Buddhism, Taoism, and Hinduism. Here, the person does not act so as to become a certain way, or to be a certain way, or to produce results, or to have evidence, or to symbolize anything. Perhaps he acts so as to *align* himself (rightly) with the deepest reality, to be aligned with this deepest reality by letting it act through him. This mode of action needs to be analyzed further, but it does not seem to involve a mode of connection to a consequence.

15. H. P. Grice, "Meaning," *Philosophical Review* 67 (1957): 377–388.

16. See John Von Neumann and Oscar Morgenstern, *The Theory of Games and Economic Behavior*, 2d ed. (Princeton: Princeton Univ. Press, 1947), appendix. An examination of philosophical issues about the Von Neumann–Morgenstern and similar sets of conditions is contained in Robert Nozick, *The Normative Theory of Individual Choice* (Ph.D. diss., Princeton University, 1963; rpt. New York: Garland Press, 1990).

17. This is how L. J. Savage treats acts within the formalism of his decision theory; cf. his *The Foundations of Statistics* (New York: John Wiley, 1954). However, an act cannot be reduced in this way, even apart from issues about its possible symbolic value. See my *The Normative Theory of Individual Choice*, pp. 184–193.

18. See, for example, Peter Hammond, "Consequentialist Foundations for Expected Utility," *Theory and Decision* 25 (1988): 25–78.

19. As a result of Newcomb's Problem, cases have been investigated where the *probability* of an outcome alters with the reasons for doing the action, thus giving rise to the literature on "ratifiability."

20. It also is worth mentioning that when the sequencing of the actions is strategically relevant, game theorists do not simply concentrate upon the matrix-representation of a game and its payoffs but need to consider the game-tree.

21. Gibbard and Harper, "Counterfactuals and Two Kinds of Expected Utility," p. 151.

22. David P. Kreps, P. Milgrom, J. Roberts, and R. Wilson, "Rational Cooperation in the Finitely Repeated Prisoner's Dilemma," *Journal of Economic Theory* 27 (1982): 245–252.

23. As one writer puts it in summary, a player might "take an out of equilibrium action to set in motion the other player's out of equilibrium beliefs and strategies." Eric Rasmussen, *Games and Information* (Oxford: Basil Blackwell, 1989), p. 111.

24. A side note in passing. In my 1963 doctoral dissertation, I saw the necessity in game-theoretic situations of levels of knowledge infinitely extended, each player knowing the structure of the game-theoretic situation, each knowing the other knows, each knowing the other knows that he knows, and so on (*The Normative Theory of Individual Choice*, p. 274). But I thought this just was a

nit-picking point. Little did I see the far-reaching interest and implications of the condition of common knowledge of rationality. See Robert Aumann, "Correlated Equilibrium as an Expression of Bayesian Rationality," *Econometrica* 55 (1987): 1–18, and Drew Fudenberg and Jean Tirole, *Game Theory* (Cambridge, Mass.: M.I.T. Press, 1991), pp. 541–572.

25. On the tit-for-tat strategy, see Robert Axelrod, "The Emergence of Cooperation among Egoists," reprinted in *Paradoxes of Rationality and Cooperation*, ed. Campbell and Sowden, and his *The Evolution of Cooperation* (New York: Basic Books, 1984).

26. I speak intuitively here, since on an interval scale of measurement, with an arbitrary zero point, there is no special significance to a measured quantity's being negative. An arbitrary unit and arbitrary zero point create problems for interpersonal comparisons of utility. For some proposals, see my "Interpersonal Utility Theory," *Social Choice and Welfare* 2 (1985): 161–179.

27. See Philippa Foot, "The Problem of Abortion and the Doctrine of the Double Effect," in her *Virtues and Vices* (Berkeley: Univ. of California Press, 1978), pp. 19–32; Judith Thompson, "Killing, Letting Die, and the Trolley Problem" and "The Trolley Problem," in her *Rights, Restitution and Risk* (Cambridge, Mass.: Harvard Univ. Press, 1986), pp. 78–116; Warren Quinn, "Actions, Intentions, and Consequences: The Doctrine of Double-Effect," *Philosophy and Public Affairs* 18 (1989): 334–351; Warren Quinn, "Actions, Intentions, and Consequences: The Doctrine of Doing and Allowing," *Philosophical Review* 98 (1989): 287–312; Frances Kamm, "Harming Some to Save Others," *Philosophical Studies* 57 (1989): 227–260.

28. For other purposes, we might want to extend such a matrix, adding a third dimension to represent the magnitude of the consequence or effect. (Extending the matrix in this way for legal contexts was suggested to me by Justin Hughes. In such contexts we might want to know how bad the effect was: how bad was the one aimed at, and how bad was the one that occurred.) But within decision theory, of course, this magnitude is already represented by the utility of the outcome.

29. Recall also the discussion above of how a meta-principle not to violate any principles might make any violation stand for all, thereby giving every principle heavy deontological weight.

30. See Amartya Sen, *Ethics and Economics* (Oxford: Basil Blackwell, 1987), pp. 80–88.

III. RATIONAL BELIEF

1. And what if the most effective *process* in reaching the goal of performing the best action does not involve anything we can call a "procedure," anything involving the conscious monitoring of steps or the application of any rules or principles or reasons?

2. For different approaches to this matter, see Isaac Levi, *The Enterprise of Knowledge* (Cambridge, Mass.: M.I.T. Press, 1980); Gilbert Harman, *Change in View* (Cambridge, Mass.: M.I.T. Press, 1986); and Peter Gardenfors, *Knowledge in Flux* (Cambridge, Mass.: M.I.T. Press, 1988).

3. See Alvin Goldman, *Epistemology and Cognition* (Cambridge, Mass.: Har-

vard Univ. Press, 1986), pp. 58–121, who offers a reliability analysis of justification rather than of rationality; Frank Ramsey, "Reasonable Degrees of Belief," in his *The Foundations of Mathematics and Other Logical Essays* (London: Routledge and Kegan Paul, 1931), pp. 199–203; William Talbott, *The Reliability of the Cognitive Mechanism* (Ph.D. diss., Harvard Univ., 1976; rpt. with a new preface New York: Garland Press, 1990); Stephen Stich, *The Fragmentation of Reason* (Cambridge, Mass.: M.I.T. Press, 1990), pp. 89–100.

4. See Thomas Kuhn, *The Essential Tension* (Chicago: Univ. of Chicago Press, 1977), pp. 320–339; W. V. Quine and Joseph Ullian, *The Web of Belief*, 2d ed. (New York: Random House, 1978), pp. 64–82.

5. John Rawls, *A Theory of Justice* (Cambridge, Mass.: Harvard Univ. Press, 1971), pp. 62, 90–95.

6. There are game-theoretic situations in which ignorance of a correct probability can be beneficial. See Eric Rasmussen, *Games and Information* (Oxford: Basil Blackwell, 1989), p. 116, "Entry Deterrence IV."

7. Compare the distinction between goals and side constraints, and the discussion of a "utilitarianism of rights" in my *Anarchy, State, and Utopia* (New York: Basic Books, 1974), pp. 28–33.

8. Amartya Sen, "Rights and Agency," *Philosophy and Public Affairs* 11 (1982).

9. It is the literature that makes the parent female and the child male. Are mothers more loving? (Sons *are* more crime-prone.) Or does the literature assume that women are more susceptible to conflicts between emotion and evidence?

10. That is the criterion, we have seen, of the best action. So suppose that she arrives at this belief through a process that reliably produces best actions.

11. On the "ethics of belief," see William James, "The Will to Believe," in his *The Will to Believe and Other Essays* (Cambridge, Mass.: Harvard Univ. Press, 1979), pp. 13–33; Jack Meiland, "What Ought We to Believe," *American Philosophical Quarterly* 17 (1980): 15–24; John Heil, "Believing What One Ought," *Journal of Philosophy* 80 (1983): 752–765. Heil makes a distinction similar to mine between the proposition that *p* being the rational thing to believe and the believing *p* being the rational thing to do.

12. See Frederick Schauer, *Playing by the Rules* (Oxford: Clarendon Press, 1991), which contains an extensive discussion of this question with regard to rules. Do they have an authority that carries weight, even in particular cases where the ultimate purposes they were designed to further clearly will not be furthered or will be retarded?

13. The traditional theorists of rationality concentrated upon reasons and reasoning, without mentioning reliable processes; some more recent theorists have focused upon the reliability aspect without emphasizing reasoning. These exclusions are understandable if certain kinds of reasoning and reliability always go together, if the only reliable processes involve those kinds of reasoning—knocks on the head do not work—and those kinds of reasoning always are reliable.

14. See Karl Popper, *The Logic of Scientific Discovery* (New York: Basic Books, 1959), and *Conjectures and Refutations* (New York: Basic Books, 1962), p. 240.

15. We might suggest here a requirement comparable to the notion of tracking in the theory of knowledge. See my *Philosophical Explanations* (Cambridge, Mass.: Harvard Univ. Press, 1981), ch. 3.

16. See Robert Nozick, "Moral Complications and Moral Structures," *Natural Law Forum* 13 (1968): 1–50; *Readings in Nonmonotonic Reasoning*, ed. Matthew Ginsberg (Los Altos, Calif.: Morgan Kaufmann, 1987); John Pollock, *How to Build a Person* (Cambridge, Mass.: M.I.T. Press, 1989), pp. 124–155.

17. Three people have been tried for a capital crime and found guilty, but only one has been sentenced to death. None of them knows which one this is, and we may assume, as each of them does, that each has a 1/3 chance of being executed. The evening before the scheduled execution, prisoner A asks the guard, who does know which prisoner will be executed, to give a note he has written to be delivered to his wife to one of the two others, one who will not be executed. As the guard leaves to deliver the note, prisoner A believes that he has a 1/3 chance of being executed the next morning. When the guard returns and truthfully says he has delivered the note, prisoner A still believes he has a 1/3 chance. He has received no relevant new information, for he knew beforehand that (at least) one of the other prisoners would not be executed and so was available to deliver the note. He now asks the guard which prisoner the note was given to, and the guard tells him it was prisoner B. It would be a mistake for prisoner A to reason that he now has a 1/2 chance of being executed on the grounds that he and prisoner C started with an equal chance of 1/3 each, the situation stays symmetrical, and so they continue to have an equal chance that now has risen to 1/2. This particular situation is not symmetrical. Either B or C could have been the recipient of the note—so the fact that C did not receive it *is* relevant to assessing his probability of execution (which now rises to 2/3)—whereas A could not have been the recipient of the note. The information could have come that C was not to be executed, but the information could not have come that A was not to be. Hence, when the actual information does arrive, it is C's probability that is increased. In contrast, prisoner A's probability of execution *would* rise to 1/2 in the following situations: prisoner A asks the returning guard, "Did prisoner B receive the note, yes or no?" and the guard answers, "Yes"; or prisoner A first asks the guard to give the note to a prisoner who will not be executed the next day, any one of the *three*, and (assuming the guard is equally likely to give it to anyone who will not be executed, including prisoner A himself) the guard returns saying he gave it to prisoner B. The crucial factor is the way in which the probability of B's receiving the note differs, depending upon whether prisoner A or prisoner C is to be executed. If A is to be executed, the probability that B receives the note is 1/2 (and the probability that C receives the note is the same). If C is to be executed, the probability that B receives the note is 1. These probability values sum to 1 and 1/2, of which the probability coming from A's being executed (that is, 1/2) is one-third of the total, while the probability coming from C's being executed (that is, 1) is two-thirds of this total. Hence the information that B receives the note leaves A with a 1/3 chance of being executed and gives C a 2/3 chance. All this is made pellucid in a Bayesian network diagram; see Judea Pearl, *Probabilistic Reasoning in Intelligent Systems:*

Networks of Plausible Inference (San Mateo, Calif.: Morgan Kaufmann, 1989), fig. 9.1, p. 417.

18. What matters is not only the particular content of *e* but also what other information could have arrived (and with what probabilities). To have tried to build this latter information into the evidence itself would have radically altered the structure of a Carnapian inductive logic. See Rudolf Carnap, *The Logical Foundations of Probability* (Chicago: Univ. of Chicago Press, 1950), and *The Continuum of Inductive Methods* (Chicago: Univ. of Chicago Press, 1952). Carnap's preferred system in the first of these books included a carefully stated version of the principle of indifference: all structure descriptions receive the same a priori probability. Perhaps at the most basic level there must be a structural reason for any difference in a priori probability. (Even here one might think this a matter for empirical support.) But there is no reason to think we have reached that level, even in our current fundamental physics, and certainly not with the properties we ordinarily consider.

19. Consider an item *I* of information from your sources of information that says "*p* is true." What does receiving *I* show? As an application of Bayes' Theorem, prob (*p*/*I* is received) = [prob(*I* is received/*p*) × initial prob(*p*)]/[prob(*I* is received/*p*) × initial prob(*p*)] + [prob(*I* is received/not-*p*) × initial prob(not-*p*)]. Let us further suppose that the sources of information will report either that *p* is true or that it is not. (To consider the possibility that they may issue no report at all will unnecessarily complicate the statement to follow.) Then prob(*I* is received/not-*p*) = 1 − prob(sources say "*p* is false"/not-*p*). Thus, the denominator in the above specification of Bayes' Theorem is equivalent to [prob(*I* is received/*p*) × initial prob(*p*)] + [(1 − prob(sources say "*p* is false"/not-*p*)) × initial prob(not-*p*)]. The latter part of this denominator, after the plus sign, is equal to initial prob(not-*p*) − prob(sources say "*p* is false"/not-*p*) × initial prob(not-*p*). Thus, the less the probability that these sources say "*p* is false," given not-*p*, the less does receiving the information *I* saying that *p* is true support the hypothesis that it is true. Bayes' Theorem tells us we also must consider what other information could have arrived and with what (conditional) probabilities.

Consider now a Bayesian analysis of how the epistemological skeptic's hypothesis *SK* fares in the face of our observation and experience *E*. Since the skeptic's hypothesis *SK* has been crafted so that prob(*E*/*SK*) = 1, it follows that, even if prob(*E*/not-*SK*) also is 1, still prob(not-*SK*/*E*) will not rise above the prior probability of not-*SK*. On a Bayesian account of posterior probability, the posterior probability of skepticism is no less than its prior probability, the posterior probability of nonskepticism is no greater than *its* prior probability. Evidence doesn't help.

20. The literature on "reflective equilibrium" between principles and cases presumes that the principles themselves have an independent and current authority on their face. See Nelson Goodman, *Fact, Fiction, and Forecast* (Cambridge, Mass.: Harvard Univ. Press, 1955), ch. 4, sec. 2, pp. 62–66, and Rawls, *A Theory of Justice*, pp. 19–21, 48–51. For a critical discussion of reflective equilibrium, see Stich, *The Fragmentation of Reason*, pp. 83–89.

21. For the framework of a theory of this sort, see John Holland, Keith

Holyoak, Richard Nisbett, and Paul Thagard's fascinating book, *Induction: Processes of Inference, Learning, and Discovery* (Cambridge, Mass.: M.I.T. Press, 1986).

22. See *Parallel Distributed Processing: Explorations in the Microstructure of Cognition*, ed. James McClelland and David Rumelhart, 2 vols. (Cambridge, Mass.: M.I.T. Press, 1986), esp. chs. 1–8, 11, 14, 26.

23. Simulations are now much more common in the physical and social sciences, but philosophers of science have not yet, to my knowledge, considered the special issues raised for the theory of explanation when a science produces not a body of theoretical statements and general laws but a program and a simulation.

24. See John Holland, *Adaptation in Natural and Artificial Systems* (1975; rpt. Cambridge, Mass.: M.I.T. Press, 1992), pp. 176–179; Holland, Holyoak, Nisbett, and Thagard, *Induction*, pp. 70–75, 116–117.

25. On isolating the contradictions of the set theoretical and semantical paradoxes and limiting their damage, see Ludwig Wittgenstein, *Remarks on the Foundations of Mathematics* (Oxford: Basil Blackwell, 1956), II 80–82, III 60, V 8–12.

26. See Paul Churchland, *A Neurocomputational Perspective* (Cambridge, Mass.: M.I.T. Press, 1989); Andy Clark, *Microcognition: Philosophy, Cognitive Science, and Parallel Distributed Processing* (Cambridge, Mass.: M.I.T. Press, 1989); Patricia Churchland and Terrence Sejnowski, *The Computational Brain* (Cambridge, Mass.: M.I.T. Press, 1992).

27. In "Simplicity as Fallout" (in *How Many Questions: Essays in Honor of Sidney Morgenbesser*, ed. Leigh Cauman [Indianapolis: Hackett, 1983]), I presented one view of how the satisfaction of a simplicity maxim might emerge from the operation of a system rather than being an evaluative component within it. The system considered there did not contain feedback in accordance with some error-correction rule.

28. The study of the scope and limits of effective learning procedures has recently undergone formal development, generating many useful distinctions (for every statement in an area, is there a time when the procedure will arrive at the truth about that statement; is there a time such that for every statement in an area the procedure will arrive at the truth about all those statements?) and many intriguing results. See Daniel Osherson, Michael Stob, and Scott Weinstein, *Systems That Learn* (Cambridge, Mass.: M.I.T. Press, 1986).

29. Notice that this measure avoids the "problem of known evidence." See Clark Glymour, *Theory and Evidence* (Princeton: Princeton Univ. Press, 1980), pp. 85–93; Daniel Garber, "Old Evidence and Logical Omniscience in Bayesian Confirmation Theory," in *Testing Scientific Theories*, ed. John Earman (Minneapolis: Univ. of Minnesota Press, 1983), pp. 99–131; Colin Howson and Peter Urbach, *Scientific Reasoning: The Bayesian Approach* (LaSalle, Ill.: Open Court, 1989), pp. 270–275; John Earman, *Bayes or Bust* (Cambridge, Mass.: M.I.T. Press, 1992), ch. 5. For even when e already is known, and the conditional probability of e on $h1$ is 1, still the prob($h1 \rightarrow e$), the probability that if $h1$ were true it would *give rise* to e, need not be 1. If it is 1, then $h1$ will gain in value along *this* measure by having its full probability enter the numerator.

30. See Gilbert Harman, "The Inference to the Best Explanation," *Philosophical Review* 70 (1965): 88–95; Norwood Russell Hanson, *Patterns of Discovery* (Cambridge: Cambridge Univ. Press, 1958), pp. 85–92.

31. Perhaps the proponents of inference to the best explanation should be interpreted as having put it forward as a defeasible principle of inference.

32. In order to assess the degree of explanatory support of a set of facts for an hypothesis, should we simply take the conjunction of these facts and treat it as the evidence *e* in our causalized Bayesian formula, or, when these facts are logically independent, should we take them individually, assess their causalized Bayes' measure one at a time, and then sum these values?

33. For the theory of a network of Bayesian conditional probabilities, see Pearl, *Probabilistic Reasoning in Intelligent Systems*.

34. Compare Charles Peirce's "method of tenacity" ("The Fixation of Belief," in *The Philosophy of Peirce*, ed. Justus Buchler [London: Routledge and Kegan Paul, 1940], pp. 5–22), Nelson Goodman's notion of "entrenchment" (*Fact, Fiction, and Forecast*, pp. 87–120, and Robert Schwartz, Israel Scheffler, and Nelson Goodman, "An Improvement in the Theory of Projectability," *Journal of Philosophy* 67 [1970]: 605–608), and the bidding system in Holland, Holyoak, Nisbett, and Thagard, *Induction*, pp. 70–78, 116–121.

35. See Holland, Holyoak, Nisbett, and Thagard, *Induction*, p. 9.

36. We might see the epistemological skeptic as proposing a more stringent rule: Do not believe a statement if its credibility value is less than it could be. This rule might be given different glosses: if the statement's credibility value is less than that of any other statement, whether or not that other statement is incompatible with the first; if its credibility value would be raised by some other evidence or reasons; if it is logically possible for some statement to have a greater credibiity value.

37. The Causalized Bayes' Theorem assesses the degree of explanatory support for an hypothesis by also considering, in the denominator, all alternative hypotheses. The result then feeds as one factor into the credibility value of that hypothesis. Rule 1 then requires us to compare the credibility of the hypothesis, not against all incompatible hypotheses, but against the most credible incompatible one. If and only if a hypothesis passes that test does it survive as a candidate for belief.

38. If further investigation shows the present worry about Rule 2' to be baseless, this additional requirement will be unnecessary.

39. Compare the danger of rule utilitarianism collapsing into act utilitarianism.

40. See Henry Kyburg Jr., *Probability and the Logic of Rational Belief* (Middletown, Conn.: Wesleyan Univ. Press, 1961), pp. 196–199, and "Conjunctivitis,"in *Induction, Acceptance, and Rational Belief*, ed. Marshall Swain (Dordrecht: Reidel, 1970), pp. 55–82.

41. See Richard Foley, "Evidence and Reasons for Belief," *Analysis* 51, no. 2 (1991): 98–102; Richard Jeffrey, "The Logic of Decision Defended," *Synthese* 48 (1981): 473–492.

42. Some psychological research indicates that certain optimistic styles of explaining personally negative events—attributing them to temporary, delim-

ited, external factors—have better personal consequences than other modes of explanation—attributing them to permanent, external factors of general applicability. Despite these beneficial personal consequences, in career success, happiness, and perhaps physical health, it may be that people with the more pessimistic explanatory style have a more accurate view of the world. See Martin Seligman, *Learned Optimism* (New York: Pocket Books, 1992); on the question of accuracy, see pp. 108–112 and the references cited on p. 298. This less accurate belief gets us close to people believing statements with a lower credibility value—that would depend upon the weights within their processing mechanism and how these arise—with (though not necessarily in order to have) beneficial effect.

43. For a discussion of these and related matters, see Daniel Dennett, *Consciousness Explained* (Boston: Little, Brown, 1991), pp. 173–182.

44. For a discussion of this, see my *Philosophical Explanations*, pp. 703–706.

45. The term "radical Bayesianism" is Richard Jeffrey's. See his *Probability and the Art of Judgment* (Cambridge: Cambridge Univ. Press, 1992), essays 1 and 4–6.

46. See Isaac Levi, *The Enterprise of Knowledge*, pp. 2–19 and *passim*, and *The Fixation of Belief and Its Undoing* (Cambridge: Cambridge Univ. Press, 1991), pp. 57–62 and *passim*.

47. To drop a belief *p* that you currently hold, and hence currently believe has no serious possibility of being wrong, opens you to the possibility of later coming to adopt a belief *q* incompatible with *p*. (This belief *q* may even be not-*p* itself.) And now you believe that to do that definitely would be an error. So shouldn't a person refuse to drop a current belief (in situations where his beliefs have not already been led into contradiction)? Levi handles this as follows (see Isaac Levi, *The Fixation of Belief and Its Undoing*, pp. 160–164). To drop a belief ("contraction") cannot by itself lead you into any error you are not already making, because no new information is added. However, dropping a belief puts you in a position to add a belief that is in error at the next stage ("expansion") because that new belief no longer is incompatible with what you then believe. Levi handles this difficulty by saying that at any moment we should look only to the results of our very next move or decision, rather than to where we might end up at the infinite limit of inquiry—he calls this latter concern "messianic." But there is much that falls between the next stage and the end of time, in particular, the stage immediately after the very next one. It is *extremely* implausible that we should not take that into account *at all*, but Levi is forced to this by his view that to believe something involves treating and using it as a standard of serious possibility in any and all contexts, that is, so treating it while one continues to hold the belief—which makes it very difficult to drop a belief, thus forcing Levi to the desperate expedient of embracing radical myopia.

48. See John W. Payne, James Bettman, and Eric Johnson, "The Adaptive Decision Maker: Effort and Accuracy in Choice," in *Insights in Decision Making*, ed. Robin Hogarth (Chicago: Univ. of Chicago Press, 1990), pp. 129–153.

49. Peirce holds that in each context there is something that is not doubted, something that is taken for granted and excludes other possibilities; yet there

need be nothing in particular that is taken for granted in every context. Levi holds that, at any given time, whatever is a belief is taken for granted in every context (although some contexts might lead you to reexamine some of these beliefs). This, I have held, is too strong. The Cartesian project was even stronger: to find some beliefs that could be taken for granted in every context and that never could rationally require reexamination. One might argue that it is permissible to take $q1$ for granted in context $C1$ by finding some context $C2$ in which $q2$ is taken for granted and concluding in $C2$ that $q1$ may be taken for granted in $C1$. For this argument to carry weight, $q2$ must be weaker than $q1$ (and $C2$ similarly weaker or more abstract). Continuing this process backward, one might hope to reach a context in which nothing is taken for granted—Descartes' situation of radical doubt—yet in which something can be justified so that it henceforth always can be taken for granted. Writers have objected that Descartes is taking for granted the reliability of his reasoning in that very situation of radical doubt. We also might wonder whether he is taking for granted the criterion that marks what he can conclude in that situation. It seems that Descartes' criterion here is: p may be accepted without doubt if a malevolent demon could not convince me that p when p is false. But this criterion is satisfied by "A demon is deceiving me" or "A demon is acting upon me." Yet surely this is not a statement we henceforth should believe and take for granted. (So at best this criterion is a necessary condition for a belief that is certain.) A more adequate criterion for establishing legitimacy of belief might be formulated, yet it too might be open to counterexamples and difficulties. It seems that Descartes not only must reason correctly and reliably that a particular criterion is satisfied, he also must reason correctly and reliably that that particular criterion is adequate.

50. Just as a belief excludes alternatives, so too does a goal. How, then, does a belief differ from a goal (which marks a structured preference or utility), given that my chosen behavior is a function of both of these? My chosen behavior B is a function of my goal g and of my belief that (probably) B will achieve g.

$$B = f(g, \, Bel \, [\text{prob}(g/B)=m]),$$

where m is high. This belief about the probability of g given B, in turn, is some function f' of my other beliefs bel (as they concern different ways of achieving that goal g). Substituting, we have

$$B = f(g, f'[bel]).$$

The function f, we can assume, will involve something like an expected utility formula; the function f' will involve some formula about the formation of beliefs in probabilistic statements, on the basis of other beliefs (and experiences). Beliefs and goals, *bel* and g, each enter into the determination of our behavior, but they enter in different ways, embedded in different functional positions. (Would this conclusion be altered if we explicitly incorporated Rule 2's decision-theoretic (partial) determination of *belief*?)

51. Does ignoring these possibilities in revising probabilities lead to violation of some of the axioms of probability theory, hence of the coherence condi-

tions? Or does the contextualist's revision take place in $1 - \varepsilon$, with the ε remaining *terra incognita*? Or does the radical contextualist have probabilities that are tied to a context also, just as his beliefs are, rather than probabilities that are invariant across contexts?

52. Amos Tversky and Daniel Kahneman, "Judgment under Uncertainty: Heuristics and Biases," reprinted in *Judgment under Uncertainty: Heuristics and Biases*, ed. Daniel Kahneman, Paul Slovic, and Amos Tversky (Cambridge: Cambridge Univ. Press, 1982), pp. 3–20. See especially their discussion of the "availability heuristic," pp. 11–14.

53. For a discussion of research on "belief perserverance after evidential discrediting," see Lee Ross and Craig Anderson, "Shortcomings in the Attribution Process: On the Origins and Maintenance of Erroneous Social Assessments," in *Judgment under Uncertainty*, ed. Kahneman, Slovic, and Tversky, esp. pp. 148–152.

54. Psychologists have worried about the continuing effects of the falsehoods they tell experimental subjects (in order to avoid contamination of the experiment's results), even though they afterward tell them the truth, for the falsehoods may have continuing effects, even after they are revealed. Our current reflections raise questions about the propriety of experiments in which the psychologist tells the *truth* from the very beginning (or which are done in natural environments, with no prior information being given about purpose). The mere fact that someone responded that way *in an experiment*, and talked about it to some researcher afterward, may give that particular information a special saliency and hence an unrepresentative force in shaping the person's later beliefs about his own character and capacities. If the truth can bias—not just falsehoods—then psychologists might have additional obligations to counteract the effects of their experimental interventions into people's lives.

55. There are other biases in the assessment of evidence that one would wish to correct for. See generally *Judgment under Uncertainty*, ed. Kahneman, Slovic, and Tversky.

56. Some suggestive material is available in the psychological literature. See ibid., articles 30–32. And recall the writings of C. S. Peirce on the self-correcting nature of scientific procedures.

57. The pursuit by selective universities of "geographical distribution" in their admissions originated in second-level discrimination by Harvard University in 1922. Its president, A. Lawrence Lowell, openly advocated quotas restricting the number of Jews to be admitted to Harvard College—a case of explicitly applying different standards to different groups. When this announcement of overt first-level discrimination produced a public uproar, Harvard University discovered the virtues of "geographical distribution." It is clear that this goal was added alongside the other traditional ones in order to limit the admissions of Jewish applicants, who tended then to be congregated in large cities. The Harvard admissions process had progressed from first- to second-level discrimination. For a detailed study of this history, see Penny Feldman, "Recruiting an Elite: Admission to Harvard College" (Ph.D. diss., Harvard Univ., 1975). See also Alan Dershowitz and Laura Hart, "Affirmative

Action and the Harvard College Diversity-Discretion Model: Paradigm or Pretext?" *Cardozo Law Review* 1 (1979): 379–424.

58. P. Bickel, Eugene Hummel, and J. W. O'Connell, "Is There a Sex Bias in Graduate Admissions," *Science* 187 (1975): 398–404.

59. Another too rapid conclusion of nondiscrimination (or of the relative nonseriousness of discrimination) based upon statistics is made by Thomas Sowell, who argues as follows. Almost all whites cannot tell the difference, or do not pause to notice the difference, among subgroups of blacks and hence can be expected to discriminate among them equally. Yet the average income of American blacks from the Caribbean islands is equal to that of white Americans. So isn't it the culturally based traits of the other black subgroups, rather than discrimination by whites, that keeps the average income of these other black subgroups below the white average? See Thomas Sowell, *Civil Rights: Rhetoric or Reality?* (New York: William Morrow, 1984), pp. 77–79.

However, there are white subgroups whose average income is above the general white average—for instance, people of Scandinavian descent and Jews. Perhaps the blacks from the islands too would have an income above the white average were it not for discrimination. There may be discrimination against all blacks, keeping their income below what it otherwise would be. The existence of a black subgroup *at* the white average does not preclude consequential discrimination against all blacks.

60. Rectifying such second-level arbitrariness—it need not be discrimination—should be distinguished from another goal sometimes put forward: to enhance the self-image or external image of particular minorities in the United States that are (or feel themselves to be) oppressed by including their products in the canon of work taught. Notice that there can be an *educational* purpose to including some writers from these groups, even were their artistic merits less than those of the very greatest writers one might include. Still, they would be far more perceptive and talented than the vast majority of the students who would be reading them. To have it borne in upon these students who don't yet acknowledge this that some women and minority members are very much more intelligent, perceptive, and talented than they themselves are would serve an important educational function.

In the final chapter of *Philosophical Explanations*, I describe a process of alternating stages of value and meaning: establishing unities, reaching out to connect with and include a further diversity of material that breaks these unities apart, establishing new and wider unities, reaching to connect still further, and so on. Adherents to a current (threatened) unity might fruitfully see "multiculturalism" as a part of this ongoing process, not its final stage.

61. See Robert Nozick, *The Examined Life* (New York: Simon and Schuster 1989), pp. 76–83, and Oliver Williamson, "Calculativeness, Trust and Economic Organization" (March 1992 preprint of a talk presented at the Conference on Law and Economics, Univ. of Chicago Law School, April 1992). That one refrains from calculation about exactly how trustworthy a friend is, simply trusting him, does not entail that sufficiently strong counterevidence could not suffice to convince one of that friend's untrustworthiness.

IV. EVOLUTIONARY REASONS

1. Could there not, however, be concatenations or extensions of these relations that would constitute reasons even though our minds could not recognize that? Might the reason relation be recursively enumerable but not recursive?

2. See Nelson Goodman, *Fact, Fiction, and Forecast* (Cambridge, Mass.: Harvard Univ. Press, 1955), pp. 65–66, which raises a similar question for the a priori view.

3. *Philosophical Explanations* (Cambridge, Mass.: Harvard Univ. Press, 1981), pp. 248–253. Others have presented views in which the degree of support is contingent. How much support is lent to the hypothesis that all P's are Q's by a number of instances of P's that are Q's will depend upon the existing belief about how variable P's tend to be with respect to Q's, that is, about the range of variation in the (relevant) kind of thing that P is with respect to the (relevant) kind of thing that Q is. See John Holland, Keith Holyoak, Richard Nisbett, and Paul Thagard, *Induction: Processes of Inference, Learning, and Discovery* (Cambridge, Mass.: M.I.T. Press, 1986), pp. 232–233, a view anticipated in Norman Campbell, *What Is Science?* (1921; rpt. New York: Dover, 1952), pp. 63–64.)

4. In view of recent debates about adaptationism, it would be desirable if this hypothesis does not demand overly much specificity in the evolutionary selection of features of the brain. See Stephen Jay Gould and Richard Lewontin, "The Spandrals of San Marcos and the Panglossian Paradigm: A Critique of the Adaptationist Programme," *Proceedings of the Royal Society of London, B* 205 (1979): 581–598; also see the various essays debating optimality in *The Latest on the Best: Essays on Evolution and Optimality,* ed. John Dupre (Cambridge, Mass.: M.I.T. Press, 1987), chs. 4–9.

5. Leda Cosmides and John Tooby, "Are Humans Good Intuitive Statisticians After All?" (forthcoming); Leda Cosmides, "The Logic of Social Exchange: Has Natural Selection Shaped How Humans Reason?" *Cognition* 31 (1989): 187–276; Leda Cosmides and John Tooby, "From Evolution to Behavior," in *The Latest on the Best,* ed. Dupre; John Tooby and Leda Cosmides, "The Psychological Foundations of Culture," in *The Adapted Mind,* ed. J. Bardow, L. Cosmides, and J. Tooby (New York: Oxford Univ. Press, forthcoming), pp. 19–136.

6. See Daniel Dennett, *Consciousness Explained* (Boston: Little, Brown, 1991), pp. 184–187, for a discussion of the Baldwin effect.

7. W. V. Quine, "Truth by Convention" (1936), reprinted in W. V. Quine, *The Ways of Paradox* (Cambridge, Mass.: Harvard Univ. Press, 1976), pp. 77–106.

8. The distinction between evidence as a factual connection and as an (almost) a priori evident connection parallels the distinction between rationality as arising from a factually reliable process and rationality as constituted by a certain kind of dense meshing together of overlapping and connected statements, arguments, and inferences. In each case we have a factual aspect distinguished from a rational aspect; in each case we want the two to go together, and we feel uncomfortable with a rational aspect that is unmoored from a fac-

tual connection. When we believe the rational aspect is attached to the factual, we feel comfortable in holding that a rational instantiation is valuable in itself. But when the two aspects come to be seen as detached, when a mode of rationality no longer seems to mirror facts or be a way of getting at them—as happened with the tradition of scholastic disputation—then that mode loses its allure, it no longer seems beautiful or intrinsically valuable.

Compare how much easier it is to rest comfortable with a deontological position in ethics when the required or right action's consequences also seem reasonably good.

9. If inductive reasoning *is* rational, then there is such a rational argument, the inductive one; this gets dismissed as circular. So the problem is held to be one of supporting one portion of Reason, inductive reasoning, by *other* portions of Reason, that is, in a noncircular way.

10. See also p. 197n.49.

11. Kant, *Critique of Pure Reason*, trans. Norman Kemp Smith (London: Macmillan, 1933), Preface to the Second Edition.

12. Compare W. V. Quine, *Word and Object* (Cambridge, Mass.: M.I.T. Press, 1960), ch. 2.

13. Kant, *Critique of Pure Reason*, Preface to the First Edition.

14. See Robert Nozick, "Experience, Theory and Language," in *The Philosophy of W. V. Quine*, ed. Lewis Hahn (LaSalle, Ill.: Open Court, 1986), pp. 340–341, and Stephen Stich, *The Fragmentation of Reason* (Cambridge, Mass.: M.I.T. Press, 1990), pp. 60–63. Stich goes on to argue that, because of such differences in the costs of error, the cognitive mechanism that evolution selects for may not be the most reliable detector of truth when this lesser reliability will be outweighed by the mechanism's other virtues.

15. The theory of population genetics, fully filled out, has the following structure, Richard Lewontin tells us (Lewontin, *The Genetic Basis of Evolutionary Change* [New York: Columbia Univ. Press, 1974], ch. 1, esp. pp. 12–15, from which I take the description in the remainder of this paragraph). It consists of genotypic descriptions G1 and G2 of the population at times $t1$ and $t2$, and of transformation laws that get from the one to the other: a set of epigenetic laws that give the distribution of phenotypes that result from the development of various genotypes in various environments; laws of mating, of migration, and of natural selection that transform the phenotypic array in a population within the span of a generation; the set of epigenetic relations that allow inferences about the distribution of genotypes corresponding to any distribution of phenotypes; and the genetic rules (of Mendel and Morgan) that predict the array of genotypes in the next generation produced from gametogenesis and fertilization, given an array of parental genotypes. Genotypes and phenotypes are state variables; population genetic theory thus maps a set of genotypes into a set of phenotypes, transforms these into other phenotypes, and then maps the result back into genotypes that then are transformed to produce the genotypic array in the next generation.

Building upon this structure, Elliott Sober construes evolutionary theory as a theory of forces acting upon a zero-force equilibrium state specified by the Hardy-Weinberg equation. (This equation states that after the first generation, the ratio of alleles at each locus within a population will remain constant unless acted upon by outside forces, and it states a formula for this ratio.) Evolutionary theory specifies how this equilibrium changes under various forces (selection, mutation, migration, genetic drift) acting singly and in combination. (See Elliott Sober, *The Nature of Selection* [Cambridge, Mass.: M.I.T. Press, 1984], ch. 1.) However, as John Beatty notes, the Hardy-Weinberg law is a consequence of Mendelian inheritance, and the mechanisms for this—sexual reproduction, male-female and female-male crosses having equivalent results, mechanisms satisfying the law of segregation and of independent assortment—are themselves a product of evolution. If evolutionary theory also is to explain how Mendelian inheritance arises, Sober's account of it cannot be complete. (See John Beatty, "What's Wrong with the Received View of Evolutionary Theory?" in *Proceedings of the P.S.A., 1980*, ed. Peter Asquith and Ronald Giere [East Lansing, Mich.: Philosophy of Science Association, 1980], vol. 2.)

We can generalize Sober's account and avoid this difficulty by seeing evolutionary theory as an historical theory that describes a sequence of *different* zero-force equilibrium states. Each such state is paired with a mechanism of heredity (and in the first generation?), and the theory of each such state specifies the forces that can disrupt this equilibrium and the laws of such disruption. Some disruptions will lead to the existence of a new mechanism of heredity, and, once existing, this new mechanism gives rise to its own new zero-force state, the laws of its disruption, and so forth. Thus we get an historical narrative of a sequence of zero-force states and associated mechanisms, each giving rise to the next in accordance with the transformation laws associated with that state and mechanism. With each new equilibrium state may come a new list of deviating forces and new laws about how these operate. So in Lewontin's schema, the output of a transformation can be a new natural (zero-force) state, with different deviating forces and laws. But even though the equilibrium state, the particular mechanism of heredity, and the deviating forces all can change—in this sense, the theory is radically historical—what makes it an evolutionary story, all the way through, is the constant role of heritable variations in fitness.

16. Susan Mills and John Beatty, "The Propensity Interpretation of Fitness," reprinted in *Conceptual Issues in Evolutionary Biology*, ed. Elliott Sober (Cambridge, Mass.: M.I.T. Press, 1984), pp. 36–57.

17. See John Beatty and Susan Finsen, "Rethinking the Propensity Interpretaion," in *What the Philosophy of Biology Is: Essays for David Hull*, ed. Michael Ruse (Dordrecht, Kluwer, 1989), pp. 17–30.

18. Robert Brandon recognizes that more than the expected value of the number of offspring in the next generation matters—increased variance can be selectively disadvantageous—so he proposes measuring fitness by subtracting from the expected number of offspring some function of the variance. See Robert Brandon, *Adaptation and Environment* (Princeton: Princeton Univ. Press, 1990), pp. 39–77. But *which* particular function is to be subtracted? Beatty and Finsen state that it is not simply a question of mean and variance; the skew of a distribution also matters. Since the particular statistics are a component of the organism's strategy in an environment, fitness in general should not be

identified with any *one* statistic. See Beatty and Finsen, "Rethinking the Propensity Interpretation," pp. 17–30.

19. See Ernest Nagel, *The Structure of Science* (New York: Harcourt, Brace and World, 1961), pp. 401–428. Nagel followed the biologist G. Sommerhoff, *Analytical Biology* (London, 1950).

20. Larry Wright, "Functions," *Philosophical Review* 82 (1973), reprinted in *Conceptual Issues in Evolutionary Biology*, ed. Sober, pp. 347–368.

21. Christopher Boorse, "Wright on Functions," reprinted in *Conceptual Issues in Evolutionary Biology*, ed. Sober, pp. 369–385.

22. These examples come from Peter Godfrey-Smith, but he offers a different account of why these are not said to be functions.

23. Rudolf Carnap, "Testability and Meaning," *Philosophy of Science* 3 (1936): 419–471 and 4 (1937): 1–45.

24. L. J. Savage, *The Foundations of Statistics* (New York: John Wiley, 1954).

25. The dutch book argument, discussed below, does not provide such an independent rationale. At best, it states why, if there are personal probabilities that a person will always act upon, these should satisfy the usual probability axioms; it does not state why there must or should be such personal probabilities that always guide (betting) choices.

26. Although I developed all the particular points of this paragraph in my *The Normative Theory of Individual Choice* (1963; rpt. New York: Garland Press, 1990), pp. 159–172 and 246–250, it was only after talking with Hilary Putnam and seeing a recent unpublished essay of his, "Pragmatism and Moral Objectivity" (forthcoming), where independently he presses the issue of why one should act upon the more probable, that I came to see this as a serious problem, not just as a finicky difficulty. (Another related issue, why should one act on the certain rather than the probable, *perhaps* can be resolved by dominance considerations, *if* these do not beg the question.)

27. Consider, finally, a problem about rationality itself. Let the statement R be: Believe statement p (or do action A) if and only if p (or A) can be shown to be rational. (Or could have been shown to be so when you first acquired that belief. To maintain it, perhaps it is enough that it not be shown to be irrational.) We have strong inductive grounds—good reasons, that is—for supposing that R itself cannot be shown to be rational—no one has done it yet, despite very serious efforts. Suppose that is so. Then if R is true, you should not believe it, since it cannot be shown to be rational. Then there is at least one truth that rationality will not lead you to. (And if that one, why not others?) On the other hand, if R is false, then there is something that is to be believed (or done) though it cannot be shown to be rational, *or* there is something that is not to be believed (or done) though it can be shown to be rational. In any of these cases, rationality seems to be limited. There are strong inductive grounds to believe that, once any specific notion of rationality is specified, R cannot be shown to be rational. By its own standards, rationality has (thus far) failed to justify itself. So it seems rational for us to believe that R cannot be shown to be rational and hence, if R is true, not to believe R. (How is the situation changed when Rules 1 and 2' are substituted for R?)

28. This does not necessarily mean that we once were better at finding out and proving, for instance, principles of induction and the existence of

other minds and the external world and that we since have become specialized to work in tandem with these facts, which now we no longer can justify or prove.

29. See Donald Norman, *The Psychology of Everyday Things* (New York: Basic Books, 1988), ch. 3.

30. Hubert Dreyfus has argued that the project of artificial intelligence has encountered difficulties due to the embedded, and embodied, nature of our rationality. See his *What Computers Can't Do: A Critique of Artificial Reason* (New York: Harper and Row, 1972).

31. This question is pressed upon us by Nelson Goodman's work on "grue" and "bleen," unusual predicates that fit the past behavior of green and blue things but diverge from the usual predicates in the future. See Goodman, "A Query on Confirmation," *Journal of Philosophy* 43 (1946): 383–385, and *Fact, Fiction, and Forecast*, pp. 73–83. This same point can be made by drawing different curves through the same past data points. Which of these regularities will continue to hold?

32. It is instructive to compare Wittgenstein's remarks in *On Certainty* (Oxford: Basil Blackwell, 1969), par. 83, 88, 94, 103, 105, 152, on the "frame of reference," "propositions that stand fast for me," and what "is anchored in all my questions and answers, so anchored that I cannot touch it" to our hypothesis of evolution instilling in us as a phylogenetic inheritance stable facts of past environments. However, Wittgenstein does not consider the ways in which these instilled framework components might operate to induce changes in each other.

33. See Douglass North, *Institutions, Institutional Change and Economic Performance* (Cambridge: Cambridge Univ. Press, 1990); Andrew Schotter, *The Economic Theory of Social Institutions* (Cambridge: Cambridge Univ. Press, 1981); Oliver Williamson, *The Economic Institutions of Capitalism* (New York: Free Press, 1985); Margaret Levi, "A Logic of Institutional Change," in *The Limits of Rationality*, ed. Karen Schwers Cook and Margaret Levi (Chicago: Univ. of Chicago Press, 1990), pp. 383–401; Thrainn Eggertsson, *Economic Behavior and Institutions* (Cambridge: Cambridge Univ. Press, 1990); Harold Demsetz and Armen Alchian, "Production, Information Costs and Economic Organization," *American Economic Review* 62 (1972): 777–795; Michael Jensen and William Meckling, "Theory of the Firm: Managerial Behavior, Agency Costs and Ownership Structure," *Journal of Financial Economics* 3 (1976): 305–360 (rpt. in *Economic and Social Institutions*, ed. Karl Brunner [Boston: Martinus Nijhoff, 1979], pp. 163–231); E. Furbotn and S. Pejovich, "Property Rights and the Behavior of the Firm in a Socialist State," in *The Economics of Property Rights*, ed. Furbotn and Pejovich (Cambridge: Ballinger, 1974), pp. 227–251; Dennis Mueller, *Public Choice II* (Cambridge: Cambridge Univ. Press, 1989); Gary Becker, *The Economic Approach to Human Behavior* (Chicago: Univ. of Chicago Press, 1976); James Coleman, *Foundations of Social Theory* (Cambridge, Mass.: Harvard Univ. Press, 1990); Richard Swedberg, *Economics and Sociology* (Princeton: Princeton Univ. Press, 1990).

34. Alternatively, might an institution function as if it maximized some objective function by the concatenation of the behavior of individuals within it, none of whom attempted to maximize that or any other objective function?

35. See Richard Dawkins, *The Selfish Gene* (Oxford: Oxford Univ. Press, 1976).

36. This claim is put forth by Gary Becker, *A Treatise on the Family* (Cambridge, Mass.: Harvard Univ. Press, 1981), p. 102, who cites supporting literature.

37. "This adaptation [of man's actions] to the general circumstances that surround him is brought about by his observance of rules which he has not designed and often does not even know explicitly . . . our actions [are] governed by rules adapted to the kind of world in which we live, that is, to circumstances which we are not aware of and which yet determine the pattern of our successful actions." The rules themselves "have by a process of selection been evolved in the society in which he lives, and which are thus the product of the experiences of generations." F. A. Hayek, *Law, Legislation and Liberty*, vol. 1: *Rules and Order* (Chicago: Univ. of Chicago Press, 1973), pp. 11–12. The process that Hayek describes is one of group selection. "These rules of conduct have thus not developed as the recognized conditions for the achievement of a known purpose, but have evolved because the groups who practiced them were more successful and displaced others" (p. 18).

38. E. O. Wilson, *Sociobiology* (Cambridge, Mass.: Harvard Univ. Press, 1975), p. 145. Chapter 7 of Wilson's book is an elaboration of this theme, distinguishing different levels of response over different time periods: organismic, ecological, and evolutionary.

For each level of frequency of change, there might be mechanisms adapted to respond to changes of (approximately) that frequency, producing things or entities that last approximately that long, with modifications through appropriate feedback rules. We can distinguish these cases: the thing produced fits the constancy of the kind it is geared to; the constancy has changed and the thing produced is changing so as to fit the new constancy—it is on the way to a new equilibrium; the constancy is changing at a more rapid rate than the feedback mechanism of change can respond to—no fit between a new thing produced and a then obtaining constancy will result.

39. And would acceptance of an argument that the selective process *is* severe and appropriate itself represent a bias in the views of itself that our society presents to its members (compare Marxist views of ideology)? Does that bias exist because it reflects some enduring robust truth about social life or because it serves the continuance of that particular (kind of) society and helps to maintain the dominance of some particular ruling group within it?

40. See Richard Dawkins, *The Blind Watchmaker* (New York: W. W. Norton, 1986), pp. 77–86.

41. Moreover, Paul David points out that the arrangment of keys on the standard English-language typewriter keyboard is technologically inefficient but that, given the existing investment in equipment and typing skills, a change to a different keyboard is economically inefficient. Hence, when a hill-climbing method does lead to what is a stable global optimum, that optimum may have specific defects of its own that it is inefficient to remedy only because of the historical adjustments that were made to dovetail with it. See Paul David, "Clio and the Economics of QWERTY," *American Economic Review* 75 (1985): 332–337.

42. Some have argued that Japanese modes of industrial relations should be a model for the United States, an argument taken more seriously because of the results of international economic competition. Similarly, the willingness in Eastern Europe and the former U.S.S.R. to experiment with great changes in the direction of market capitalism stems from the demonstrated and visibly greater economic prosperity in the capitalist world.

V. INSTRUMENTAL RATIONALITY AND ITS LIMITS

1. Notice that we already have *within* the network *two* pieces of apparatus: the standard Bayes' formula, which uses evidential conditional probabilities; and the causalized version, which uses causal probabilities. Is there some way these can be combined, along with symbolic considerations? As a rough approximation—the actual processing network will fit a far more complicated description—we might see the degree of credibility of h on the basis of e, cred(h,e), as a weighted sum of the causalized Bayesian ratio (with subjunctive conditionals), the standard Bayesian ratio (with conditional probabilities), and a symbolic component sym(h,e). (It is unclear, however, what the appropriate symbolic component would be here—what believing h on the basis of e symbolizes. The degree to which it symbolizes believing the truth?) And might these weights be the very ones we use also in our decision theory, in our DV formula? A person then will use *these* credibility values to eliminate some statements as unworthy of belief, namely, those for which some incompatible statement has a higher credibility value. And then the person will use the further rules to decide which of these still admissible statements to believe.

2. David Hume, *A Treatise of Human Nature*, ed. L. A. Selby-Bigge (1888; Oxford: Oxford Univ. Press, 1958), bk. II, pt. III, sec. III, p. 416. Hume continues, "It is not contrary to reason for me to choose my total ruin, to prevent the least uneasiness of an Indian or person wholly unknown to me. It is as little contrary to reason to prefer even my own acknowledged lesser good to my greater."

3. See John Von Neumann and Oscar Morgenstern, *Theory of Games and Economic Behavior*, 3d ed. (Princeton: Princeton Univ. Press, 1953), appendix; R. D. Luce and Howard Raiffa, *Games and Decisions* (New York: John Wiley, 1957), pp. 12–38.

4. Alternatively, one might attempt to describe a (normative) *process* of forming and modifying preferences, individually and together, and see if this process, if carried out indefinitely, would result in a Von Neumann–Morgenstern utility function. Von Neumann–Morgenstern utility theory then might be seen as an end-state description of the result of a particular process, at least at the limit. It then might turn out that we have no particular reason always to carry that process to its limit.

5. Should we distinguish two conceptions of desires mandated by rationality: desires it is rational to have, and desires it is rational to have *if* rationality is itself desirable or valuable? Could it be argued that the second cannot be dismissed without making it unclear why it is desirable to have the desires it is rational to have?

6. For discussion of second-order preferences, see Harry Frankfurt, "Free-

dom of the Will and the Concept of a Person," *Journal of Philosophy* 68 (1971): 5–20; Amartya Sen, "Choice, Orderings and Morality," reprinted in his *Choice, Welfare and Measurement* (Oxford: Basil Blackwell, 1982), pp. 74–83; and Richard Jeffrey, "Preferences among Preferences," *Journal of Philosophy* 71 (1974): 377–391. See also Gilbert Harman, "Desired Desires," in *Value, Welfare, and Morality*, ed. R. Frey and C. Morris (forthcoming).

7. William Talbott and Amartya Sen independently suggested this point to me.

8. For a discussion of difficulties in delineating this disposition, see Robert Nozick, *The Normative Theory of Individual Choice* (1963; rpt. New York: Garland Press, 1990), pp 39–48, 70–78.

9. Formulating this condition as a presumption that holds in the absence of reasons for its not holding avoids the objections presented in my "On the Randian Argument," *The Personalist* 52, no. 2 (1971): 285–286, to a stronger principle.

10. I owe this point about identity to Howard Sobel.

11. One mark of an irrational desire or belief may be that it does not go through holistic controls and modification. It just sticks out all by itself, resistant to integration with other desires and beliefs. See David Shapiro, *Neurotic Styles* (New York: Basic Books, 1965). I conjecture that the same would be the case with posthypnotic suggestion: it will not merge with or get modified within the holistic network of beliefs and desires.

12. See my *Philosophical Explanations* (Cambridge, Mass.: Harvard Univ. Press, 1981), pp. 348–352, 714–716. Some writers have formulated further conditions relating preferences and desires to knowledge; these concern knowledge not just of their causes but of their consequences and their interrelations with everything else. See, for example, Richard Brandt, *A Theory of the Good and the Right* (Oxford: Oxford Univ. Press, 1979), pp. 110–129, 149–162; and in criticism see Allan Gibbard, *Wise Choices, Apt Feelings* (Oxford: Oxford Univ. Press, 1990), pp. 18–22.

13. For an extremely illuminating discussion of many issues that arise about goals and their functions, see Michael Bratman, *Intention, Plans, and Practical Reason* (Cambridge, Mass.: Harvard Univ. Press, 1987). Bratman discusses many of these issues under the topic of "intentions."

14. See Helmut Jungermann, Ingrid von Ulardt, and Lutz Hausmann, "The Role of the Goal for Generating Actions," in *Analysing and Aiding Decision Processes*, ed. P. Humphreys, O. Svenson, and A. Vari (Amsterdam: North Holland, 1983), esp. pp. 223–228.

15. See my *The Examined Life* (New York: Simon and Schuster, 1989), pp. 40–42.

16. Is there something further that stands to goals as goals do to desires and desires do to preferences, involving still another level of processing and filtering?

17. Recall Isaac Levi's treatment of belief as a standard of serious possibility, so that one need not assign probabilities to or consider situations where that belief is false (see p. 96 above). Levi's rule for coming to believe something can decide this on the basis of a small marginal difference; but once something is made a *belief*, that has large effect. Whereas if we went back to the situation

before it was made a belief by that rule, its difference from another hypothesis, another possible belief, would have been small, apparently not sufficient to yield directly any such large difference in effects.

18. See Henry Montgomery, "Decision Rules and the Search for a Dominance Structure," in *Analysing and Aiding Decision Processes*, ed. Humphreys, Svenson, and Vari, pp. 343–369, and "From Cognition to Action," in *Process and Structure in Human Decision Making*, ed. Henry Montgomery and Ola Svenson (New York: John Wiley, 1989), pp. 23–49. Montgomery considers the rule of maximizing expected utility to be a different matter, since it takes into account all information. But notice that the formula is a way of combining (amalgamating?) information into one attribute, the Expected Utility, and thereby saying that one action beats and dominates another on all relevant attributes, for now there is only *one* such attribute, Expected Utility, and (at that level) there no longer are reasons against the maximal action or reasons for another.

19. See Bratman, *Intentions, Plans, and Practical Reason*.

20. It would be too strong to run the condition in the other direction; not every preference we have need imply being a different kind of person when that preference is satisfied.

21. Notice that this condition does not bar desires that are guaranteed to lead to false or even inconsistent beliefs. (In Chapter 3, in the section "Rules of Rationality," we said that a procedure that led to a set of inconsistent beliefs need not be irrational.) It is another matter if there is a desire *for* such beliefs.

22. I am grateful to Gilbert Harman for pointing this out.

23. See John Broome, *Weighing Goods* (Oxford: Basil Blackwell, 1991), pp. 100–107; Susan Hurley, *Natural Reasons* (Oxford: Oxford Univ. Press, 1989), chs. 4–6.

24. Note the parallel between this discussion of the testability of decision theory, which we interpret as containing an existential quantifier ("there exists a set of aspects specifying alternatives such that . . . "), and our earlier account of fitness, which employed an existential quantification over heritable genotypic traits.

25. See W. V. Quine, *Word and Object* (Cambridge, Mass.: M.I.T. Press, 1960), pp. 57–61; Donald Davidson, *Inquiries into Truth and Interpretation* (Oxford: Oxford Univ. Press, 1984), essays 9–13; David Lewis, "Radical Interpretation," in his *Philosophical Papers*, vol. 1 (Oxford: Oxford Univ. Press, 1983), pp. 108–121; Ronald Dworkin, *Law's Empire* (Cambridge, Mass.: Harvard Univ. Press, 1986), ch. 2; Hurley, *Natural Reasons*, ch. 5.

26. For versions of this proposal, see David Lewis, "Radical Interpretation," pp. 108–118; Richard Grandy, "Reference, Meaning and Belief," *Journal of Philosophy* 70 (1973): 439–452.

27. See *Judgment under Uncertainty: Heuristics and Biases*, ed. Daniel Kahneman, Paul Slovic, and Amos Tversky (Cambridge: Cambridge Univ. Press, 1982); Lee Ross and Richard Nisbett, *Human Inference* (Englewood Cliffs, N.J.: Prentice-Hall, 1980); and Paul Thagard and Richard Nisbett, "Rationality and Charity," *Philosophy of Science* 50 (1983): 250–267, which discusses the implications of these psychological results for the formulation of a principle of interpretation. But see also the contrasting view of the research of Tversky and Kahneman in Gerd Gigerenzer, "How to Make Cognitive Illusions Disap-

pear," *European Review of Social Psychology* 2 (1991): 83–115, and in Leda Cosmides and John Tooby, "Are Humans Good Intuitive Statisticians After All?" (forthcoming).

28. Thagard and Nisbett, "Rationality and Charity," mention Zen masters and Hegel as examples.

29. See Jack Goody and Ian Watt, "The Consequences of Literacy," *Comparative Studies in History and Society* 5 (1963): 304–345; Jack Goody, *The Domestication of the Savage Mind* (Cambridge: Cambridge Univ. Press, 1977), pp. 36–51, 74–111; Goody, *The Logic of Writing and the Organization of Society* (Cambridge: Cambridge Univ. Press, 1986), pp. 1–20, 171–185.

30. See Donald Davidson, "On the Very Idea of a Conceptual Scheme," in his *Inquiries into Truth and Interpretation* (Oxford: Oxford Univ. Press, 1984), pp. 183–198.

31. See Susan Hurley, "Intelligibility, Imperialism, and Conceptual Scheme," *Midwest Studies in Philosophy* (forthcoming).

32. See Alasdair MacIntyre, *Whose Justice? Which Rationality?* (Notre Dame, Ind.: Univ. of Notre Dame Press, 1988).

33. See Dworkin, *Law's Empire*, pp. 46–68, 76–86.

34. See Stephen Jay Gould and Richard Lewontin, "The Spandrals of San Marcos and the Panglossian Paradigm: A Critique of the Adaptationist Programme," *Proceedings of the Royal Society of London, B* 205 (1979): 581-598. Daniel Dennett not only has drawn the analogy between the interpretative task and the one of evolutionary explanation but has maintained these are really the same task and must both be guided by an optimality assumption! See Dennett, *The Intentional Stance* (Cambridge, Mass.: M.I.T. Press, 1987), pp. 237–321.

35. For one early example of such a notion of conditional utility, see my *Normative Theory of Individual Choice*, pp. 144–154.

36. On the points of this paragraph, see my *Normative Theory of Individual Choice*, pp. 94–98.

37. Independently, Gilbert Harman has objected that the past probabilities should not bind, though he does not address the intertemporal dutch book argument. See his "Realism, Antirealism and Reasons for Belief" (forthcoming).

38. The strict Bayesian may hope that the person also shows "good judgment" in her particular personal probabilities, but no further specific normative condition demarcates this.

39. See Paul Teller, "Conditionalization and Observation," *Synthese* 26 (1973): 218–258, stating an argument attributed to David Lewis. Bas Van Frassen notes that this argument depends upon the person who violates conditionalization following some other particular rule; he claims therefore that violating conditionalization is permissible so long as it does not follow a rule. Bas Van Frassen, *Laws and Symmetry* (Oxford: Oxford Univ. Press, 1989), pp. 160–176.

40. See John Earman, *Bayes or Bust* (Cambridge, Mass.: M.I.T. Press, 1992), pp. 195–198. For further criticisms of Bayesian conditionalization, see F. Bacchus, H. E. Kyburg Jr., and M. Thalos, "Against Conditionalization," *Synthese* 85 (1990): 475–506.

41. This, I believe, is the conception of Nicholas Rescher: "Rationality consists in the intelligent pursuit of appropriate objectives." Rescher, *Rationality* (Oxford: Clarendon Press, 1988), p. vii.

42. Herbert Simon and Allen Newell, *Human Problem Solving* (Englewood Cliffs, N.J.: Prentice-Hall, 1972), pp. 71–105.

43. The most prominent exponent of the problem model for intellectual history is Karl Popper. In his later writing, Popper placed this approach within his framework of "three worlds": world I of physical objects, world II of states of consciousness, and world III of objective contents of thought, where this includes scientific and poetic thoughts (and, Popper says, works of art). Among the denizens of world III, Popper says, are problem situations, consisting of a problem, its background (that is, the language used and the theories embodied in the problem's structure), and the framework of concepts and theories available to use on the problem. In addition, world III contains critical arguments, theoretical systems, and states of discussion of an argument. The history of science, Popper maintains, should be a history not of theories alone but rather of problem situations and how they are modified through attempts to solve the problems—these attempts being the theories. (See Karl Popper, "On the Theory of the Objective Mind," in his *Objective Knowledge* [Oxford: Oxford Univ. Press, 1972], pp. 153–190, esp. p. 177.) Historical understanding, Popper says, grows from analysis of world III relations, not of world II thought processes (p. 178). The intellectual historian will study intellectual products, their structural features, compatibilities, and theoretical relations, and will also study these products as responses to the problem situation. A "situational analysis" is an idealized reconstruction of the problem situation in which the agent found himself that makes his action or theory rationally understandable (to the extent this can be done), showing how it is adequate to the situation as he saw it.

Does this mean adequate to the situation as that person saw the *situation*, or adequate to the situation as that person saw *adequacy*? (Or both?) The first would have the historian describe the situation as the person saw it and then try to show that the person's action or theory was adequate to that situation, whether or not the person himself saw adequacy that way. In doing this, the historian can import other standards of adequacy, that of her own time or whichever ones she takes to be correct. It is an interesting question whether that thinker's response in that situation was an adequate one. But what that person was trying to do was to come up with a solution (in that problem situation as he saw it) that was adequate by *his* standards of adequacy, or by those of his discipline at the time (as he saw those), not by later standards or by ours. To explain why Galileo did not accept Kepler's laws of planetary motion, Popper answers that Galileo was justified in not accepting Kepler's laws then and in working with a bold oversimplification instead (p. 173). Now this fits *Popper's* methodology; but only if it fit Galileo's (and he was following it then) will we have an explanation of why Galileo did not accept those laws.

John Passmore describes one mode of the history of philosophy—the one he favors—as a *problematic* history. This mode seeks to understand the problems a philosopher was facing, the questions he was trying to answer, and it then seeks to trace the steps of his theoretical construction as an attempt to solve these problems and answer these questions. (John Passmore, "The Idea of a History of Philosophy," *History and Theory* 4 [1964–65]: 3–32.) How constant are the problems and questions philosophers have faced over time? Can questions be similar enough for the answers proposed to one to count also as possible answers to another when there are different reasons for asking them, even if the reasons are similar. For the *questions* to be the same, must the (implicit) range of possible *answers* also be the same, or at least largely overlap? The question "Why this?" often is an inexplicit form of the question "Why this rather than that?" When two historical periods ask about the same "this" but in contrast to very different "thats," are their questions sufficiently similar for their answers to compete or to illuminate each other? The question "How is that possible?" is an inexplicit form of the question "How is that possible, given that this holds true?" When two historical periods puzzle over the possibility of the same "that" but in the face of different "thises" that seem to exclude it, are they asking the same question—are they even then talking about the same "this"? When two theorists worry about the possibiity of free will, one because he takes as given divine foreknowledge, the other because she takes as given univeral causal determinism, are they investigating the same question or speaking about the same thing? Even when the problems are not constant, problem-oriented histories can study how the theorists of the past were trying to solve *their* problems, and why the philosopher's problems have changed over time.

In art history, Michael Baxandall has proposed seeing the maker of a picture as addressing a problem, his product being its finished and concrete solution. To understand the product, we need to reconstruct the specific problem it was designed to solve and the specific circumstances out of which the painter was addressing it. (See Baxandall, *Patterns of Intention* [New Haven: Yale Univ. Press, 1985].) Earlier, E. H. Gombrich described the history of representational painting in the West as a series of experiments designed to solve particular changing problems in accordance with a pattern of schema and correction. (See Gombrich, *Art and Illusion* [New York: Pantheon, 1960]. Gombrich acknowledges the influence of Karl Popper's thought.)

In a well-known manifesto, the English historian of political thought Quentin Skinner sets forth a program for historical investigation that rejects the problem model. Do not, he says, see political theorists as offering answers to perennial questions or positions on timeless topics, or even as attempting to solve *intellectual* problems of the moment. Rather, their writings are interventions in particular controversies, and we should see their main intent, their illocutionary act, as *doing that*, namely, supporting one side in a particular social and political controversy, arguing for that faction's position, and so forth. (See Skinner, "Meaning and Understanding in the History of Ideas," *History and Theory* 8 [1969]: 3–53.) The writer's intention is a particular one, specific to the particular occasion. (Skinner grants that other things may be studied also, but he makes central to his mode of intellectual history the identification and study of particular interventions into specific controversies.)

Thousands of people have taken different sides on each particular controversy, however. The reason we are interested in *these* writers is not that they
took a side but that they said something interesting, indeed something that
seems to transcend that particular controversy and apply more generally. If
this were not so, it would not be a task of such delicacy to identify the particular controversy into which the writer (supposedly) meant to be intervening.
Indeed, which controversy a writer is seen as having taken a stand upon may
depend upon the precise dating of his writing. A different year, a different
controversy, a different intervention.

Of course, at most times there is some social or political controversy or other
going on, so it is not surprising that intellectual historians can find a controversy to tag the writing onto. If a writer says something of wide applicability,
it will have implications for many different possible controversies. That he
says his content at a particular time, with implications for a controversy raging
then, does *not* mean his intention (or illocutionary act) is to take a side in *that*
controversy, certainly not that his intention is *only* to take a side. For the writer
may intend to propound a general theory or truth of wide relevance and applicability. His illocutionary act, if we need to introduce that category, may be
theorizing. The political theorists might be trying to say timeless things that
apply to (many) other contexts and times, so to treat them as speaking only
about one particular context and controversy would be to distort their aim.

Even in a case where we agree with the sociologist or historian that one aim
of a writer was to advance a particular cause or side of a controversy, we still
must ask why the writer did so by presenting abstract theoretical content, by
presenting general principles. To win others to his side or to make more firm
their position there, he cannot simply announce his preference for that side; he
must produce reasons convincing to them. Reasons might be particular, but
they also can be general theoretical considerations that apply well to a wide
range of cases and also point to one side in this instance. If the other cases they
apply to are cases the other person already accepts, then (by the general reasoning) these other cases will be recruited as evidence and support for the
proposed judgment in the case at issue.

So even if a writer does mean to intervene in a particular controversy, even
if his major intention is not to *theorize*, *we* will be interested in his work not
because it intervenes on a side but because it manages to present a general and
possibly persuasive theory that applies to a wide range of cases, historical situations, and so on. The extent of *our* interest will be due to the extent of his
success in presenting an appealing and apparently compelling general theory
of wide applicability. (Remember, there are thousands of other people who
simply lined up on one side or the other, people we do not study in the same
detail.) What interests us in the theorist, what makes him important, is not the
fact that he too lined up—*if* he did—but the theory he developed. Even if the
writer is not simply trying to theorize, he is trying to justify through abstract
and general reasoning, so we cannot understand what the writer is doing without focusing upon what *he* is concentrating upon, the structure of supportive
reasons for a general position as it affects the adequacy and acceptability of the

position. If the writer's illocutionary act is justifying, one of our prime concerns will be to investigate whether and to what extent he *did* justify. Intellectual history, then, must be in large part a history of ideas, theories, and reasoned positions, rather than a history of identified intellectual moves in a power game. (In another article, Skinner does note that even if a theorist is cynical, his public justificatory reasons will constrain what else he can endorse and do. See Quentin Skinner, "Some Problems in the Analysis of Political Thought and Action," in *Meaning and Context: Quentin Skinner and His Critics*, ed. James Tully [Princeton: Princeton Univ. Press, 1988], pp. 110–114.) We are back, then, to the realm of intellectual problems and attempts to solve or advance them.

It is useful to have a general classification of the broad kinds of factors that intellectual historians use to understand what sets and shapes a problem. Peter Gay, *Art and Act* (New York: Harper and Row, 1976), pp. 1–32, lists three types:

1. *Culture*: social and economic factors, social needs and problems, religious and political pressures, often institutional.

2. *Craft*: the techniques, traditions, and tools of a subject or discipline. We can use a term of Thomas Kuhn's and call this the "disciplinary matrix": those tools, techniques, inherited problems, body of knowledge, and current state of discussion that are widely known or available to those in the discipline, and the standards and evaluative criteria participants are expected to apply.

3. The *private sphere*: the person's family, inner psychological life, anxieties, fantasies, defenses, unconscious needs, and *biography* more narrowly considered.

To these three factors we can add two more:

4. The individual's *personal intellectual standards* for judging a theory or detecting a problem. (Einstein, for example, thought the equivalence of gravitational and inertial mass was something that needed explaining. A symmetry where there seems no reason to expect one, an asymmetry where it seems symmetry should reign—these and similar factors, bordering on the aesthetic, may set a problem for a thinker to ponder.) Those personal standards need not be widespread in the discipline, although they may *become* so if following them has led to a powerful theory that then makes these standards salient to others.

5. *General modes of thought* in the society, not necessarily institutionally based. This includes: a framework of beliefs, such as P. F. Strawson's descriptive metaphysics; a framework of general causal and explanatory principles; a marking of which kinds of thing need explaining and which kinds do not; and a marking of the kinds of factors that can be appealed to as explanatory factors or as evidence for a theory.

Given a specification of the components of a particular problem situation (its goal, initial state and resources, admissible operations, and constraints), we can go on to investigate which of the five types of factors have shaped these particular components. We can form a matrix of the possibilities of influence, and for a particular problem we can investigate how each column has shaped each row (for example, how the disciplinary matrix has fixed or shaped the constraints, how the culture has shaped the goals, and so on). This is not a *theory* of problem setting; it is a categorization of the various kinds of influence, a structure within which historical investigation can be organized, a checklist of questions to be asked. We can ask: What made *those* the goals, initial states and materials, admissible operations, and constraints *for him*? And how did that person give structure to his situation and come to think of himself as facing that particular problem, however smudged or fuzzily defined its components were?

Disciplinary history concentrates upon how the disciplinary matrix affects the problem situation and hence the resulting intellectual products. Broader histories may look to all five factors. But since the makers of intellectual products often position their work in relation to earlier products, criticizing or modifying or developing them and so differentiating their new work, one guiding theme of intellectual history is that the disciplinary matrix will play some significant role. The intellectual historian's task does not end with studying the creation of a theory or idea; she also will study how it spreads and the impact it has both within a discipline and in the wider society, including its impact upon each of the five factors in the matrix (culture, craft, and so on). What helps make room for a new idea so that it is viewed as even possible? (See Hans Blumenberg, *The Legitimacy of the Modern Age* [Cambridge, Mass.: M.I.T. Press, 1983], pp. 457–481.) What determines how much attention the idea is paid, who assists in its propagation within the discipline, within other disciplines, and in the wider society, and what social and personal incentives lead them to do this? Who places microphones in front of certain ideas, and why do they choose these to amplify? (See Bruno Latour, *Science in Action* [Cambridge, Mass.: Harvard Univ. Press, 1987], on the process of forming a network of allies in science.) How is an idea modified or diluted as it spreads? The intellectual historian also can investigate what determines how an idea fares in competition with other ideas in the discipline or in the society. In particular, were there rational and objective standards according to which the victor in a competition was superior to the loser? Even if there were objective disciplinary standards indicating that one competitor was superior to all others, the wide range of possible standards means that we must still investigate why those particular standards were invoked then.

44. Even these he may have edited and "cleaned up." This was the case with Michelangelo and the letters and drawings he left behind, a corpus designed to support his view of himself as untaught by others and as uniformly successful in his projects.

45. See Pat Langley, Herbert Simon, Gary Bradshaw, and Jan Zytkin, *Scientific Discovery* (Cambridge, Mass.: M.I.T. Press, 1987), pp. 3–36, 49–59; D. N. Perkins and Gavriel Salomon, "Are Cognitive Skills Context-Bound?" *Educational Researcher* 18, no. 1 (January-February 1989): 16–25.

46. See Frank Ramsey, *The Foundations of Mathematics and Other Logical Essays* (London: Routledge and Kegan Paul, 1931), pp. 115–116.

47. For a discussion of asymmetry and symmetry within the thought of Ein-

stein, see Gerald Holton, "On Trying to Understand Scientific Genius," reprinted in his *Thematic Origins of Scientific Thought* (Cambridge, Mass.: Harvard Univ. Press, 1973), pp. 353–380.

48. John Holland, Keith Holyoak, Richard Nisbett, and Paul Thagard, *Induction: Processes of Inference, Learning, and Discovery* (Cambridge, Mass.: M.I.T. Press, 1986), pp. 286–319.

49. On this point, see Howard Gardner, *The Creators of the Modern Era* (forthcoming).

50. Simon and Newell, *Human Problem Solving*.

51. See Georg Polya, *Patterns of Plausible Inference*, 2d ed. (Princeton: Princeton Univ. Press, 1986).

52. See Kenneth Arrow, *Social Choice and Individual Values* (New York: John Wiley, 1951); Amartya Sen, "Social Choice Theory," in *Handbook of Mathematical Economics*, ed. K. J. Arrow and M. Intriligator (Amsterdam: North Holland, 1985); John Milnor, "Games against Nature," in *Decision Processes*, ed. R. M. Thrall, C. H. Coombs, and R. L. Davis (New York: John Wiley, 1954), pp. 49–60; Luce and Raiffa, *Games and Decisions*, pp. 286–298.

53. For a very modest example, see the discussion of the r×H structure for retributive punishment in my books *Anarchy, State, and Utopia* (New York: Basic Books, 1974), pp. 59–64, and *Philosophical Explanations*, pp. 363–380, 388–390. The point is that even such a trivially simple structure can generate interesting results. The entitlement theory of justice in *Anarchy, State, and Utopia* is another example of a modest model built in analogy to the general structure of a formal system (with axioms, rules of inference, and resulting theorems).

54. See Langley, Simon, Bradshaw, and Zytkin, *Scientific Discovery*.

55. See my "Newcomb's Problem and Two Principles of Choice," in *Essays in Honor of C. G. Hempel*, ed. N. Rescher et al. (Dordrecht: Reidel, 1969), pp. 135–136.

56. For recent discussions of thought experiments in science, see Nancy Nersessian, "How Do Scientists Think?" in *Cognitive Models of Science*, ed. Ronald Giere (Minneapolis: University of Minnesota Press, 1992), esp. pp. 25–35, and David Gooding, "The Procedural Turn," in *ibid.*, esp. pp. 69–72.

57. See Thomas Kuhn, "Objectivity, Value Judgment, and Theory Choice," in Kuhn, *The Essential Tension* (Chicago: Univ. of Chicago Press, 1977), pp. 331–332.

58. F. A. Hayek, *The Constitution of Liberty* (Chicago: Univ. of Chicago Press, 1960), ch. 2.

59. On alertness being limited, see my *The Examined Life*, pp. 40–42. It was Hayek who defined the degree of civilization as the extent to which we benefit from knowledge we do not ourselves possess.

60. See R. Boyd and P. J. Richerson, *Culture and the Evolutionary Process* (Chicago: Univ. of Chicago Press, 1985); John Tooby and Leda Cosmides, "Evolutionary Psychology and the Generation of Culture," *Ethology and Sociobiology* 10 (1989): 29–49; Allan Gibbard, *Wise Choices, Apt Feelings*.

61. In learning from others, we seem to presume that they are rational—rational enough for us to understand what they are up to. Is there this evolutionary basis to the principle of charity in translation that we already have

critically discussed? Such a principle, however, need not be so general as to apply to everyone; it would be enough to presume rationality in one's own group.

62. See Ludwig Wittgenstein, *Philosophical Investigations* (Oxford: Basil Blackwell, 1953); Quine, *Word and Object*; Hilary Putnam, "The Meaning of 'Meaning,'" in his *Mind, Language and Reality: Philosophical Papers, vol. 2,* (Cambridge: Cambridge Univ. Press, 1973), pp. 215–272.

63. Adam Smith, *The Wealth of Nations*, bk. 1, ch. 2.

64. Max Weber, *Economy and Society* (New York: Bedminster, 1968).

SUBJECT INDEX

INDEX OF NAMES